AFRO~AMERICAN ENCYCLOPEDIA

Book 1

Thoughts, Doings, and Sayings of the Race

Copyright © 1992 by Winston~Derek Publishers, Inc.

Published by Winston~Derek Publishers, Inc.
Nashville, Tennessee 37209

ISBN: 1~55523~538~7
Printed in the United States of America

PUBLISHER'S NOTE

THOUGHTS, DOINGS, AND SAYINGS OF THE RACE was the first African American encyclopedia compiled and published in the United States. This celebrated document of African American history first appeared in 1895, the same year in which the honorable Frederick Douglass, the father of the abolitionist movement, died; therefore, many addresses and articles in these two books are dedicated to this distinguished African American.

As these volumes are read and studied it is important to keep in mind that only thirty years have lapsed since the emancipation of a people who were confined to captivity for more than four hundred years. The many hundreds of facts presented in this work describe the legendary accomplishments of a recently freed people. It is important that these volumes be accessible to every classroom, church, and home. This resource is a beacon that will shine forth to assist the millions of descendants of slaves to find a new direction of faith, hope, and victory.

In light of the praises and discoveries on every page, many may find it difficult to believe that so much progress could have been made during such oppressive times. Nevertheless, with the help of the Almighty Creator these milestones were reached. Here is evidence of what a tormented and downtrodden people achieved without a government to care whether they lived or died.

This rare and precious work has been reprinted as it was almost a hundred years ago; not a single page has been altered, save for the front and back covers. Readers will feel a renewed pride at discovering the accomplishments of African Americans. These pages describe the sacrifice and anxieties, happiness and wisdom, and most of all the love for God and one another.

To all who read the words within these two books: pray for the blessed souls already departed and that future generations of African Americans will use this as a bridge to reach their dreams—a foundation to build even greater pyramids that will remain for millenniums to come.

WINSTON~DEREK PUBLISHERS, INC.
1992

JAMES W. PEEBLES, PH.D.
PUBLISHER

AFRO-AMERICAN ENCYCLOPÆDIA

ENLIGHTENING THE RACE

Afro-American Encyclopaedia;

OR, THE

THOUGHTS, DOINGS, AND SAYINGS OF THE RACE,

—— EMBRACING ——

Addresses, Lectures, Biographical Sketches, Sermons, Poems, Names of Universities, Colleges, Seminaries, Newspapers, Books, and a History of the Denominations, giving the Numerical Strength of Each. In fact, it teaches every subject of interest to the colored people, as discussed by more than one hundred of their wisest and best men and women.

ILLUSTRATED WITH BEAUTIFUL HALF-TONE ENGRAVINGS.

Compiled and Arranged by James T. Haley.

No man has a right to bring up his children without surrounding them with good books if he has the means to buy them. A library is one of the necessities of life. A book is better for weariness than sleep; better for cheerfulness than wine; it is often a better physician than a doctor, and a better preacher than a minister.—*Beecher.*

First Published By:
NASHVILLE, TENN.:
HALEY & FLORIDA.
1896.

"TO SOW THE FALLOW SOIL"

WINSTON-DEREK
Publishers, Inc.

PENNYWELL DRIVE . P.O. BOX 90883 . NASHVILLE, TENNESSEE 37209

Entered according to act of Congress, in the year 1895, by HALEY & FLORIDA, in the office of the Librarian of Congress, Washington, D. C.

All rights reserved.

PREFACE.

Twenty years ago we commenced the subscription book business. Our canvass was usually from door to door, embracing both white and colored. The scarcity of books by negro authors suggested the idea of the compilation of this book. The labor connected with such a work as this none can fully appreciate but those who have performed it. We have tried to compress within a few hundred pages the momentous events connected with the Afro-American race during the nineteenth century. The utmost care has been taken in the collation of the matter in this work, and no expense has been spared to make it not only acceptable to the colored people, but to all classes of readers as well. We can scarcely hope that each article our book contains will be found strictly accurate, since authors of the highest repute differ greatly; where there is a difference of opinion we have endeavored to give the explanation which appeared to be the best supported. We hope and believe the book is free from serious error, but if any should be discovered we shall feel under obligation to those who detect the same, if they will kindly communicate with us, so that in future editions they may be corrected. The book, however, is one of reference rather than one of criticism, an accumulation of facts rather than of opinions. It furnishes the most authentic information concerning the race, and we trust it will awaken a more appreciative spirit of enterprise among them. It has aimed to direct attention to their vast capabilities and resources, many of which are yet undeveloped. We have endeavored to meet the wants of the negro, who is desirous of knowing more of the history of his race, and the achievements of its great men and women (but who are without the assistance of books that bear upon this subject), by compiling these subjects, believing that it will incite a more cheerful reading and deeper research, as the best means of obtaining general information. An effort has been made to render it so generally interesting that it may "be dipped into here and there with the certainty of something being found capable of giving instruction to all classes of readers." The matter contained in this volume can be accumulated only by years of labor and research from sources not easily accessible to the general reader, to say nothing of the vast amount that is fresh from the pens of the most eminent men and women of the race.

Our object throughout has been to produce a useful book, therefore, as far as was consistent with our plan, we have carefully gleaned whatever was of value wherever it could be found. If at any time we have failed to give credit, it has been because we did not know to whom credit was due. It would have been impossible to render this volume as complete as it now appears, without the sanction of living authors, publishers and owners of copyrights to make extracts; for their courtesy, and for all information from whatever source we tender our most grateful acknowledgments. With this preface, we launch our boat, trusting, hoping and praying that it may accomplish some good.

J. T. HALEY.

NASHVILLE, TENN., Sept. 1, 1895.

DEDICATION

To all, of whatever nationality, who desire to know more of the progress and achievements of the race, and especially to Afro-Americans, old and young, but more especially to those noble, consecrated Christian men and women, who have rendered me such valuable assistance in the preparation of this work, is this volume dedicated.

By the Compiler.

CONTENTS.

A Black Moses,	35
A Careless Word,	550
Advice to Young Ladies,	276
A Model Church,	417
A Negro Bank,	532
A Temperance Lecture, by Rev. J. C. Price,	190
A Valuable Remedy for Diphtheria and Throat Disease,	75
A Wise Negro Editor,	532
Africa and the Africans,	1
African Methodist Episcopal Church, The	434
African Methodist Episcopal Zion Church, The	442
Africanize,	339
Africanization,	339
Afro-American vs. Negro,	369
Albino,	230
Alexander, Rev. Charles E.,	326
All Things Else,	557
Ambition (sermon),	500
Americanisms Pertaining to Afro-Americans,	339
An Educational Sermon on the Needs of the Negro,	451
Anti-Negro,	339
Anti-Slavery,	339
Anti-Slaveryist,	339
Arnett, Bishop B. W.,	570
Atwood, W. Q.,	200
Barksdale, Rev. Jas. D.,	594
Barnes, Hon. Robert C.,	595
Baulden, Rev. J. F.,	222
Baylor, Rev. R. W.,	609
Benjamin Franklin on the Analysis of Beer,	189
Bethel A. M. E. Church,	418
Black Douglass,	228
Blyden, Rev. Edward W., A.M., D.D., LL.D.,	38
Boyd, Dr. Robert Fulton,	59
Brown, Dr. T. A.,	602
Brown, Miss Hallie Q.,	581
Bryant, Jas. E.,	209
Business Enterprise,	199
Business Men Among the Race,	202
Canons of Interpretation (sermon)	491
Causes of Color,	11

CONTENTS.

Centennial of Modern Missions, The (sermon),	477
Central Tennessee College,	294
Christ Bringing us to God by Reconciliation and Glorification, (sermon)	463
Christmas,	547
Christian Truth in Slave Songs,	254
Choice Thoughts and Utterances of Wise Colored People,	526
Church History,	414
Clark, Rev. G. V.,	615
Clifford, J. R.,	352
Clinton, Rev. Geo. W., D.D.,	118
Colored,	339
Colored Catholics,	415
Colored Congregational Statistics for the South,	640
Color of the First Man,	15
Color of the First Woman,	17
Colored Missionary Baptists in the Southern States,	427
Colored Bar Association,	50
Colored Methodist Church in America, History of,	418
Congregational Methodist Church, Colored,	414
Contrabands,	339
Crummell, Rev. Dr. Alex.,	561
Curtis, Dr. T. A.,	76
Darkness,	551
Davis, Rev. J. A., B.D.,	584
Darky,	340
Deshong, Rev. J. M. W.,	593
Dixie and Dixie Land,	340
Douglass, Hon. Frederick, in Memoriam of,	579
Douglass, Associated Press Dispatch,	379
Douglass, As an Orator,	384
Douglass, As a Talker,	392
Douglass, By Wm. Lloyd Garrison,	381
Douglass, Dead,	548
Douglass, Extracts from the Press,	398–413
Douglass, The Grand Old Hero,	394
Dupee, Rev. Geo. W.,	611
Duty of the State to the Negro,	142
Duty of the Hour,	332
Emancipation Day,	228
Experience,	556
Extracts from the Colored Press,	530
Extravagance,	283
Farris, Samuel,	207
First Race Newspaper in the South,	237
Flirting Women,	534
Fortune, T. T., on His People,	537
Free States,	341
Freedman's Bank,	360
Freedmen's Bureau,	237
Fugitive Slave Law,	227

CONTENTS.

Gaddie, Rev. D. A.,	476
God Avenging the Wronged (sermon),	470
God's Problem for the South,	20
Goodnight, Douglass,	397
Grand United Order of Odd Fellows in America,	236
Gray, Dr. Ida,	84
Habits and Associations,	540
Haines' Normal and Industrial Institute,	110
Harper, Mrs. F. E. W.,	592
Harrington, W. R.,	597
Harrison, Rev. Zechariah,	597
Have a Bank Account,	194
Have Courage,	214
History of Lane College,	328
History of Livingstone College,	316
Holsey, Bishop L. H.,	599
Hooks, Mrs. Julia A.,	563
Humane Education,	267
Improving Negro Homes,	174
Industrial Education for the Negroes,	170
Influence (sermon),	509
In Gladness,	556
In Memoriam—The Grand Old Man,	549
Jenifer, Dr. J. T.,	562
Johnson, Rev. Wm. D., D.D.,	590
Jones, Madam Sisseretta,	575
Jones, Dr. Sarah G.,	75
Kennedy, Rev. Paul H,	613
Lacks Race Pride,	356
Lane, Bishop Isaac,	352
Laney, Miss Lucy,	108
Langston, Hon. John M., A.B., A.M., LL.D.,	40
Last Sale of Slaves,	345
Lewis, Edmonia,	413
Lewis, Rev. W. A., B.D.,	572
Liberia,	5
Liberty,	281
Life's Struggles,	548
Lovinggood, Mrs. Lillie England,	270
Lucifer and His Angels Cast Out of Heaven,	546
Maroon,	341
Marooner,	341
Maxims, Proverbs and Phrases,	243
McCurdy, Mrs. M. A.,	137
Meharry Medical College,	301
Mental and Physical Culture (sermon),	458
Mind and Matter,	87
Mitchell, John, Jr.,	206
More Negro Than White,	536
Mortality of the Colored People, and How to Reduce It,	64

x.   CONTENTS.

Mother's Treasures,	558
Mulatto (see Negro),	341
Music and Morals,	222
Names and Authors of More than 100 Race Publications,	164
Nature,	265
Nearing Home,	555
Negro,	341
Negro Catcher,	341
Negro Cloth,	341
Negro Corn,	341
Negro Driver,	341
Negro Exodus,	343
Negro Fellow,	341
Negro Hate,	341
Negro Head,	342
Negro Hound,	342
Negro Minstrels,	342
Negro Progress,	203
Negro Worshiper,	342
Newspapers (names and locations),	129
"Nigger,"	342
Objects of Education, Morally and Physically,	280
Opportunities and Responsibilities of Colored Women,	146
Our Duties as Concerns the Future of Boys and Girls,	277
Our Fallen Heroes,	372
Payne, Bishop Daniel A., D.D., LL.D.,	556, 578
Peculiar Institutions,	342
Penn, Prof. I. Garland,	560
Phelps, Mrs. Mary R.,	113
Philosophy,	284
Poems,	544
Population of the World,	622
Population of each State and Territory in the U.S.—Arranged in Alphabetical Order,	622
*Population, White and Colored, of each State and Territory in the United States, Arranged by Counties, in Alphabetical Order,	623
Porter, Troy,	306
Prayer (sermon),	455
Price, Rev. J. C., D.D.,	553
Pro-Slavery,	342
Prosperous Colored People in Richmond,	211
Quadroon,	342
Race Co-operation,	532
Race Facts Worth Knowing,	224
Randle, C. S.,	210
Robinson, Hon. Geo. T.,	620
Rowe, Rev. Geo. C.,	589

*The following States which have less than 1,000 colored population are excepted: Montana, New Mexico, New Hampshire, Nevada, North Dakota, South Dakota, Utah, Vermont, Wyoming.

CONTENTS.

Sambo,	342
Searcy, Rev. T. J.,	574
Self-Culture,	354
Sermonic Department,	450
Settle, Hon. J. T.,	42
Seventeen reasons Why the Negro Should be Proud of His Race,	357
Shall I Take a Paper?	127
Shall Our Women Extract Teeth?	82
Silver and Gold,	551
Slave Breeder,	342
Slave Code,	342
Slave Dealer,	342
Slave Driver,	342
Slave Hunt,	342
Slave Labor,	342
Slave Liberator,	342
Slave Lord,	343
Slave Owner,	343
Slave Pen,	343
Slave Power,	343
Slave Ships,	343
Slave State,	343
Slaver,	343
Slavery Abolished,	228
Slavery in England,	228
Slavery in the North,	359
Smith, Hon. H. C.,	124
Status of the Negro,	348
"Stonewall" Jackson,	544
Sunshine,	177
Taylor, Rev. Preston,	215
Taylor, Mrs. Georgia Gordon,	222
Temperance,	186
Temperance Resolutions by the A. M. E. Church,	189
Tennessee,	554
The A. M. E. Zion Church on Temperance,	188
The African Ostrich,	252
The Colored Cumberland Presbyterian Church,	414
The Colored Man in Medicine,	70
The Crucifixion,	555
The Derivations and Nicknames of the States,	238
The Duty of the Hour,	332
The Emancipation of Women,	274
The Farm House by the River,	547
The Fleetness of Time,	549
The Free-Will Baptist Denomination,	423
The Future of the Negro,	162
The Good Jesus Factory,	227
The Grand Old Man, In Memoriam,	549
The Great Need of Negro Farmers,	251
The Greatest Negro Scholar in the World,	228
The Jubilee Singers,	237

CONTENTS.

The Lord's Anointed,	552
The Low Percentage of Mortgaged Property in the South and its Relation to the Negro Population,	368
The Myrtle-Hill Gate,	551
The Negro as an Economist,	173
The Negro in Dentistry,	78
The Outlook for Colored Cumberland Presbyterians,	414
The Penitent Thief on the Cross (sermon),	474
The Possibilities of the Negro,	33
The Power of the Press,	167
The Presbyterian Church in the United States and the Colored People,	429
The Providence of God in the Historical Development of the Negro,	25
The Reason Why,	545
The Responsibility of Women as Teachers,	114
The Richest Colored Man in the United States,	213
The Richest Colored Man in Georgia,	212
The River of Death,	554
The Song of Believers (sermon),	483
The Source of all True Courage (sermon),	450
The Sunshine Girl,	534
The "Tennesseans,"	234
The Value of the Soul,	518
The White Man and the Colored Man as Christian Citizens,	361
Timothy and Clover,	555
Thompson, Clarissa M.,	566
Tobacco,	193
Trades for Your Children,	204
Trap for Young Girls,	535
True Christianity,	183
Turner, Rev. Wm. L.,	579
Turner, Rev. James H.,	603
Tuskegee Normal and Industrial Institute,	102
Union American Methodist Episcopal Church,	414
Underground Railroad,	234
Universities and Colleges,	291
University, Fisk,	322
University, Tougaloo,	307
Value of Old Coins,	195
Vann, Rev. M., D.D.,	605
Vaughn, Rev. C. C.,	617
Virginia's First Woman Physician,	75
Wade Hampton Defending the Negro,	371
Washington, Prof. Booker T.,	84
We Are Rising,	552
Wealthy Colored New York Men,	212
Wealth of Southern Negroes,	213
Winter, Lewis,	205
Woman's Work in the Elevation of the Race,	271
Woods, Granville T.,	576
Worthy the Lamb That Was Slain,	558
Write Thy Name,	547

LIST OF ILLUSTRATIONS.

A. M. E. Church, Bethel, Detroit, Mich	441
A. M. E. Church, St. John, Nashville, Tenn	435
African Warrior	xvi.
Afro-American Encyclopædia, Enlightening the Race—Frontispiece	
Barksdale, Rev. Jas. D., Detroit, Mich	594
Barnes, Hon. Robert C., Detroit, Mich	595
Baylor, Rev. R. W., Columbia, S. C	610
Blyden, Hon. E. W., Liberia,	39
Boyd, Dr. R. F., Nashville, Tenn	60
Boyd, Dr. R. F., Residence of, Nashville, Tenn	63
Brown, Dr. T. A., Memphis, Tenn	602
Brown, Miss Hallie Q., Wilberforce, Ohio	582
Bryant, Jas. E., Paducah, Ky	209
Rev. H. D. Cannady, Georgia	588
Cassedy Industrial Hall, Tuskegee, Ala	99
Church, R. R., Residence of, Memphis. Tenn	176
Clark, Rev. G. V., Memphis, Tenn	616
Clinton, Rev. Geo. W., Salisbury, N. C	119
College, Central Tennessee, Nashville, Tenn	295
College, Lane, Jackson, Tenn	329
College, Livingstone, Salisbury, N. C	317
College, Meharry Medical, Nashville, Tenn. (Four Illustrations)	301, 304, 305, 306
Cotton Picking in Mississippi	253
Crummell, Rev. Alex., D.D., Washington, D. C	561
Curtis, Dr. T. A., Montgomery, Ala	77
Davis, Rev. J. A., Nashville, Tenn	584
Deshong, Rev. J. M. W., Fayetteville, Tenn	593
Douglass, Hon. Frederick, Washington, D. C	395
Dupee, Rev. Geo. W., Paducah, Ky	612
Farris, Samuel, Memphis, Tenn	208
Haines' Normal Institute, Augusta, Ga	110
Harrington, W. R., Nashville, Tenn	596
Harrison, Rev. Z., Mount Vernon, Ind	598
Holsey, Bishop L. H., Augusta, Ga	600
Hut of a Slave in "Old Kentuck"	639
Johnson, Rev. Wm. D., Athens, Ga	591
Kennedy, Rev. Paul H., Henderson, Ky	614
Landing Fish at Appalachicola, Fla	201
Lane, Bishop Isaac	353
Langston, Hon. John M., A.B., A.M., LL.D., Washington, D. C.	41

LIST OF ILLUSTRATIONS.

Lee Avenue Christian Church, Nashville, Tenn.	621
"Mammy" and Her Pet	182
McCurdy, Mrs. M. A., Rome, Ga.	138
Negro Exposition Building, Atlanta, Ga.	559
Phelps Hall, Tuskegee, Ala	103
Phelps, Mrs. Mary R., Augusta, Ga.	112
Plymouth Congregational Church and Parsonage, Charleston, S. C.	640
Price, Rev. Dr. J. C., Salisbury, N. C.	553
Randle, C. S., Nashville, Tenn.	210
Robinson, Capt. Geo. T., Nashville, Tenn.	620
Rowe, Rev. Geo. C., Charleston, S. C.	589
Searcy, Rev. T. J., Memphis, Tenn.	574
Settle, Hon. J. T., Memphis, Tenn.	43
Settle, Hon. J. T., Residence of, Memphis, Tenn.	48
Smith, Hon. H. C., Cleveland, Ohio	125
Taylor, Dr. Preston, Nashville, Tenn.	217
Taylor, Mrs. Georgia Gordon, Nashville, Tenn.	223
Taylor, Dr. Preston, Residence of, Nashville, Tenn.	219
Taylor & Co., Funeral Directors, Nashville, Tenn.	221
Thompson, Clarissa M., Fort Worth, Texas	566
Trinity Church, C. M. E., Augusta, Ga.	419
Turner, Bishop Henry M., Atlanta, Ga.	36
Turner, Rev. James H.	604
Turner, Rev. Wm. L., Russellville, Ky.	579
Turpentine Farm Near Savannah, Ga.	185
University, Fisk, Nashville, Tenn. (Three Illustrations)	323, 325, 327
University, Tougaloo, Tougaloo, Miss. (Nine Illustrations)	307–315
Vann, Rev. Dr. M., Chattanooga, Tenn.	606
Vaughn, Rev. C. C., Russellville, Ky.	618
Washington, Prof. Booker T., Tuskegee, Ala.	85
Williams, Mrs. Fannie Barrier, Chicago, Ill.	147
Winter, Lewis, Nashville, Tenn.	205

AFRICAN WARRIOR.

Africa and the Africans.

AFRICA is one of the great divisions of the globe—the second in point of size, but the least important as regards civilization and progress. Until recently, this continent, so long a land of mystery, was inhabited by wild and barbarous tribes and untrodden by the foot of civilization. This great continent of the globe lies in the Eastern Hemisphere, South of Europe, and is separated from that continent by the Mediterranean Sea. No other land division of the globe has such a rounded and complete outline. The explorations of travelers within the present century have revealed all the leading topographical features of the country, and enabled us to form a fairly accurate knowledge of its configurations. Lying almost wholly in or near the equatorial regions, its torrid climate and enormous deserts render explorations perilous.

It is southwest of Asia, with which it is connected by the Isthmus of Suez. It may, however, be described in brief as an insular continent, since it has of recent years been disconnected from Asia by the Suez Canal.

The continent lies between 37 degrees 20 minutes north, and 35 degrees south latitude, and 17 degrees 33 minutes west, and 51 degrees 22 minutes east longitude. It is, therefore, almost wholly in the tropical regions. The greatest length of this mysterious land, when we measure from Cape Aquehas, just east of Cape of Good Hope to Cape Bon, which is near Bizerta in Tunis, is about 4,330 geographical miles; while the greatest width, taking Cape Verd on the Atlantic side and Cape Gardafin on the Indian Ocean, is 4,000 geographical miles. Figuring the entire length of the country, excluding Madagascar and other African islands, we have about 11,300,000 statute square miles. The explorations of the continent are slowly advancing year by year, but with earnest and unceasing progress.

The southern portion of Africa is a vast tableland not generally elevated, sloping on its northern side to the equatorial plane of Soudan, and thence to the lowland region which constitutes the greater part of Northern Africa. Senegambia on the west and Abyssinia on the east are characterized by mountaneous ridges and plateaus, which "stretch from the southern tableland like rocky promontories into a sea of level country." The only other elevated region of importance is the Atlas range in the northwest. The coast line is about 16,000 miles in extent, or about two-thirds of the entire distance around the globe. The bodies of water which surround Africa are the Mediterranean Sea on the north, the Red Sea and the Indian Ocean on the east, the Southern Ocean on the south, and the Atlantic Ocean on the west.

This country has been looked upon as pre-eminently the land of deserts. The great Sahara stretches almost across northern Africa. It is not an unbroken sandy expanse, but full of variety, broken up by great oases and green stretches of land. Some of them are 120 miles in length and from three to five miles broad. In Southern Africa is another desert known as Kalahari. The plateaus of Southern Africa are fertile and thickly populated.

The extent of the mineral wealth of the continent is unknown, but the precious metals are only found in a limited area. Gold is found in Guinea, iron and copper are found in inter-tropical Africa, coal has been discovered along the Zambesi, and salt is everywhere abundant.

Dense forests with rankest vegetation, teaming with animal and insect life, pervade the equatorial regions. The most valuable productions of the vegetable kingdom are dates, oranges, olives, rice, cotton, indigo, bananas and grains.

The quadrupeds found in Africa cover a wide range of natural history. The chimpanzee and the gorilla, baboons and monkeys abound in great numbers. The elephant, rhinoceros, hippopotamus, buffalo, giraffe, camelopard, zebra, quagga, antelope, lion, leopard, panther, tiger, hyena, jackal and camel are all at home on the "Dark Continent." The camel is used as the principal beast of burden. There are five great mountain systems. The climate is more equable in the distribution of heat than that of America. There are many large and important rivers: The Congo, the Limpoppo, the Niger, the Nile, the Senegal, and the Zambesi. The Nile is the most famous and wonderful of all. Many of the lakes are vast inland seas, whose existence have been verified by recent explorers. The general form of Africa is triangular, the northern part being the base, and the southern extremity the vertex.

In the northern part of Africa the Mohammedan religion prevails, numbering perhaps two-thirds of the entire population. There are about 700,000 Jews, principally in the cities. Christianity pervails in Madagascar, Liberia, the British possessions of Southern Africa, Algeria, parts of Abyssinia and Egypt.

In the providence of God it seems that this great and glorious country is chiefly for the *colored races,* and especially for the negro. Centuries of effort and centuries of failure demonstrate that white men cannot build up colonies there. That portion of the continent lying between the Mediterranean Sea and latitude 20 degrees north, is settled principally by tribes not indigenous, such as Arabs, Turks, Moors and Frenchmen. They have gained possession of the country by conquest. Egypt is partly peopled by Copts, supposed to be descended from the ancient Egyptians, but they are probably a mixed race. The greater portion of Africa's population belongs to two races, the Berbers and the Negroes of Ethiopia. The former are nomadic occupying the mountainous regions of Barbary and the Sahara. They are sometimes called the Kabyles. The Berber nation is one of great integrity. They are warlike and predatory. Their religion is Mohammedism. In South Africa there are many Hottentots, entirely different from all the negro race. Central Africa is inhabited by the Ethiopic race. Mohammedanism and Fetishism are the prevailing religious of the continent. Some tribes offer human sacrifices. The principal negro nations are the Mandingoes, the Foolahs, the Yolofs and Ashantees. It is estimated by some writers that 150 languages are spoken in Africa, and that the population is about 200,000,000.

The principal divisions of the continent are as follows:

Algeria, Tripoli, Morocco, Tunis, Bambara, Senegambia, Liberia, Ashantee, Dahomey, Gando, Bornoo, Adamawa, Loango, Congo, Angola, Beuguela, Cape Colony, Orange Free State, Madagascar, Mosambique, Zanquebar, Adel, Cazembe, Abyssinia, Darfoor, Kordofan, Waday, Soudan, Sennar, Neubia, Egypt, and Haussa.

The word negro is a name given to a considerable branch of the human family possessing certain physical characteristics which distinguish it in a very marked degree from the other branches or varieties of mankind.—*International Cyclopedia.*

The term negro is properly applied to the races inhabiting that part of Africa lying between latitude 10 degrees north, and 20 degrees south, and to their descendants in the old and new world. It does not include the Egyptians, Berbers, Abyssinians, Hottentots,

Nubians, etc., though in popular language, especially in the older writings, it comprises these and other dark skinned nations, who are not however characterized by the crisp hair of the true negro.

The negroes are said to occupy about one half of Africa, excluding the northern and southern extremities, but including its most fertile portions. They have less nervous sensibility than the whites, and are not subject to nervous afflictions. They are comparatively insensible to pain, bearing severe surgical operations well; they seldom have a fetid breath, but transpire much excrementious matter by means of glands of the skin, whose odorous secretion is well known. His skin is soft and silky; hair, though called wool, does not present the characters of it, and differs but little from that of the other races except in color and in its curled and twisted form. He flourishes under the fiercest heats and unhealthy dampness of the tropics, where the white man soon dies.

In addition to Africa, negroes are found in the United States, Brazil, West Indies, Peru, Arabia, and the Cape Verd Islands. They are rare in Austria, Europe, and Polynesia.

Negroes were almost unknown to the Hebrews. They were unknown to the Greeks until the seventh century B.C. About twenty-three hundred years B.C. the Egyptians became acquainted with negroes, who helped them on their monuments as early as 1,600 years B.C.

The African negroes display considerable ingenuity in the manufacture of weapons, in the working of iron, in the weaving of mats, cloth and baskets from dyed grasses, in the dressing of the skins of animals, in the structure of their huts and household utensils, and in the various implements and objects of use in a barbarous state of society.

Some of them worship idols, and believe in good and evil spirits, in witchcraft, charms and spells, omens, lucky and unlucky days. They make prayers and offerings to their idols, and have sacred songs, and festivals. They sacrifice animals and sometimes human victims. They have priests who are their doctors. They believe generally in an after life, without any distinct idea of retribution. They have great fears of ghosts and apparitions. They become ready converts to foreign religions. All tribes are passionately fond of music, and have many ingeniously contrived musical instruments. They have a keen sense of the ridiculous, and are of a cheerful disposition. Naturally they are kind-hearted and hospitable to strangers, and are ready to receive instruction, and profit by it. They are quick to perceive the beauty of goodness, and hence they generally appreciate the services of missionaries in their behalf, and but for intoxicating drinks brought by traders, they would probably soon become Christianized.

LIBERIA.

LIBERIA is a negro republic in Western Africa, on the upper coast of Upper Guinea. The boundaries are not definitely fixed, but provisionally the River Thebar has been adopted as the northwestern, and the San Pedro as the eastern frontier. The republic has a coast line of 600 miles, and extends back 100 miles, on an average, but with the probability of a vast extension into the interior as the tribes near the frontier desire to conclude treaties providing for the incorporation of their territories with Liberia. The present area is estimated at 9,700 square miles. The republic owes its origin to the "American Colonization Society," which was established in December, 1816, for the purpose of removing the negroes of the United States from the cramping influences of American slavery, and placing them in their own fatherland. The first expedition of emigrants, 86 in number, was sent out in February, 1820.

About 36 miles along the coast, with an average breadth of two miles, of the Mesurado territory was purchased in December, 1821. For a hundred years the principal powers of Europe, in particular France and England, had repeatedly tried to gain possession, but the native chiefs had invariably refused to part with even an acre, and were known to be extremely hostile to the whites. On the 7th of January, 1822, the smaller of the two islands lying near the mouth of the Mesurado River was occupied by the colonists, who called it Perseverance Island. They remained here until April 25th, when they removed to Mesurado Heights, and raised the American flag. The colony henceforth grew, and expanded in territory and influence, taking under its jurisdiction from time to time the large tribes contiguous. In 1846 the board of directors of the American Colonization Society invited the colony to proclaim their independent sovereignty, as a means of protection against the oppressive interference of foreigners, and a special fund of $15,000 was raised to buy up the national title to all the coast from Sherbro to Cape Palmas, in order to secure to the new nationality continuity of coast. In July, 1847, the declaration of independence, prepared by Hilary Teoge, was published. Representatives of the people met in convention, and promulgated a constitution similar to that of the United States. Soon after the new republic was recognized by England and France; in 1852 it was in treaty stipulations with England, France, Belgium, Prussia, Italy, the United States, Denmark, Holland, Hayti, Portugal, and Austria.

The constitution of Liberia, like that of the United States, establishes an entire separation of the church from the State, and places all religious denominations on an equal footing, but all citizens of the republic must belong to the negro race.

The most important tribes within and near the republic are the following:

1. The Veys, extending from Gallinas, their northern boundary, southward to Little Cape Mount: they stretch inland about two days' journey. They invented some twenty-five years ago an alphabet for writing their language and, next to the Mandingoes, they are regarded as the most intelligent of the aboriginal tribes. As they hold constant intercourse with the Mandingoes and other Mohammedan tribes in the interior, Mohammedism is making rapid progress among them.

2. The Pessehs, who are located about 70 miles from the coast, and extent about 100 miles from north to south, are entirely pagan. They may be called the peasants of West Africa, and supply most of the domestic slaves for the Veys, Bassas, Mandingoes, and Kroos. A missionary effort was attempted among them many years ago by the Presbyterian Board of Foreign Missions, but it was abandoned shortly after in consequence of the death of the first missionary, Geo. L. Seymore.

3. The Barline tribe living about eight days' journey northeast from Monrovia, and next interior to the Pessehs, has recently been brought into treaty relations with Liberia. The Barlins are not Mohammedans.

4. The Bassas occupy a coastline of sixty miles or more, and extend about the same distance inland. They are the great producers of palm oil and camwood, which are sold to foreigners by thousands of tons annually. In 1835 a mission was begun among these people

by the American Baptist Missionary Union, whose missionaries studied the language, organized three schools, embracing in all nearly a hundred pupils, maintained preaching steadily at three places, and occasionally at a great many more, and translated large portions of the New Testament into the Bassa language. Notwithstanding this promising commencement, the mission has been abandoned for many years, but the Southern Baptist convention has resumed missionary operations among the Bassas.

5. The Kroo, who occupy the region south of the Bassa, extend about 70 miles along the coast, and only a few miles inland. They are the sailors of West Africa, and never enslave or sell each other. About 50 years ago a mission was established among them by the Presbyterian Board of Foreign Missions at Settra Kroo, but it has long since ceased operations.

6. The Greboes, who border upon the southeastern boundaries of the Kroos, extend from Grand Sesters to the Cavalla River. In 1834 a mission was established among them by the American Board of Commissioners for Foreign Missions, which continued in operation for seven years. A church was organized, the language reduced to writing, and parts of the New Testament and other religious books translated into it.

7. The Mandingoes, who are found on the whole eastern frontier of the republic, and extend back to the heart of Soudan, are the most intelligent within the limits of Liberia. They have schools and mosques in every large town, and, by their great influence upon the neighboring tribes, they have contributed in no little degree to abate the ignorance and soften the manners of the native population of Liberia.

Agriculture is carried on with increasing success. Sugar is the principal article of produce, also of manufacture. Arrowroot, rice, cocoa, cotton and coffee are cultivated. Lime is made from burnt shells. Trade is rapidly extending. Palm oil, ivory, gold dust, cam-wood, wax, coffee, indigo, ginger, arrowroot and hides are among the principal articles of export. The capital and largest town is Monrovia, a seaport on Cape Mesurado, with about 15,000 population. Liberia has a population of 1,050,000. But speaking of Liberia to-day, in his excellent work, "Christianity, Islam and the Negro Race," Mr. E. W. Blyden says: "No agency has yet been tried for Africa's regeneration, which promises so much and is capable of so much for the permanent welfare of the people as the method of the American Colonization Society in the establishment of Liberia. The United States has furnished Africa with the most effective instrument of unlimited progress and development in the Republic of Liberia. The basis of the Liberian political life is the American constitution and laws. But the earlier legislators of the new State very soon discovered that American precedents, in not a few important respects, would have to be set aside; and it is creditable to their statesmanship that they were able to introduce with prudence such modifications into the American system as made it applicable to their new circumstances and practicable for their purposes. Their successors are finding more and more that as they advance into the continent and develop national life, new modifications will be necessary. These must take place if there is normal growth—if the nation is to be the true expression of the race. The friends of Liberians abroad cannot help them to national or racial expression. They must fight their own battles and achieve their own victories, if they are not to be overawed, depressed and overcome, not so much by the merits and virtues as by the vices and failings of foreigners, whose literature they read and whose commodities they purchase.

The theory upon which Liberia was founded has thus far stood the test. It is a theory with definite practical consequences, which every one who is earnest in the desire for African regeneration and acquainted with the facts must accept, and which no one in these days, however antagonistic to the negro in exile, will strenuously oppose.

In Liberia, the people, with all the drawbacks incident to their necessarily isolated life, have the legislative control of at least 500 miles of coast, and of an indefinite interior. They recognize the necessity—the prime necessity—of the moral and religious emotions. Their minds are strengthened and expaned by the wide and glorious prospects which their independent nationality and the vast continent on which they live with its teeming millions of their blood relations open before them; and they stretch out their hands to the United States for the return of their exiled brethren, to increase their civilized and Christian force. They ask for greater educational and religious facilities. They could have greater material prosperity; but they look upon the life as more than meat, and the body as more than raiment. For more than half a century they have resisted the appeals of Europeans for an indiscriminate trade in the country, and have thus kept an extensive region both on the coast and in the interior in a virgin state waiting for their brethren from the United States, who will know how to protect themselves against the influence of a vicious foreign trade, and who will be able to introduce in a regular and healthful form the blessings of freedom and civilization. As an example of the work in promotion of a genuine Christian civilization which Liberia, as an independent nation, whose laws are final, has the power of performing, see the recent law enacted against Sabbath breaking, which applies only to the seaboard and to the proceedings of foreign vessels. You would understand the import of this fact and its bearing upon Christianity in this country if you could see how all along the coast out of Liberia the Sabbath is disregarded by foreign traders, while the missionaries look helplessly on. In course of time, Liberia will banish the traffic in spirits from the whole of her domain; and in this effort she will be sustained by the great Mohammedan trading community on the east and north.

Now, here is an instrument—indigenous, sympathetic and permanent—for the aggressive work of the American church. If American Christians will deal with this question earnestly and wisely, they can in a few years revolutionize the migration countries. America possesses the elements—the human instruments—now needed for the work in Africa, and they are anxious to come. Rev. H. N. Payne says: "Much as the colored people are attached to the places where they grew up, thousands of them would gladly go to Arkansas, to Texas, or *to any other place* where they would better their condition; but they cannot raise the money to emigrate, and must stay and suffer where they are." Now here is disinterested testimony, put not half so strongly as the facts warrant. The *any other place* is Africa; and if these helpless creatures do not name Africa in the utterance of their tearful longings, it is because thousands do not dream that there is any possibility of ever getting to this distant country. I found, during my travels in the South, in 1882, that hundreds were turning their faces to Arkansas and Texas, who had never heard of Liberia or the American Colonization Society.

Do not wait until you have trained the negroes up to your ideal—in your peculiar modes of thinking. You cannot make them Anglo-Saxons. You never will make them so in spirit and possibilities, if I interpret the providence of God aright. The Hebrews of Egypt remained illiterate and ignorant, though surrounded for 400 years by the splendors of a brilliant civilization. That civilization was not for them, though they had, by providential direction, been brought into contact with it. It was not suited for the peculiar work for which they were destined. So the children of Africa in the United States have the possibilities of a great work in the fatherland. Remove them from the pressure in your country to the freedom and congeniality of their ancestral home, and so open a wider sphere, for the play and development of their social, moral and spiritual nature. It is not the best plan to rely upon college training to fit them for work in Africa.

The fugitive Hebrew slaves, without the learning of the schools, received the law for their guidance—found the truth for their race—in the solitudes of the desert. In Africa, the merest rudiments of Western learning will have more power upon the negro than the highest culture in America. There is something in the atmosphere, in the sunshine, the clouds, the rain, the flowers, the music of the birds, that makes the a b c of your culture more valuable to him than all the metaphysics and philosophy you can possibly give him in America.

The Republic of Liberia now stands before the world. The nations of the earth are looking to her as one of the hopeful spots on the continent of Africa. Travelers in Syria tell us that Damascus owes its fertility and beauty to one single stream—the River Abana. Without that little river, the charm and glory of Damascus would disappear. It would be a city in a desert. So the influence of Liberia, insignificant as it may seem, is the increasing source of beauty and fertility, of civilization and progress to West and Central Africa.

We do not ask that all the colored people should leave the United States and go to Africa. If such a result were possible it is not, for the present, at least desirable; certainly it is not indispensable. For the work to be accomplished much less than one-tenth of the eight millions will be necessary. The question is not whether certain rich men will choose to remain behind, but whether there will be found worthy men who will choose to lead the return. Plenty of prosperous Jews remained in Babylon when Ezra marshalled his band of 40,000, and began a new, glorious epoch in the history of his race, making the preparation for that epoch in the history of the the world which has been held glorious enough to be dated from for evermore.

There are negroes enough in the United States to join in the return—descendants of Africa enough, who are faithful to their instincts of the race, and who realize their duty to their fatherland. There are many who are faithful, there are men and women who will go, who have a restless sense of homelessness which will never be appeased until they stand in the great land where their forefathers lived; until they catch glimpses of the old sun and moon and stars, which still shine in their pristine brilliancy upon that vast domain; until, from the deck of the ship which bears them back home, they see visions of the hills rising from the white margin of the continent, and listen to the breaking music of the waves—the exhilarating laughter of the sea as it dashes against the beach. These are the elements of the great restoration. It may come in our own life time. It may be our happiness to see those rise up who will formulate progress for Africa—embody the ideas which will reduce our social and political life to order; and we may, before we die, thank God that we have seen this salvation; that the negro has grasped with a clear knowledge his meaning in the world's vast life—in politics, in science, in religion.

CAUSES OF COLOR.

THE various colors seen in the natives in Africa, where amalgamation with other races is impossible, has drawn forth much criticism, and puzzled the ethnologist not a little. Yet nothing is more easily accounted for than this difference of color among the same people, and even under the same circumstances. Climate and climate alone, is the sole cause. And now to the proof. Instances are adduced, in which individuals, transplanted into another climate than that of their birth, are said to have restrained their peculiarities of form and color unaltered, and to have transmitted the same to their posterity for generations. But cases of this kind, though often substantiated to a certain extent, appear to have been much exaggerated, both as to the duration of time ascribed, and the absence of any change. It is highly probable that the original characteristics will be found undergoing gradual modifications, which tend to assimilate them to those of the new country and situation.

The Jews, however slightly their features may have assimilated to those of other nations among whom they are scattered, from the causes already stated, certainly form a very striking example as regards the uncertainty of perpetuity in color. Descended from one stock, and prohibited by the most sacred institutions from intermarrying with the people of other nations, and yet dispersed, according to the divine prediction, into every country on the globe, this one people is marked with the color of all; fair in Britian and Germany; brown in France and in Turkey; swarthy in Portugal and in Spain; olive in Syria and Chaldea; tawny or copper-colored in Arabia and in Egypt; whilst they are "black at Congo, in Africa."

Let us survey the gradations of color on the continent of Africa itself. The inhabitants of the north are whitest; and as we advance southward towards the line, and those countries in which the sun's rays fall more perpendicularly, the complexion gradually assumes a darker shade. And the same men whose color has been rendered black by the powerful influence of the sun, if they remove to the north gradually become white, (I mean their posterity), and eventually lose their dark color.

The Portuguese who planted themselves on the coast of Africa a few centuries ago, have been succeeded by descendants blacker than many Africans. On the coast of Malabar there are two colonies of Jews, the old colony and the new, separated by color, and known as the "black Jews" and the "white Jews."

The old colony are the black Jews, and have been longer subjected to the influence of the climate. The hair of the black Jews is curly, showing a resemblance to the Negro. The white Jews are as dark as the Gypsies, and each generation growing darker.

Dr. Livingstone says:

I was struck with the appearance of the people in Londa and the neighborhood; they seemed more slender in form and their color a lighter olive than any we had hitherto met.

Lower down the Zambisi the same writer says:

Most of the men are muscular, and have large, ploughman hands. Their color is the same admixture, from very dark to light olive, that we saw in Londa.

In the year 1840, the writer was at Havana, and saw on board a vessel just arrived from Africa some five hundred slaves, captured in different parts of the country. Among these captives were colors varying from light brown to black, and their features represented the finest Anglo-Saxon and the most degraded African.

There is a nation called Tuaricks, who inhabit the oases and southern borders of the great desert, whose occupation is commerce, and whose caravans ply between the Negro countries and Fezzan. They are described by the travelers, Hornemann and Lyon.

The western tribes of this nation are white, so far as the climate and their habits will allow. Others are of a yellow cast; others again are swarthy; and in the neighborhood of Soudan, there is said to be a tribe completely black. All speak the same dialect, and it is a dialect of the original African tongue. There is no reasonable doubt of their being aboriginal.

Lyon says they are the finest race of men he ever saw, "tall, straight and handsome, with a certain air of independence and pride which is very imposing." If we observe the gradations of color in different localities in the meridian under which we live, we shall perceive a very close relation to the heat of the sun in each respectively. Under the equator we have the deep black of the Negro, then the copper or olive of the Moors of northern Africa; then the Spaniard and Italian, swarthy compared with other Europeans; the French still darker than the English, while the fair and florid complexion of England and Germany passes more northerly into the bleached Scandinavian white.

It is well-known that in whatever region travelers ascend mountains they find the vegetation at every successive level altering its character and gradully assuming the appearances presented in more northern countries; thus indicating that the atmosphere, temperature and physical agencies in general, assimilate as we approach Alpine regions to the peculiarities locally connected with high latitudes.

If, therefore, complexion and other bodily qualities belonging to races of men depend upon climate and external conditions, we should expect to find them varying in reference to elevation of surface; and if they should he found actually to undergo such variations, this will be a strong argument that these external characteristics do, in fact, depend upon local conditions.

Now, if we inquire respecting the physical characters of the tribes inhabiting high tracts in warm countries, we shall find that they coincide with those which prevail in the level or low parts of more northern tracts.

The Swiss, in the high mountains above the plains of Lombardy, have sandy or brown hair. What a contrast presents itself to the traveler who descends into the Milanese territory, where the peasants have black hair and eyes, with strongly-marked Italian and almost oriental features.

In the higher part of the Biscayan country instead of the swarthy complexion and black hair of the Castilians, the natives have a fair complexion with light blue eyes and and flaxen or auburn hair.

In the inter-tropical region, high elevations of surface, as they produce a cooler climate, occasion the appearance of light complexions. In the higher parts of Senegambia, which front the Atlantic, and are cooled by winds from the Western Ocean, where, in fact, the temperature is known to be moderate, and even cool at times, the light copper-colored Fulahs are found surrounded on every side by black Negro nations inhabiting lower districts; and nearly in the same parallel, but on the opposite coast of Africa, are the high plains of Enared and Kaffa, where the inhabitants are said to be fairer than the inhabitants of Southern Europe.

Do we need any better evidence of the influence of climate on man than to witness its effect on beasts and birds? Æolian informs us that the Eubaea was famous for producing white oxen. Blumenbach remarks that "all the swine of Piedmont are black, those of Normandy white, and those of Bavaria are of a reddish brown. "The turkeys of Normandy," he states "are all black; those of Hanover almost all white. In Guinea the dogs and the gallinaceous fowls are as black as the human inhabitants of the same country." The lack of color in the northern regions of many animals which possess color in more temperate latitudes—as the bear, the fox, the hare, beasts of burden, the falcon, crow, jackdaw, and chaffinch—seems to arise entirely from climate. The common bear is differently colored in different regions. The dog loses its coat entirely in Africa, and has a smooth skin.

We all see and admit the change which a few years produce in the complexion of a Caucasian going from our northern latitude into the tropics.—*The Rising Sun.*

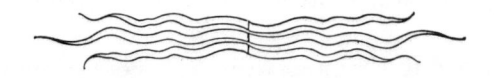

Color of the First Man.

BY REV. J. F. DYSON, B.D.

THOSE who are conversant with the Hebrew language will agree with me in the statement that the Hebrew word Adam, the name given to the first man, means reddish or auburn color, as well as man; or better, perhaps, red man; the name designating the color. I therefore claim two points, which, to any reasonable person, are sufficient proof of Adam's color, namely: The color of the material out of which he was made, and this indicated his name. Is it not more reasonable to believe that a man made out of red colored material, and having a name signifying red color, was red, than to believe that he was white? And is it not strange that many men who seem consistent in making expositions on other weighty matters will agree that the first man was made of red clay, that his name signified red color, that it was given him because of his red color, yet he was white? Mystical inference! If the first man had been made out of chalk, and called *Chivvah*, which is the Hebrew for white, what rational man is there under the sun who would presume to gravely assert that, notwithstanding his formation from chalk, and his name which implies the color of chalk, yet the first man was red? But I must not cross the Rubicon before I come to it. Perhaps when I have presented my whole argument some opinions will have undergone a change. Was the first woman of the color of the first man? This is a question whose answer will determine my cause of procedure.

1. Is it *possible* that the color of the first woman was not of the same color of the first man? To say that it is *impossible* is to limit omnipotence and omniscience. The same wisdom that produced one color in man, could produce a different color in the woman.

2. It is *probable* that the first woman was not of the same color of the first man, from the presumption that God having manifested variety of color throughout the several kingdoms of nature would not make an exception of this rule in the heads of creation. To begin with, there is the black earth and the white light of the sun; and

there is the black crow and the white crane; the black and polar bear; black and white beasts; the black dolphin and white fish. There is chalk, limestone and lead; coal, granite and iron; black and white stone and minerals; ebony trees and sycamore trees; blackberries and white cap berries; the dun pansy and the white rose, and so forth.

3. It is *probable* that the first woman and man were not of the same complexion, from the fact of the existence of divers colors in their offspring, to time whereof the history of man runneth not to the contrary, and the total silence of history, sacred and profane, at the surprise of any race, or individual of any race, in meeting another race, or individual of another race of a different complexion, justifies this probability yet more.

4. It is *probable* that the first man and woman were of different complexions, from the fact that all of Noah's children were not of the same color. The words alchemy and chemistry preserve in our own language this meaning of Ham or Cham. They literally mean the "black art," from Kemia, chem—black. They came to us through the Arabs from Egypt. That Ham in Hebrew means swarthy or darkish all linguists are agreed and, as we have before intimated, that in the early history of mankind names given men frequently indicated peculiar physical features possessed by those who bore them, we are therefore to conclude that Noah's second son was of a complexion darker than that of either the oldest or youngest son.

Japheth, the name of the youngest son, was no doubt derived from Yaphah, which means "to be beautiful," hence fair, that complexion being thought the ideal of beauty among the ancients. But for the children to be of different colors, it is necessary that the parents be of different colors, and again their parents must have been of different colors, and so on back to the diversity of color between Adam and Eve.

What was Eve's color? She could not have been red like Adam, otherwise their posterity would have all been red. If she were darker than red, or even Adam's color, their descendants, according to physiological law, would have been yet darker. If she was jet black, their children, by the same law, would have been a brown next to black. These results would have been as stated, *provided* their offspring had taken color after Adam, admitting Eve to have been red, brown or black, and thus, too, accounting for the yellow, brown, red and black races of those who hold that there are five distinct races of man. But how about the white race? It seems to have been left entirely out of the enumeration. There can be but one conclusion regarding it. If Adam was of a reddish color—as I think I have clearly shown him to have been—and Eve was of a color which was neither yellow, red, brown nor black, and as some of their posterity are a complexion different from either of these just named, and that complexion is the only one that she could possess, if we agree with Blumenback that there are but five races of men distinguished by their color, then we must conclude that Eve, the first woman, was white. The argument upon which this conclusion is founded is both scriptural and scientific, and from this basis, and none other, it proposes to declare a hitherto hidden truth. Having established the color of the first man by a draft on Scripture narrative, etymology and mental philosophy, I shall, in another chapter, establish the color of the first woman by the same means, perhaps using the argument of two or three affinitive sciences in addition thereto.—*The Unity of the Human Race.*

Color of the First Woman.

BY REV. J. F. DYSON, B.D.

LET us first consider Gen. ii. 21–23, wherein Moses, Israel's great law-giver, gives the world the only trustworthy history it has of the creation of woman and the beginning of the world. "And the Lord God caused a deep sleep to fall upon the man, and he slept; and he took one of his ribs, and closed up the flesh instead thereof. And the rib, which the Lord God had taken from the man, made he a woman and brought her unto the man. And the man said, this is now bone of my bone and flesh of my flesh; she shall be called woman, because she was taken out of man."

I attach more importance to the fact that woman was made out of man's rib than others do, yet no more than the fact deserves. If Adam was made out of red clay, which made his color red, it is unreasonable to believe that as Eve was made out a white rib she therefore naturally received her color from it, or received no color at all, if it be contended that white is no color. In all candor, is not this a more reasonable, a simpler theory than the unscriptural ones that are thrust into notice of the reading public? It puts an end to many theories heretofore advanced, and silences forever Ariel's bray, and brands his infamous assertion that the negro is a brute, a malicious falsehood; it withholds from the murderer Cain and a she ape in the land of Nod the ancestry of the black race; it shows that the color of Ham's descendants is not the result of Noah's cursing Canaan, by proving that the source of their color was in Eden. In a word, it turns a full light upon the Scripture declaration, "God hath made of one blood all nations of men for to dwell on all the face of the earth," traces it to its true source, and keeps to the text in contending with those who inadvertently overlook this truth, pervert, or willfully deny it. It does not require nearly as great a stretch of faith to believe that Eve took her color from the rib out of which she was created as to believe that she was created out of the rib; therefore let us bow at the shrine of reason and consistency. In proving the color of Adam I resorted to the etymology of his name. Does not the etymology of Eve's name also have reference to her color? Beyond a doubt it has. The word which we translate Eve is Chavvah in Hebrew, and means simply life, and no one who is familiar with Holy Writ will deny that life and immortality are symbolized by white, from the Pentateuch of Moses to the Apocalypse of John, and in human experience from Nimrod until now. Therefore Eve's *color* indicated that she was the "mother of all living," or the source of all living, as much as her name. In order for the woman to engage the attention of the man she must have been attractive. What color is more attractive than white? For her to claim his protection she must have had a delicate appearance. What color is more delicate than white? To draw upon his affection she must have been fair, or, in other words white; and I do not think it more poetic than truthful for me to say that Eve's color denoted virtue, the brightest gem in the diadem of her priceless womanhood, and the most glorious and most valuable legacy left by her to her posterity.

It would be unwise for me to multiply these subsidiary arguments in support of the fact of Eve's color being white, which has been already made plain, for in doing so I would underrate the mental ability of the reader to grasp ordinary truth, and see by the clear light of analogy, illustration and reason.

Next we will consider the complexions of the descendants of father Adam and mother Eve. At once the important question is proposed: "If Eve was white and Adam was red, none of their immediate descendants could have been white or entirely black. Some of them must have approximated a white color, some a color medium between white and red, and others must have approximated Adam's color, or the colors must have graded from nearly, or quite red, up to nearly white, in several fine shades. Where then is the source of full white and full black people?" This question is not difficult of solution. In answering it I shall show, however paradoxical the proposition may seem, that it is easier to account for the black and white children from a red Adam and a white Eve than it is to account for yellow, red, brown and black children from a white Adam and a white Eve, white and yellow children from a red Adam and a red Eve, or white, yellow, red and brown children from a black Adam and black Eve.

Knowing that there are different opinions as to the universality of the flood, I shall not insist that all human beings save Noah, his wife, his three sons and their wives, perished therein. My agreeing with those who affirm or those who deny this theory would neither strengthen nor weaken my argument asserting the divergence of color in the first human pair, and per force of reason in their descendants whether they were roaming the tableland of Nod during the flood, or rocking in the Ark upon the billows above Shinar. I have often stated that Noah's three sons, saying nothing of his wife or his son's wives, differed in complexion. The names of two of them indicate this. Ham (Hebrew Cham) means swarthy. Japheth (Hebrew Yaphar) means fair or whitish. Between Ham's swarthy complexion and Japheth's fair complexion it is not unreasonable to believe Shem's auburn complexion had place.

The Scriptures teach that Noah lived after the flood three hundred and fifty years, but giving no account of his having any other children than those who survived the flood with him and his wife in the Ark. As the Scriptures are mute on this subject I shall be also. Not denying that Noah had other sons and daughters born unto him after the flood, but basing my theory of the re-peopling of the earth upon the fruitfulness of Shem, Ham and Japhet, and the fruitfulness of their children and their children's children, whose geographical distribution alone I shall notice.

I assume as a matter of course that the white complexion did not exist after Eve's death until centuries after the confusion of tongues at Babel, and the dispersion of the three grand divisions of mankind thence "upon all the face of the earth," as the Hebrew has it, nor was the very black complexion known until the people distinguished thereby had subordinated themselves to the circumstances which produced it. To what do these statements lead? They lead to the inevitable conclusion that all the complexions except the white and black were the naturally direct result of the union of Adam's and Eve's complexions, but that these were produced by the "influences of the chemical solar rays, the altitude or depression of the general level, the difference of geological formations, the varying agencies of magnetism and electricity, as atmospheric peculiarities, miasmatic exhalations from vegetable and mineral matter, difference of soil, proximity to the ocean, variety of food, habits of life and exposure."

God's Problem for the South.

BY REV. A. L. PHILLIPS, TUSCALOOSA, ALA.

GOD is the greatest of all problem makers. Neither nature nor metaphysics nor grace contains a single problem that is not his by origination and proposal. The mystery of the milky way or the doctrine of perception or the method of reconciliation between God and man are not human. Since no human mind has ever fully understood them, it is but just to infer that they are super-human in origin. When God sets a problem before the human mind he usually indicates general principles by which it is to be solved. He never ciphers out the details for any man. God told Moses to go lead his people out of Egypt. "Come now, therefore, and I will send thee unto Pharaoh, that thou mayest bring forth my people, the children of Israel, out of Egypt." (Ex. iii. 10.) When Moses had insisted upon Jehovah's telling him something about the details of the work, he was at last asked, "What is that in thine hand? And he said, A rod. Cast it on the ground. He cast it on the ground and it became a serpent, and Moses fled from before it. And the Lord said into Moses: Put forth thine hand and take it by the tail. And he put forth his hand and caught it and it became a rod in his hand; that they may believe that the Lord God of their fathers hath appeared unto thee." (Ex. iv. 3–5.) Moses' problem was *to lead out the people;* his method of solution was to be *miracles.* Jesus stood in the midst of his disheartened disciples on the mount in Galilee, and gave them the greatest problem ever committed to human head, heart and hand. "Go ye into all the world and preach the Gospel to every creature." Such a problem had never been given to men in the past history of the church; it has not been modified one jot or one tittle since its first announcement. It was original, startling, overwhelming. It gave the world a new estimate of the power of the human soul, that it could embrace with loving solicitude the entire human family. The problem carried within its depths its own solution as a granite mass bearing its imbedded dynamite. The problem was *Go:* its solution lay in one word—*preach.* The problem is now before us. It is divine; so is its solution. The church must, and, by God's good grace, will work it out.

In working it out, the church in the United States has some peculiar conditions to meet. It is better equipped in brains, in money, in spirituality than ever in its history. More people are easily accessible than ever before. Cries for the preached word come from every quarter of our own country and in tumultuous mobs beneath our windows alarm our sleeping consciences. Mute appeals of unnumbered millions of heathen call us irresistibly to their help. The Syro-Phœnician woman in the coasts of Tyre begs for crumbs from the spiritual feast that our Lord spreads before us. Poor Lazarus, outcast, sore-covered, dog-licked, lies at our door piteously pleading, "Give, or I die!" Let us attend to this cry from Lazarus for a little while. We'll not stop to speak of the Chinaman, for he is removed from us by law, nor the Indian, who is fast being removed by powder, rascality, and liquor. Our problem in the South is how to reach the negro with the gospel. It may be solved perhaps by first reaching the *white man.* For until his brain is cleared and his conscience aroused, very little can be done. What are the conditions of the problem? 1. Many millions of white and black people live in the same territory. 2. The whites once owned the blacks. 3. The whites are vastly in the majority, have infinitely more money, education and spirituality. 4. Against the will of the intelligent majority, the minority was freed. 5. By law both black and white are equal citizens of the same government. 6. Powerful influences have for years been at work causing ill-will between the two races. The question that we have to answer is, can these two races live in peace on the same soil as equal citizens of the same government? If so, how?

What does history say about it? Before the general diffusion of Christianity when two alien races came into contact, one or the other was exterminated or enslaved. Rome and Carthage fought until it was written *Delenda est Carthago*. But what lesson do the records of nations since our Lord's ascension *even down to the year* 1891 teach us? An elaborate experiment was made in Spain. But the Moors were expelled in spite of their superior science and art. Spain and Portugal came into contact with the natives of Mexico and South America only to enslave and destroy them. The Puritan and the cavalier met the proud red man on his own soil and have killed him until only a small remnant remains to build the camp-fire and recall the deeds of ancient braves, with no hope for the future except his ration of blue beef and abuse. Slave and Hebrew, though not even of different races, cannot live together unless the Jew will submit to oppression nearly as galling as slavery. What says history? She says emphatically that the experiment that we are making in this country is a crime against humanity—that either slavery or death must be its end.

What says the Constitution of the United States? Before the adoption of Article XIII. of the amendments of the Constitution abolishing slavery, its existence had been simply ignored by that immortal document. Perhaps no greater experiment in making laws has ever been attempted than the adoption of the last three amendments, making citizens out of slaves up to that time kept ignorant by law. Questions as to the wisdom of their enactment or perpetuation are purely theoretical. They are there, and nothing short of a revolution can remove them. What does the Constitution, our highest and most unchanging law, say about these two races living together? It simply says to all alike, "You shall live together in peace!" This may not be the voice of conscience, but it is the fiat of authority. The Constitution therefore says to us, say we yea or say we nay, "I know that history declares it can't be done, but my voice is louder and my arm is stronger than history. Let there be peace!" The Constitution sought to create peace and interject it between the discordant and warring elements of society. As loyal citizens of our land and as staunch defenders of the Constitution, we must *obey the law*.

What says the gospel of God? "As ye would that men should do to you do ye even so to them likewise." "Follow peace with all men." "Thou shalt love thy neighbor as thyself." We are perhaps too prone to apply these wholesome precepts to the lives of others, forgetting for the time their direct bearing upon our own consciences and lives. It is to no purpose that we say that we once did our religious duty to the negroes. Satifying reflections on our past performances may soothe us into present neglect. Energetic resolutions to do our duty in the future may be a subtly delusive way of calming the cryings of an urgent conscience to-day. A shifting of responsibility that God has laid, is impossible, for the only method of discharging responsibility to God is by doing the duties demanded.

A condition of society exists to-day in the South the like of which has never before been seen. Ignorance and intelligence, poverty and plenty, have always existed side by side everywhere. But when in the history of the ages has a people who were never in bondage to any man, conferred on an alien race, once their slaves, the equal legal rights and privileges which they themselves have created and enjoy?

When we have set aside all political considerations and social fears, we find that the essence of the whole matter lies in the question of, How shall two men, equal before the law, behave towards one another? History is eloquent with illustrations, and the Constitution speaks with the voice of authority. But to consider this question, neither history nor the Constitution is sufficient. For the Christian, there is but one code of morals, but one yard-stick for measuring this cloth, but one voice—and that of law and love united —that has inherently the power of solution. Political expedients are, at best, mere temporary aids. The law is useful as an educator, but it has no power of producing in its own subjects sympathetic obedience. We must have a solvent more permanent than party platforms, more powerful than all law. Something is needed to arouse the conscience, engage the heart, and direct intelligent effort. There are three persons concerned in this matter—the white man, the negro and Almighty God. The [white man knows his weakness, the negro is expectant, and, unless the Lord show the strength of his right arm, the pessimism taught us by history and aggravated by the demands of an unfailing law, will soon change to discord and open strife. A learned divine once said, "Unless the gospel solve this matter, then it will be *bang! bang!*" Says the apostle "I can do all things in him that strengtheneth (*endynamites*) me." What says the gospel? "Go ye into all the world and preach the gospel." "For it is the power of God unto salvation to every one that believeth"—"Christ the power of God and the wisdom of God." So long as we walk in such light as that, there is no pessimism, not even a shade of doubt.

Again, says this same gospel, 1 Thess. ii. 3, 4, For our exhortation is not of error nor of uncleanness, nor in guile; but even as we have been approved of God to be entrusted with the gospel, so we speak; not as pleasing men, but God, which proveth our hearts. That is, we were made by Christ, at his ascension, trustees of his Gospel, for the benefit of all mankind. Shall not this stir up our consciences? A trustee must be *faithful*. Have we, as individuals, or as a church of Jesus Christ, done our duty to the negroes? At the judgment seat of Christ it will be too late to attempt an answer. It is called to-day. "The Spirit of the Lord is upon me," said Jesus, "because he hath anointed me to preach the gospel to the poor; he hath sent me to heal the broken-hearted, to preach deliverance to the captives, and recovering of sight to the blind, to set at liberty them that are bruised, to preach the acceptable year of the Lord." Man can have no higher duty, he can enjoy no more sanctifying privilege than to do the works and speak the words of God to men everywhere. Is there a finer field in our South-land for preaching Christ than is afforded by the negroes? Humble, bound by Satan in chains of lust, enslaved to sin, blinded by the god of this world, ignorant of the time of God's calling—among such, surely ought the gospel to be preached.

The Southern Presbyterian Church is just entering upon the great evangelistic period of its history. For the coming of this time God has been patiently preparing us. He has endowed us with a pure doctrine and an adaptable polity. He has enlarged our borders. He has filled our barns with plenty. He has unstopped our ears to the cry of the heathen. He has opened our eyes to the destitution at home. He has been perfecting us by the sufferings of persecution, dissension and discord from within and from without. Uniform and unified we stand before him to-day. In his own hand-writing he gives us our ploblems. The great home-problem is how to evangelize our colored fellow-citizens, who are our friends and neighbors. Surely, God's people will not halt now. To halt will be to retreat. With heart and head and hand, intelligently, wisely, humbly, patiently, cheerfully, sympathetically, for God's own glory, let us now do our whole duty *to the negro*. Let North, East and West be patient and charitable, while aiding us to adapt the gospel to these hitherto untried conditions. Let all the people conscientiously introduce God into this mighty problem. It will soon be solved then, and, until then, *never*.

The Providence of God in the Historical Development of the Negro.

BY REV. A. F. BEARD, D.D.

THE orginal condition of the Negro people was heathenism in Africa. Then came two and a half centuries of American slavery with the evils which it bred and fostered. In the dreadful discipline of slavery, there had yet been a great gain in condition over the estate of their ancestors. The race had ceased to be absolutely African; there remained few with wholly African blood.* Not only by the amalgam of race but in other ways, all had gained something from contact with civilization. Those who had lived in towns and cities had taken on certain of the blessings of civilization. The great majority who lived on remote plantations had nevertheless seen something of civilization. Mentally and morally children, their heathenism had been modified by living among white people. The speech of heathenism had been exchanged for the rudiments of the English tongue. Besides this they had learned needful lessons in their hard school of servitude. The spirit of obedience, the consequent reverence for law and respect for authority, in the providence of God, were preparations for the

---

*A Southern authority, in a careful work entitled: "The Resources and Population of South Carolina," published in 1883 with the State imprint, speaking of the Negro people uses the following words, viz.: "One-third has a large infusion of white blood. Another third has less, but still some; and of the other third it would be difficult to find an assured specimen of pure African blood. If the lineage of these Negroes whose color and features seem most unmistakably to mark them as of purely African descent be traced, indisputable evidence may often be obtained of white parentage more or less remote."

day of emancipation. While most of them imperfectly apprehended the meaning of a religion which meant character and conduct, yet nearly all had absorbed a sense of the government of God, which was strong and in some ways controlling. All this was progress in condition over the estate of their African ancestors; a great gain over naked barbarism. This was not the purpose of man, but it was in the providence of God.

When Christian faith and love said this redeemed people must now be educated and helped into worthy Christian manhood and womanhood, this was another step in the movement of divine providence.

When the race history began, it began at zero. Four millions of people had existed, but as yet there could be no history. That there may be history, there must be legal marriage, family name, continuity of family life, and possession of property. The Negro had none of these.

A score and a half years have passed and the Negroes number seven millions of people. Two millions have learned to read. Many have pushed on beyond elementary education, and a small percentage have made attainments which are prophetic of power and position for the race in the times to come.

While it is true that those who cannot read to-day are in excess of the original four millions when they were set free, and that the Negro left to himself has even degenerated from the Negro of slavery, it is also true that a single generation has witnessed in the life of hundreds of thousands a wonderful evolution in manhood and womanhood. The growth of the race in honorable self-hood has been for such, like the story of Narcissus in the myths of the ancients. Narcissus, you remember, had fallen from the knowledge of his high birthright as a descendant of the gods, and was living low down unmindful of his high origin. But one day at the water side for the first time he saw his own image reflected back to him as from a mirror. It was not a clear vision, but to him it was a revelation. He saw that he was not like the brutes. He felt that he ought to be more than he was. His thoughts within him were stirred. The sense of his high origin and birthright slowly came to him. One thought quickened another, and he found himself rising to his thought until he felt the fire of his divinity. He grew in his purpose toward that which he held in his mind. He cast aside what was low, and he resolutely left all that pulled him down. Thus leaving the things that were behind, he pressed forward, and so became transformed in thought, in character and in life, passing from achievement to permanent possession, until the glory of the gods was his, and he took his place among them.

Thousands upon thousands of the Negro people have had this vision and revelation. The idea of self-hood, and the reaching forth to it, in a single generation of the Negro race has been a wonderful prophecy of possibility in the significance and quality and nobility of life. This is seen to be the master key to unlock the door of caste and hindrance for their entrance to the rights of manhood and womanhood, and to the dignities of life. This is the power that is to settle at last the standing and the recognition of race. This is a gain greater than that which can be tabulated in statistics. This is the highest achievement of this generation of the Negro race. It means a people who are capable of storing strength and character. It means the uplift of race life.*

We are not to conclude, however, that a true and living progress of the race is to come easily or in a short period of time.

The fact that millions are in degradation and are not getting out of it, and that more children are growing up in ignorance than are being educated, is one of gravity, and must excite concern. It will trouble future generations more than it does the present one. It must not only qualify the progress of those who would rise, but it must also make the question of white and black people living side by side in peace and in respect for civil and Christian rights more difficult of solution, and more uncertain in respect to time.

We may expect no little trouble in such conditions. The alienation between the white and black people will be likely to widen and

---

*When the race history began there was not a school for the Negro; there are now more than 25,000 schools.

Then there was not a Negro pupil; now there are enrolled 1,309,251 pupils in schools.

Then the number of Negro people who could read "were not worth the counting;" now 2,000,000 people have learned to read since 1865.

But elementary education is not all. There are 25 colleges, 8,396 professors and students; there are 25 schools of theology with 755 students; there are 5 schools of law, and 5 schools of medicine.

Where a Negro teacher would have been a subject for jest and also of arrest, there are now 20,000 such teachers in common schools.

Where their churches had the ministry of ignorant and immoral preachers these are being displaced by those who are intelligent and worthy. Purer churches are being organized. We sometimes think the progress is slow. It is no slower than Christianity is.

The Negro who possessed nothing is acquiring property. The estimate of taxable property gained since emancipation for 7,000,000 of people is 264,000,000 of dollars.

deepen. True peace and cordial relations depend upon conditions which as yet exist but in very small degree.

The moral evolution of mankind is a very slow process. The development of purity of mind and heart is a long way from perfection yet, in peoples most powerfully affected by Christianity. The development of conscience so that it shall rule the life of man has not been such as to make the best communities unduly elated. The development of civil society which depends upon the development of man, upon the expansion of his mind and the regulation of his moral nature, is slow even when the hindrances are fewer than the helps.

Consider now a people among whom chastity was an almost unknown virtue, among whom superstition overlaid conscience, among whom conscience was in the alphabet of development, among whom the first principles of civil society and duties were never thought of, and he would be unreasonable who should even in favorable environments expect any permanent progress which shall come in other than in long and patient years. Then remember that for the most part the environments are not favorable. There is the prejudice of race to be overcome—prejudice which lives cruelly and dies slowly.

The Negro people have not to make their first acquaintance with oppression and injustice, and no one can tell when they and their wrongs will part company. It will be a long time before the Negro race will have even-handed justice. The race will be tolerated, perhaps, and some Christian souls will cherish friendliness and give helpfulness. But to most the Negro will be a social and political burden. He will be discriminated against. If recent events in the South teach anything the negro may not expect his civil rights and perhaps not the protection of equal laws for many a year. We may hope for gradual amelioration with gradual education. We may hope that brute force and violence and personal cruelties will not long continue, but we have no reason to expect that the time of discipline is nearly over. This people are to remain a separate race, who cannot be absorbed with the people by the side of whom they are to live, and yet to live without a separate national existence—always in the minority—always the weaker among the stronger. Here, on the same soil the struggle of life must go on, are two races—the juxtaposition of two nationalities—that differ in physical externals, in distinctive characteristics and in sympathies; the weaker condemned to the discouragements which grow out of their weakness, and with no alternative but the generosity of the stronger when any conflict of interest may arise. Until Christ shall possess the hearts of men as he does not yet, it requires no prophet to tell us that the history in many respects must be sad, and it may be fearful. There are difficult facts to meet when we consider the development of this race.

What shall we say as to the providence of God in this history?

Let us get our bearings. For the sake of comparison suppose we recall the history of the development of some other peoples during this period of two hundred and fifty years, peoples who were civilized when the first shipload of slaves landed in Virginia.

Our Anglo-Saxon people. It has not been always a sunny day and an excursion of pleasure in the forward movements of our own race. During this same period of time more people in England have lost their lives in their struggles to come where they now are, than have perished in this land through slavery. Not to mention ruder days, two hundred and fifty years past have witnessed stormy times in old England. The dethronement and beheading of a king, bloody wars under Cromwell, persecutions for opinions' sake; imprisonments and executions in the restored monarchy; insurrections in Scotland, conspiracies in Ireland, massacres in all three islands, and that on a large scale. How people suffered for their opinions! How property was taken from them! How families were exiled and scattered! It is a crimson history.

If we take France, e.g., in the same period, there are the Huguenot persecutions, the revocation of the Edict of Nantes and its attendant horrors, St. Bartholomew's day and its murders, and for centuries men hunted down like beasts and driven from their country to keep their lives; the French Revolution; the Reign of Terror; the Goddess of Reason and the Scourge of Unreason. Germany with its continuous wars poured blood of men on the soil like water.

All this and more in many lands became history while the Negro was in the tobacco plantations and in the cotton fields. There is in the lesson of history certainly no ground for discouragement for the Negro people in the fact that struggle means struggle, and that struggling up means time, a long time. Said the apostle, "For we know that the whole creation groaneth and travaileth in pain together, until now." This is what other peoples have been doing all the ages "until now." The stages of advancement and attainment in the history of peoples are, if you please to call them so, the evolutions in these processes God's providence. The kingdom of truth, of order, of reason, of justice and, finally and supremely, of love, that is, the kingdom of God comes in these processes; in and through the conflicts of human thought and the struggles of human will not only, but most often by means of them. The philosophy of the history which records the movement of men's minds through darkness into light, through obstacles and painful transformations, over oppositions and adversaries, the errors and the evils, the discordances and distractions are all in evidence that these very conditions in the providence of God, furnished not only the occasions, but the reasons and methods for growth out of weakness into strength, for the expansion of intelligence, for better laws, for better and larger life. History is full of movements which themselves were big with injustice, and from which were painfully envolved the very arguments to overcome them, and to deliver the people from their evils. The progress of mankind has thus been through storms and against head winds. The course has seldom been a straight one as men planned, but a crooked one as men made it, like a ship beating its way against hard and furious weather. When the evils in one form had come to be at last too grevious to be borne, then under the impulsion of necessity there is a new course of thought and action, and the ship tacks about. She does not point to the goal always but there is a gain in the stretch. The movement is zig-zag, and often apparently away from what is desired, but the resultant of these movements is progress toward the final good. From every century and every race comes this same story. It is this, the law of struggle is the law of life, a severe law, but in the providence of God, and in the long run the law through which comes all human achievement and progress. The peoples who are welded are welded in the fire.

Now the Negro people will prove to be no exception to this law, unless they are always to be a subject class. If in their hard conditions God has some better things for them they cannot get this in an easy way nor in a short time. They are taking now their first step in their historic life as a people. No people ever got as far as their advanced guard has, more easily or more rapidly.

If now under the dispensations of God's providences these who have moved up from the lowland to highland look back into the bogs to see millions of people there with little movement to better life and get discouraged, or if they see the difficulties and dangers, the inevitable hostility to which they are subjected, and get apprehensive, we can say to these, other people have been through floods and under the waters. Governments and institutions and races are but human nature on a great scale, and what the word of the Lord says to persons is true for aggregations of persons, "Beloved, think it not strange concerning the fiery trial which is to try you, as though some strange thing happened to you." It must needs be that peoples which have not been through the fiery ordeal, which is God's school of development for the accumulated strength of trial, must remain in weakness. The accumulated strength of a patient overcoming on the part of a soul or on the part of a people, is a permanent possession, and in the end is worth all the cost. Ideas that have been wrought in by pain and wrought out by patience are those which are permanent. The working and the waiting, the injustice and reactions to the confirmations of justice, the wandering in the wilderness on the way to the promised land, and the dying without the sight of it; the violence of opposers as well as the hand of Christian sympathy, the hostility of caste as well as brotherly kindness, these are all in the process. This discipline, development, evolution, all in the end make for the regeneration of the generations. If the process is hard, it is yet a process in the providence of God, and it prevents weakness. No people who have a history have been exempt. All have found in this way their inheritances. If this stumbles you, does it stumble you any more than the fact of sin in the world?

Again, if the missionary, or the philanthropist, or patriot, is likely to be discouraged or disheartened because that which will surely take many generations is not secured in one generation, he may call to mind the fact that the providence of God is a continuous providence, and as the great historian of France says, "its logic is not the less conclusive for reasoning slowly." As Christians we may not forget that the first fact of history is sovereignty of God. Men may oppose this, and suffer and cause others to suffer, but they cannot hinder it. The Omnipotent will is ceaselessly working. It has neither change of purpose nor repose. Every detail of history, every attempt to hinder and destroy that which God has purposed, works on and all work together in combination and dependency until God's clock of time shall strike the hour of his providence.

Very truly did Ex-Governor Bullock, of Georgia, recently testify as to the present avowed purpose in our Congress to practically annul the fourteenth and fifteenth amendments to our Constitution, which confirm to white and black alike the rights of freedmen and the privileges of citizenship, in saying, "this is not only unpatriotic, but for our section is bad politics." Yes it is, and it is one more of those false movements intended to reverse the providence of God and to secure the will of man, but which always turn out for the furtherance of the divine purposes. The brethren of Joseph took counsel together to hinder the purposes of God. The stronger sold the weaker a slave in another land. But as time moved on, these sinners and brothers must needs go "way down into Egypt land." Then conscience extorted the confession from them, "We have verily been guilty concerning our brother." The one whom they proposed to degrade in servitude God had highly exalted. "Ye thought evil against me, but God meant it unto good." Man is free, but God rules.

What God in his purposes may have in store for the people whom his providence brought from the jungles of Africa, and whom his providence prepared for the emancipation which he himself ordained and brought to pass, we cannot know until his providence shall have ripened. But this we have learned, that God has overturned the purposes of man. When men proposed to make the chains stronger, God snapped them. Enough already has been concluded to give us a pledge of God's purpose that he intends this people to be at least really and truly free, and to have their opportunity for manhood and womanhood. That which has been settled in heaven will not be unsettled on earth. Prividence takes no step backward. The chariot wheels of God turn only one way. On man's part possession may wait, must wait upon preparedness. The fullest manhood, the truest brotherhood, the best life, is not a gift which one may take and say, "I have it." It is a salvation which one must needs work out with fear and with trembling, as God works it in. As to time, this salvation of a people will move on with the movement of Christianity and Christian faith in our land.

Finally, we who are working together with God are engaged in that which is assured. There is no uncertainty as to the result. The prayers of good men and good women, the schools and the teachers, the churches and the preachers, the forces that make for righteousness, the promises of God for the accomplishment of his purposes among men, "the stars in their courses," will bring forth judgment unto truth. There may be oppositions, hindrances, and what are to us discouraging delays, but he who came "to bring forth judgment unto truth will not fail, nor be discouraged." And when God shall explain his providences and justify his ways to man, it shall be seen that human history is something more than the fact that men can choose, and that one event thus follows another coming and going, but that while they choose there is One who both governs and judges. To the degree that we believe this we shall be faithful and we need not fear.

Whatever happens on the way to this day of God, it is for us to labor on, confident in his redeeming grace, in the certainty of his holy government, in the pledge of his omniscience, in the help of his omnipotence, and in the amen of his accomplishments.

The Possibilities of the Negro.

BY THE LATE SENATOR LOGAN.

Extracts from His Washington City Address in the A. M. E. Church.

AFTER dwelling at length upon the marvelous progress of the colored race in the United States, he then pointed out the negro's faults:

If there is any one thing that will clog the wheels of your material progress it is the fact that some of you try to overreach yourselves. Do not become dazzled at the splendor and magnificence of those who had hundreds of years to make this country what it is today. No man is a success who has not a fixed object as a sign-post—an aim in life to attain unto. A man should get that kind and that amount of education that will best fit him for the performance and the attainment of his object in life. Too much Greek will do you no good; what does a man want with Greek around a table with a white apron on? I do not say that you should not study Greek if you intend to fill a chair in some institution of learning; I do not say that you should not read medicine if you desire to become a physician, or law if you wish to follow that profession. But I tell you our white people are fast growing indolent and lazy. If you watch your chances and take timely advantage of the opportunities offered you, your race will be the wage workers, the skilled artisans, and eventually the land owners and the wealthy class of this country. I advise you to learn trades; learn to become mechanics. You have the ability and capacity to reach the highest point, and even go further in the march of progress than has yet been made by any people.

I predict that the time will come and it is not far off when we will have a negro poet from the South. He will set the magnificent splendor of the "Sunny South" to music. His muse will touch the lyre and you will hear the sweet murmur of the stream, the rippling waters, and we shall see the beauty of that country as it was never seen before. It will come; and after him other still greater men. But it takes labor to become a great man just as it takes centuries to make a great nation. Great men are not fashioned in heaven and thrown from the hand of the Almighty to become potentates here on earth, nor are they born rich. I admit that there is, in some parts of this country, a prejudice against you on account of your color and former condition. In my opinion the best way to overcome this is to show your capability of doing everything that a white man does, and do it just as well or better than he does. If a white man scorns you, show him that you are too high-bred, too noble-hearted to take notice of it; and the first opportunity you have do him a favor, and I warrant you he will feel ashamed of himself and never again will he make an exhibition of his prejudice. The future is yours and you have it in which to rise to the heights or descend to the depths.

A BLACK MOSES.

BY THADEUS EDGAR HORTON.

BISHOP HENRY M. TURNER, of the A. M. E. Church, who has stood for many years as one of the foremost representatives of the negro race in this country, has attracted attention of late by his advocacy of the return of the black man to his native land. His published views on this subject have been extensively discussed, and because of the bishop's prominence and his reputation as a student of the Afro-American problem, have had great weight attached to them.

The bishop is himself an interesting personality. He was born in Newberry, S. C., in 1834. His parents were free, but while a boy he was "bound out" to a slave owner and worked side by side with slaves in the fields until his fifteenth year. Then, tiring of the hard labor and ill treatment, and with restless longings for something higher than the farm hand's fate, he ran away from his master and entered the service of a firm of attorneys in Abberville, S. C., where John C. Calhoun once practiced law. His employers, attracted by his aptitude, especially in spelling, taught him the elementary English branches, and in the intervals of his duties as office boy he read law, often pouring over his books late at night, when his "bosses" had gone home.

At twenty years of age young Turner became a liscensed minister of the M. E. Church, South. After a few years of itinerant service, during which his fame as an eloquent preacher spread through the surrounding country, he determined to go to Africa as a missionary. About the same time he transferred his allegiance to the A. M. E. Church, and entered Trinity College, in Baltimore, where he studied for four years, completing the courses in divinity, Latin, Greek and Hebrew.

The war was in full blast when he ended his college term and he was assigned to the pastorate of Israel Church, in Washington. His

BISHOP HENRY M. TURNER,
Of the A. M. E. Church.

reputation and his congregation grew rapidly, and when the enlistment of negro troops was decided upon, on the recommendation of Chief Justice Chase and Secretary Stanton, President Lincoln made him chaplain of the first regiment of colored troops that was mustered into the service of the Government. He was the first negro chaplain ever appointed and possibly the first colored officer to receive a commission. At the close of the war, so excellent had been his record, he was recommissioned a chaplain in the standing army by President Johnson. Later, he was detailed for Freedman's Bureau service and sent to Augusta, Ga.; but finding so much religious and educational work to be done among his people, he resigned that place and re-entered the regular ministry of the A. M. E. Church, delivering lectures on educational and industrial subjects, and advising the negroes how to adapt themselves to their new condition of freedom.

During the reconstruction period he became known as one of the most powerful stump speakers in Georgia. He was elected from Bibb County as a member of the Constitutional Convention, and was afterward chosen to two successive Legislatures. When Congress passed the Civil Rights Bill he resolved to abandon active participation in politics and has never since been an aspirant for an elective position. He was made postmaster at Macon, Ga., being the first Negro postmaster in the State; but resigned on account of the bitter opposition of the white people, and was appointed custom house officer at Savannah.

In 1876 he was chosen by the General Conference of the A. M. E. Church, publisher-in-chief, with headquarters at Philadelphia. Four years later the General Conference held at St. Louis elected him bishop. During all his other duties he had preached regularly, and had become known as perhaps the greatest revivalist of his race. He often preached three times on Sunday and every night in the week for three or four months at a time, and he has a record of thirty thousand additions to the church to his credit.

Bishop Turner is one of the best informed men on the Negro question in this country. He has three times visited Africa., once on a flying trip and twice in his official capacity. In 1891 he went to the Dark Continent to look after the missions of his church there, and organized conferences in Sierra Leone and Liberia. The past spring he visited Africa and spent several months on the west coast. The bishop is the general consular representative of the Republic of

Liberia to the United States, regularly accredited by President Cheesman and Secretary of State Gibson.

The bishop believes that his race will ultimately return to Africa and that it is the duty of the government to help them do so. He regards slavery not as a divine but as a providential institution of temporary duration, brought into existence for the purpose of bringing the negro in contact with the Caucasian—the great race of the world. He thinks the black man will rise faster in a republic to himself, and that that alone will bring peace and quiet to this country. He declares that for two races of people to be living in the same country, under the same institutions and subject to the same laws with no social contact, is an anomaly and can be productive only of evil results.

Bishop Turner's home is in Atlanta, Ga., where he is held in high esteem by the best people of both races. He was married a few weeks ago for the second time.—*Once A Week.*

REV. EDWARD W. BLYDEN, A.M., D.D., LL.D.

BY HON. SAMUEL LEWIS.

EDWARD WILMOT BLYDEN was born in the Danish Island of St. Thomas, West Indies, and is of the purest Negro parentage.

Inspired in early youth with a love for the fatherland, and a desire to labor for its amelioration, he went to the United States in his seventeenth year, with a view of pursuing certain studies to fit himself to work in Africa. Influential friends endeavored to secure for him admission to some institution of learning there, but so strong was the prejudice against his race at that time that the effort proved unavailing. He was advised to proceed at once to Liberia, where the Board of Foreign Missions of the Presbyterian Church in the United States was about to establish a high school under the care of Rev. David A. Wilson, M.A., a graduate of Princeton College, now Dr. Wilson, of Missouri. After a few months' residence in Liberia, young Blyden entered the new institution among its first pupils. By diligence and perseverance he soon rose to the headship of the school, and, after filling that office for three years to the satisfaction of all concerned, was, in 1862, elected to a professorship in the newly-founded college of Liberia. In 1864 he was appointed Secretary of

State by the President of Liberia, and managed for two years to combine the duties of that office with his educational work. In 1869 he made a journey to the East, visiting Egypt and Syria, chiefly with the view of studying the Arabic language in order to its introduction into the curriculum of the college.

In 1871 he resigned his professorship and after a brief visit to Europe spent two years in Sierra Leone, during which time he was

REV. EDWARD W. BLYDEN, A.M., D.D., LL.D.

sent by the Governor of this Colony, which was then under the administrations successively of Sir Arthur Kennedy and Sir John Pope Hennessy, on two diplomatic missions to the powerful chiefs of the interior. His report on one of those expeditions was published at length in the Proceedings of the Royal Geographical Society.

In 1877 he was appointed Minister Plenipotentiary of the Republic of Liberia at the Court of St. James', and was received by Her

Majesty at Osborne, July 30, 1878, being introduced by the Marquis of Salisbury, then Secretary of State for Foreign Affairs. He was soon after elected an honorary member of the Athenæum Club. In 1880 he was elected a Fellow of the American Philological Association. In 1882 he was made a corresponding and honorary member of the Society of Science and Letters of Bengal. In 1884 he was elected Vice President of the American Colonization Society. The honorary degrees of Master of Arts, Doctor of Divinity and Doctor of Laws have been conferred upon him by different American colleges. In 1885 he was nominated by the Republican party of Liberia a candidate for the Presidency of the Republic.

Dr. Blyden has in the course of his labors been brought into contact—epistolary or personal—with some of the most remarkable literary men of his day. Among them may be mentioned Lord Brougham, Mr. Gladstone, Dean Stanley, Charles Dickens, Charles Sumner.

He seems from his earliest years to have had a central idea, a dominant conviction about the Negro and his country, which has, all along, guided and sustained him in his efforts. He believes his views to be true, and he is only gradually elaborating the exact method by which they may be brought home to others.

The following articles, though written at different times, will appear, when read carefully, to be linked together. They are not only the sentiments of a careful observer and diligent student, but they are the exponents of a purpose, the patriotic purpose of a lover of the race.—*Christianity, Islam and the Negro Race.*

Hon. John M. Langston, A.B., A.M., LL.D.

ONE of the greatest negroes in America is the subject of this sketch. He was born upon a plantation in Louisa county, Virginia, on the 14th of December, 1829. He was born in slavery, and takes the name of his mother. His father was his owner, and upon his death, John was set free and sent to Ohio where he grew up to manhood, receiving in the meantime a fine education, graduating at Oberlin College in 1849. He chose the law as a profession, and graduated in that department at Oberlin College in 1853. He was

HON. JOHN M. LANGSTON, A.B., A.M., LL.D.

elected clerk of the township of Russia in 1856; in 1857 he was elected City Councilman, and two years later he became one of the Board of Education of Oberlin. In 1867, through the influence of Hon. Salmon P. Chase, Chief-Justice of the Supreme Court, he was made inspector of the colored schools, and in July of this year he made a trip through the South, speaking at every prominent place. This same year he was admitted to practice in the United States Supreme Court. In 1869 he accepted a professorship in the Law Department of Howard University, Washington, D.C. He was dean of this department for several years, receiving in the meantime the degree of LL.D. He was appointed by President Grant a member of the Board of Health of the District of Columbia in 1871. In 1877 he was appointed minister to Hayti by President Hayes. Here he remained until July 1885, when he was elected President of the Virginia Normal and Collegiate Institute. This school was founded by the government in 1882, and "supported by popular appropriations of twenty thousand dollars annually." This duty he performed with credit to himself and his people until December 1887 when he resigned much to the regret of the students for all held him in the highest esteem. He was elected a member of the Fifty-first Congress to represent the people in the Fourth Congressional District of Virginia in 1888, the first and only colored representative in Congress from the "Old Dominion." Mr. Langston is among the most scholarly men of his race. He is a man of wealth and lives in luxurious style in his "Hillsdale Cottage" in Washington, D. C.

Hon. J. T. Settle, Memphis, Tenn.

JOSIAH T. SETTLE was born among the mountains of "East Tennessee," September 30, 1850, while his parents were "in transitee" from North Carolina to Mississippi. His father was Josiah Settle, of Rockingham County, North Carolina, his mother belonged to his father, who unlike many prominent slave holders of that period, had a deep and sincere affection for his children and their mother. After several years residence in Mississippi he manumitted the mother and her eight children according to the laws of the State. He feared, however, that their freedom even then,

HON. J. T. SETTLE,
Memphis, Tenn.

might not be secure, and in 1856 he moved the family to Ohio and located them at Hamilton. It was at this time the highest evidence of his Christian manhood and nobility of character were shown, when in the presence of his family and many prominent citizens of Hamilton he lawfully married the mother of his children, giving the children a legal right to their name and their mother a right to the sacred name of wife. Giving them all the tardy justice which the conditions of slavery had until then rendered impossible.

He spent his summers with his family in Ohio and the remainder of the year upon his Mississippi plantation until the war came on, when being a "Union man" he came North and remained with his family until his death in 1869 in the 70th year of his age, he having been born in 1799. Josiah T. Settle, the subject of this sketch, attended the public schools in Hamilton and vicinity until 1866, when his father sent him to Oberlin where he prepared for, and entered college in 1868. He was one of three or four colored boys in a class of forty or fifty, yet he was chosen as one of the eight class orators to represent the class when he entered college, an honor much sought by all students. He completed his Freshman year and entered the Sophomore Class at Oberlin. In 1869 having lost his father, who had indeed been a father to him in the broadest sense of the word, he left Oberlin and went to Washington City and entered the Sophomore Class of Howard University, where he pursued his college studies and taught in the preparatory department. During a portion of his "college course" he was a clerk in the Educational Division of the "Freedmen's Bureau." In the latter part of his Senior year he was elected Reading Clerk of the House of Delegates, (the District of Columbia then being under a territorial form of government).

He graduated from the College Department of Howard University in 1872 together with James M. Gregor, now professor, and A. C. O'Hear, theirs being the first class to graduate from that department. At the time of his graduation he was performing the duties of Reading Clerk of the Legislature, teaching a class in Latin and one in mathematics daily at the University and pursuing his own studies at the same time. Immediately upon his graduation from college he entered the law department of the same institution, then under the control of Hon. John M. Langston, from which he graduated in 1875.

While a citizen of the District of Columbia, Mr. Settle took an active part in politics and held many positions of honor and profit.

these generational challenges by returning to the source

ORDER FORM ORDER FORM ORDER FORM ORDER

Name _____
Address _____
City _____ State _____ Zip _____
Telephone ( ) _____ Fax ( ) _____

Rearing African Children Under American Occupation $7.95 per book. $1.50 Shipping and Handling + .50 each additional book. Inquire about bulk rates. Quantity ____

Family Matters $9.95 per book. $2.00 Shipping and Handling + 1.00 each additional book. Inquire about bulk rates. Quantity ____

** <u>MAKE CHECK OR MONEY ORDER PAYABLE TO: PREPARE OUR YOUTH</u>

Mail Order Form To:
Prepare Our Youth, Inc.
6856 Eastern Avenue NW Suite 207
Washington, D.C. 20012 (202) 291-5040 (202) 291-5042 Fax

Introducing
KWAME RONNIE VANDERHORST
A fresh, new author of creative, solution-oriented books for families

REARING AFRICAN CHILDREN UNDER AMERICAN OCCUPATION
and
FAMILY MATTERS: HOPE and HEALING

REARING AFRICAN CHILDREN UNDER AMERICAN OCCUPATION

"Rearing African Children Under American Occupation is a little handbook of the heart. Honor and respect are the passwords, and the author teaches parents of African descent that culture as well as charity begins at home. Brother Vanderhorst calls us back to the African village where the legacy of communal Black love kept our children safe and sound." - Dr. Gwendolyn Goldsby Grant, psychologist, author and advice columnist for Essence magazine.

FAMILY MATTERS: HOPE and HEALING

FAMILY MATTERS addresses those not-so-positive traits of character that

On July 9, 1873, he was appointed a clerk in the Board of Public Works of the District of Columbia at $1,200 a year by Governor A. R. Shepherd, which he held until some time in 1874 when the Board having ceased to exist, he was on August 29, 1874, appointed clerk in the "Board of Audit," a Board consisting of the first and second comptrollers of the United States Treasury, to adjust the indebtedness of the late Board of Public Works. He continued in this position until the Board had completed its work and expired by act of Congress. He was also trustee of the public schools of the District of Columbia, serving in that capacity several years.

During the presidential campaign of 1872 he canvassed several counties of Maryland and Virginia in the interest of the Republican ticket, where his youth and brilliancy created considerable attention; he also made speeches for the ticket in Ohio, speaking at Hamilton, Dayton, Cleveland and other places. Upon his graduation from the law department he was selected as one of the orators to represent his class. He was admitted to the bar of the Supreme Court of the District of Columbia, but having determined to practice his chosen profession in the South, he left Washington in the spring of 1875 and located in North Mississippi and at once began the practice of law. He returned, however, the same year and married the refined and cultured niece of Mr. J. C. Bishop, of Annapolis, Miss Therese T. Vogelsang, and again made his home in Mississippi. In August of the same year he was unanimously nominated by the Republican convention for the position of District Attorney of the then Twelfth Judicial District of Mississippi in which there was, at that time 2,000 Republican majority. The result of the elections in Mississippi in 1875 was a revolution in the politics of the South, and the virtual death of Republicanism in that part of the country. Mr. Settle was of course defeated with all the rest.

In 1876 he was one of the delegates from Mississippi to the National Republican Convention which met in Cincinnati. He was the only delegate from Mississippi who voted for the nomination of Roscoe Conkling for president, and continued to vote for him as long as his name was before the convention. This same year he was chosen one of the presidential electors for the State-at-large on the National Republican ticket, and made the canvass of his State for Hayes and Wheeler.

In 1880 he was presidential elector on the "Garfield and Arthur" ticket. In 1882 he was strongly urged to become a candidate for

Congress in the Second Congressional District of Mississippi, but in the convention declined the nomination and himself placed General James R. Chalmers in nomination. He was made chairman of the Republican Congressional Executive Committee, and made a thorough canvass of the district which resulted in the election of General Chalmers by a handsome majority.

In 1883 Mr. Settle was nominated and elected to the Mississippi Legislature. He was elected upon an independent ticket, being strongly opposed to the fusion his party made with the Democracy. It was during this canvass that he made the most brilliant efforts of his life. He was met by the ablest speakers of both of the old parties; but before the people he was irresistible and was triumphantly elected by more than 1,200 majority. Though elected upon an independent ticket, for local reasons he never swerved from his Republicanism, and was one of the recognized leaders of the Republican members of the Legislature. Though his party was in a hopeless minority in that body, his ability and genius were fully recognized, and upon the adjournment of the Legislature he was presented with a gold-headed cane as a token of the esteem in which he was held by his fellow members. The correspondent of the St. Louis Globe-Democrat writing from Jackson, Miss., Jan. 4, 1884, of the personnel of the Mississippi Legislature said of him:

"A colored orator—but the palm for natural ability as an orator—is borne by a colored man, J. T. Settle, of Panola County. He comes of the famous North Carolina family of that name, is well educated and a lawyer by profession. He is of spare figure, light of color and good looking. When he gets the floor he speaks in a manner to command the attention of the entire house."

Upon his return from the Legislature he determined to abandon active participation in politics and devote his time and energies to the practice of law, and left Mississippi and located in Memphis, Tenn. About two months after his location in Memphis his success in practice having won for him the respect and admiration of Gen. G. P. M. Turner, the Attorney General of the Criminal Court, he appointed him Assistant Attorney General, which position he held for more than two years. During this time he conducted the greater portion of the public prosecutions. The manner in which he discharged the responsible duties of prosecuting attorney is thus put in a letter written by the Hon. Addison H. Douglas, who was at that time upon the bench of the Criminal Court:

"It is at all times a pleasant duty to offer commendation to those whose exemplary professional deportment has been such as to challenge attention. This is peculiarly appropriate in reference to those who have had the good fortune to be admitted to practice in the courts of the country; for in that capacity, with all its surroundings, of contact and associations, a man more readily and certainly develops his true character than almost anywhere else. I am led to these observations in part by closely scrutinizing the general deportment of members of the bar, both from the bench and as an associate practitioner. A remarkable instance occurs to me at present in this connection in the character and conduct of J. T. Settle, Esq. He settled in Memphis about the year 1885, having recently served in the Legislature of the State of Mississippi, and shortly after locating in the practice in this city he was appointed Assistant Attorney General, which position he continued to fill two or three years with marked ability and fidelity. His uniform attention to official business, his manly courtesy and amiability won for him the esteem and respect of the bench, the bar and litigants, and went very far to break down the existing prejudices against his color in the profession. His talent is fully recognized, and his integrity has in no instance been in the least questioned from any source.

"He prosecuted without acerbity and with fairness, but neglected no legitimate resources to fix conviction upon the really guilty.

"He is such a master of elocution and displays such fluency and indeed brilliancy, that he invariably captivated those who listened to him.

"He is remarkably simple in his manners and utterly without ostentation, and an honor to his profession. Respectfully,

"A. H. DOUGLAS."

In the spring of 1888 Mr. Settle lost by death his devoted wife, who had indeed been a helpmate to him in every sense of the word. She left him no children, their only child, a little girl, having died years before in infancy.

This same year he was made a member of the Republican State Executive Committee of Tennessee and served continuously for six years. In 1892 he was a delegate to the Republican National Convention at Minneapolis.

Though Mr. Settle takes some part and interest in politics, such as he believes the interests of his race demand, he is by no means

Residence of Hon. J. T. SETTLE, Memphis, Tenn.

what may be called a politician, and seeks no political preferment. He prefers to devote his entire time and energies to his profession and by his success demonstrates the capacity of his race to successfully measure arms with the Anglo-Saxon in the professional walks of life. Mr. Settle's course at the bar demonstrates the fact that it is possible for a colored American to succeed in the practice of law, if he will thoroughly prepare himself for his professional work and then give it his whole time and energy. He enjoys the confidence and esteem of the entire bench and bar; his practice is large and lucrative, and he is rapidly accumulating a competency. He is now in easy circumstances.

In 1890 he married Miss Fannie A. McCullough, one of the most beautiful and accomplished ladies in Memphis. She was distinguished for her superior vocal qualities, and at the time of her marriage had charge of the musical department of LeMoyne Institute. This position she resigned upon her marriage. Mr. Settle owns a beautiful house in one of the most desirable localities in Memphis where their friends always find a cordial welcome. Their marriage has been blessed by two extremely intelligent and handsome boys, Josiah T. Settle, Jr. and Frances McCullough Settle, both of whom give great promise for the future. This man's life, thus far, demonstrates what the colored American can do, and is doing in the South.

COLORED BAR ASSOCIATION.

[An address of the Hon. J. T. Settle, delivered at Greenville, Miss. Some stirring, new and novel thoughts advanced by an eloquent Memphis lawyer before the first State Bar meeting of his race held in the South.]

GENTLEMEN of the Colored Bar Association of Mississippi, I have listened with pleasure and profit to your excellent addresses on different legal topics, and I can pay you no higher compliment than to say you are an honor to the profession. I look upon this meeting as the dawn of a new era in the history of our race. It is no new thing for us to meet and participate in the public assemblages of men; in fact one of the misfortunes of our people has been a too great love for meetings and conventions of every kind, out of which little if any permanent good has ever accrued to us. The emotional side of our nature has ever been so easily reached that we have been too often used as instruments in the hands of others in promoting their own selfish ends.

This organization, of which this is the first annual meeting, marks the advent of the colored citizen into a new field of labor. It evidences the existence of a sufficient number of colored lawyers in Mississippi engaged in active practice of the law to form a State organization to promote their interests individually and collectively and in doing this they cannot fail to promote the interests of the entire race and to contribute to the general welfare of our common country, for we are as much a part of our composite nationality as any element it contains. It is no new thing for the residents of this beautiful delta to see gatherings of colored men. Politics and religion have given us conventions and conferences at short intervals until some have come to believe that we take to them as naturally as birds to the air and fishes to the sea. But whoever thought that here in this beautiful city—queen of the valley—beside this great inland sea, would meet the first colored bar association ever organized in the United States? And I think I may safely say that never in the history of the race has there been a meeting fraught with more significance. It shows that the various and trying ordeals through which we have passed during the last fifteen or twenty years in this beautiful southland, have envolved a class of men—educated, thoughtful and conservative—indeed, men who are alive to the present and prepared to meet the demands of the future.

To be members of this "Bar Association," you must be members of the bar of Mississippi, and this means a great deal; it means that you bear the great seal of the State to a good moral character, and to your possession of sufficient learning in the law to be admitted into the professional brotherhood of her greatest sons, and no State in this beautiful galaxy of States can point with greater pride to her bar than our own beloved Mississippi. Among jurists and advocates, her Sharkey and her Prentiss have few equals, and no superiors, and a long list of those who have emulated their greatness has distinguished Mississippi in the highest courts of our country and of the national legislature. Each member of this association has subscribed to the same oath and presented the same qualifications as were required of Sharkey and Prentiss, of Walthall and George. We are all equals in the world of intellect; though some of us may be small and some great, here there are no distinctions of race or color; circumstances may control the use of our attainments, but our acquisitions of learning are only circumscribed by the limitation which Deity placed upon our minds in the hour of our creation. Most of us here have spent many years in the practice of our chosen profession, many of us began the practice under adverse circumstances; none of us probably had fathers or kinsmen in the profession who could take us into their offices and induct us into the practice; then there were few if any members of the race old enough in the profession to render us much if any material assistance.

Many of our friends and all of our enemies discouraged us by saying that this was the one profession in which we could not hope to succeed. We have been compelled to realize that we are the representatives of that race which has labored in mental and physical servitude and suffered from political and social degradation since the planting of civilization on this continent. We realized in the beginning that the undertaking to become practical lawyers, and to acquire such a mastery of the law as to enter favorably upon its practice, was a serious one and doubly so to us.

We have met unreasoning prejudice which denied us excellence of any kind—which declared that we were without intellectual vigor and inventive power, and destitute of strength to grasp, and persistency to retain and master any complex and profound proposition. In many instances we have commenced our trial before a jury whose pre-formed judgment would disqualify them from sitting in any other case. We have often found, not our client, but ourselves on trial, and not ourselves alone, but the whole race with us—a race which is condemned for the failure of its individuals, while the success of every member of it is pronounced exceptional and due to incidental conditions.

We have made good soldiers and successful teachers, we have produced some great preachers and distinguished speakers, and this meeting demonstrates the fact that we are equal to the hard, tough and long-continued struggles of the bar, in some respects the severest test that can be applied to a man; and yet the world may be slow to admit our success until, perhaps, we have produced an attorney-general or a justice of the supreme court. We have met these and many other trying difficulties. Most of us here began our professional career alone and unaided, and such success as we have won has come, as come it will, through years of diligent application and earnest endeavor. We find many obstacles in our professional paths, but they are not insurmountable; they are rather crucibles into which we have been placed where the dross is purged away and the best elements of professional manhood refined and elevated.

I do not mean to say that every young man of color who has begun the practice of the law has succeeded; no, not by any means. Nor is this true of the young men of any race, for along life's highway, in all of the professions, are many wrecks which mark the weakness and frailty of human character; and here I think I may safely say that one of the principal causes of failure in the legal profession is the want of sufficient preparation. Some persons unwisely think that all that is necessary to constitute a successful lawyer is an oily tongue, a vivid imagination and a great capacity to lie; in fact some people profess to think lawyer and liar synonymous terms. Such persons, it is needless for me to say, know but little of the law and still less of the lawyer. They forget, or do not know, that the contests of lawyers are not "ex parte." They confront each other before learned and astute courts and in the presence of the world, where lies and frauds have the least possible chance of success and where exposure would usually prove fatal to a cause.

No lawyer can build a splendid professional career upon an insufficient education any more than he can build a monument of stone upon a foundation of sand. I do not mean to say a collegiate education is absolutely necessary to a successful career, but it is a great help. Few men ever reached distinction in the law who were not thorough scholars. Many also fail who are well equipped intellectually because they depend upon the oily tongue and vivid imagination rather than real earnest work. I know that there are many prejudices against our profession. It has been said that it is full of pettifoggers, who pervert the law to purposes of trickery; with quacks, who sacrifice their clients through ignorance, and with hungry hangers-on, who are continually stirring up law-suits. It is also said that lawyers delight in tricks and chicanery, that they will argue as strenuously for the wrong as the right, for the guilty as well as the innocent, and hire out their conscience as well as their ability to any one who is willing to pay a fee. I, for one, am ready to admit, to some extent, this truth. Ours, above almost any other profession, abounds with opportunities and temptations to abuse its high functions, and it would be strange indeed if it had not some, nay many unworthy members.

We see many unworthy members of other professions, and therefore take no particular shame to ourselves that some are found in ours. We also take refuge behind the maxim that the supply simply meets the demand. Were there no dishonest clients there would be no dishonest lawyers. Our profession, therefore, does but adapt itself to the community in which it is exercised. Blackstone says "that the law employs in its theory the noblest faculties of the soul," and further he declares "that it exercises in its practice the cardinal virtues of the heart." Let no man make the fatal mistake of entering our profession as a sinecure, for lawyers dearly earn all they obtain, whether of honor or emoluments. Genius may sometimes distinguish a man in some other walk of life, but not here. Here he must toil unceasingly; here there can be no drones; here no fertile imagination can supply the place of patient investigation. A well-balanced mind might easily suggest what the law ought to be, but actual investigation alone must determine what the law is.

An eminent jurist addressing a class of law students once said: "Let those who would prepare themselves for untying the knots and solving the problems of jurisprudence first of all make up their minds to hard work. Let them weigh well the fact that to scorn delights and live laborious days is the indispensable condition of professional eminence; on somewhat easier terms they may prepare themselves to prowl in courts of law for human prey, but nothing short of resolute, emulous study can raise him to that height which alone should satisfy a generous ambition."

When we examine for a moment the popular impressions against lawyers they resolve themselves into popular delusions. The law rightly practiced is one of the noblest professions that can command our time and employ our faculties. Its effects upon the mind and soul of the practitioner are at once to enlarge and exalt, whatever the world may say or think. Its practice calls into constant exercise his best qualities of intellect, and familiarizes him with the use only of the most honorable means, while as a result of his contests in the presence of the world, those contests are necessarily of the most honorable, and often of the most chivalrous character. As one consequence there is almost a total absence of feuds, animosities and jealousies among the members of the profession, and few tales or slanders concerning its practitioners find inventors or bearers in the atmosphere of the law.

The rule of absolute integrity is the rule of the first-class lawyer, and he may (as he frequently is) be entrusted with the dearest possessions, and the most sacred of human confidences, with the certainty that good faith will govern his entire conduct in the discharge of all his duties. The practice of the law enlarges and strengthens all the faculties of the mind, and naturally leads to various attainments. The constant dealing with the business and affairs of men makes him an adept and expert in all the varied branches of industry and enterprises. His habit and business of advising in difficult and complex transactions makes him a cautious, safe, and skillful counselor. His constant intercourse with men renders him a master of human nature, the working and weaknesses of the human heart, the play of human passions, and the springs and motives of human conduct. He sees rather the worst of men, and would grow cynical and misanthropic, if he was not constantly surrounded with the illustrations and manifestations of man's better qualities in the persons of his professional friends. His habit of investigating everything and of taking things only on proof, makes him incredulous, and hence he is seldom imposed upon and is never visionary. His love and veneration for the law render him somewhat conservative, while his skill and ability as a public speaker—a real power in a free community—always attract to him the popular admiration, and open to him the highest position his ambition may covet.

The successful lawyer unites in his person more of the elements of a popular leader than are usually found in another, and necessarily the members of the bar, although numerically smaller than any other trade, calling or profession, can, and usually do, directly exercise a larger influence among a given people than any other, and by concert could do much to control its affairs and shape its destinies, and it is certainly no discredit to them that the aggregate of his power and influence has always been exercised to promote and build up those institutions that advance civilization, extend the field of human effort, encourage education, promote science and the arts, purify the morals, extend the franchises of the citizen, protect virtue and secure religious toleration.

The bar has necessarily exercised the whole judicial power of this country. It has furnished the controlling influence in its varied legislation, and contributed out of all proportion to the executive officers. In the main this influence has been enlightened, liberal and patriotic; and in no instance has it attempted to advance its own interests as distinguished from the masses of our people.

This, gentlemen, is a subdued and colorless sketch of our profession from the modest standpoint of one of its humble members. The law, as a profession, comes to us with the commendations of a remote antiquity. Sages have heaped upon it lofty panegyrics. It has been said not only to embody "the gathered wisdom of a thousand years," but also in sober truth "the perfection of human wisdom;" and he who would win her favors must consecrate himself to her and to her alone, for she is indeed a jealous mistress, and never flirts or coquettes. She will have nothing to do with the danglers, and reserves her favors for those who woo in good faith and with the most honorable intentions. And here I trust you will pardon me if, from practical observation, I refer briefly to some of the elements of character absolutely necessary to every lawyer who would succeed. In this, above all other professions, is honesty the most essential element to a successful career. He who begins his practice with the idea that anything is permissible by which he can secure a fee, may as well stop among the sharks and pettifoggers, for he will never rise above them. No profession demands of its members a higher standard of honesty and integrity, and no man ever became a great or moderately successful lawyer who was not an honest and upright man. Yet honesty is one of the first elements of character which ambition is likely to overthrow; to sophisticate the truth for any purpose in the practice, breeds rottenness at the foundation of all personal power. Sooner or later the career based on dishonesty will crumble and fall. Nature is against dishonesty. God is against it. All the conservative and restorative forces of society are against it; it vitiates all the currents of power that flow out of it. The history of this country is full of instruction on this point. Memory does not have to reach far back to recall a list of eminent men who built themselves up by honest endeavor into positions of great personal power and lost such positions by intrigues and compromises into which they were tempted by the desire of place and power.

A great man turned demagogue presents the pitiable spectacle of a Samson shorne of his locks. Will is another element which cannot be overestimated. No man can be called a strong man who is not strong of will. Will may indeed be called the backbone of power, into which all the other elements of character articulate, and to no character is this element more essential than to the lawyer. The will power of Martin Luther was the most potent factor in the reformation of the sixteenth century. It was the indomitable will of Stanley that revealed the secrets of the "dark continent," and gave to mankind a new world to Christianize. When Disraeli, afterward Lord Beaconsfield, attempted to make his first speech he was openly laughed down; he turned, and shaking his fist in the face of his revilers, hissed in their teeth that the time would come when they should hear him, and the influence of this wonderful man upon the history of Europe does but show how powerful was his will.

Will has the same office in every walk of life. It may indeed be called a spark struck from Divine might. So long as it flows through honest channels there is nothing more truly divine. Willfulness is not will, it is simply a form of obstinacy. Will is positive and projects a current of vital force, which we break up into words or shape into actions. No weak, easy-going, yielding, good-natured man ever succeeded at the bar, and never will. Courage, moral and physical, are both necessary elements of character. It is the especial privilege of a lawyer never to give up a case. Lord Erskine, confessedly the first of English advocates, had not the courage to defend Hastings, and absolutely failed in the House of Commons through fear of Pitt. It is said that Cicero lost the case of Milo for the want of nerve; he had not the courage to deliver his argument in the spirit in which it was prepared, and Milo in exile said that if it had been pronounced with courage he had not been banished.

There is probably no element of character that inspires so much admiration and creates so quick and enthusistic a following as this. A man who is afraid of nothing in the discharge of his duty, afraid of no consequence personal to himself, has his battle half won before he strikes a blow. So great is the popular admiration of courage that it has always been surrounded by a halo of romance.

In the common thought the test of courage is the test of manhood. In multitudes of minds there is no unpardonable sin but that of cowardice. The truth is that he who plants courage of any kind raises friends. Earnestness and enthusiasm are also so essential that I cannot refrain from mentioning them in this connection. I name them together because they are so nearly akin; indeed, enthusiasm is only earnestness carried to white heat; they are the only qualities that can take the place of personal magnetism in compelling sympathy. Earnestness comes from strong conviction and strong feeling; enthusiasm rising out of it is the fusion and sublimation of all the elements of power within a man, and is strong in proportion as it is rational; the moment it becomes mere passion it becomes weakness.

The world refuses to be moved by men who are not in earnest. Human nature is very much like iron—if you would bend it or shape it you must heat it. Earnestness is the furnace; enthusiasm the fire whose flames need only to envelop other minds to make plastic or ductile. Truth is often unpalatable and offensive, but borne in the menstrum of a strong enthusiasm, we accept the draught which would otherwise have been refused. These are some of the elements of character most essential to success in any sphere of life, but especially so to those of us who are engaged in the practice of the law. Coming, as you do, from every part of the state, you are indeed a representative body of men. You represent the intellectual and moral worth of the race, which has survived the political revolutions which have swept over the state during the past few years.

We have learned in the hard school of adversity that we are not the wards of any political body; that the improvement of our condition in life is not the solicitude of any particular section of our country, and that the days of our political bosses are over forever; that we are the architects of our own fortunes and the arbiters of our own destinies. That with the various walks of life thrown open to us we are to enter and win victories or defeats upon equal conditions with every other race or condition of people.

We are citizens of this country by nativity, not by choice or adoption, and here, under God's providence, we mean to stay, and strike glad hands with all lovers of justice, work out our own destinies and vie with every other nationality in developing the material resources and contributing to the greatness of our beloved southland. Agitators may discuss the so-called race problem, but in the busy, active duties of life we have no time for theories. We should prepare ourselves by every energy of mind and soul to solve the problem put to us by those by whom we are surrounded, and with whom we live, viz.: "The survival of the fittest." Citizens by nativity, we have no other land to love. To this we have given our labor for more than 100 years; in defense of her flag we have given our lives; to sustain her integrity we have contributed whatever was demanded of us. At all times have we been faithful and reliable.

We have never been numbered among our country's enemies. We have never been found in the ranks of the Socialists and Anarchists in their attacks upon social order and our free institutions. Yet we have lived under a condition of things at times unequaled in the history of civilized government. We see the political party to which we have given a blind devotion for a quarter of a century growing tired of our allegiance. We see our rights in Mississippi, together with those of some of our unfortunate white fellow-citizens, diminished and taken away. I must confess these are not incentives to awaken sentiments of "armor patriae" in our hearts. Though sometimes discouraged we are not despondent, and behind the clouds that overhang our horizon we think we can see the silver lining, and challenge any race or condition of American citizenship to a greater love of country.

Erin's sons were never truer to the Emerald Isle, nor the Highlander to Scotland's cliffs and crags than we to the land of our birth. What member of any race ever gave expression to loftier sentiments of patriotism in the American Congress than the distinguished lawyer and scholar, Hon. John M. Langston, of Virginia, when from his seat in that august body he said: "Ah, my white fellow citizens on the other side of the house, and on every side, black as we are, no man shall go ahead of us in devotion to this country, in devotion to its free institutions, for we hold our lives, our property and our sacred honor in pledge to the welfare of our country and of all our fellow citizens. Do you want us to fight for your flag? Call on us and we will come. Do you want men to tarry at home and take care of your wives and children, to take care of your homes and protect your interests? Call on us and we will sacredly keep and perform every trust and obligation." Every member of the race echoes these sentiments, and in the years to come, when man's passions and prejudices have subsided, impartial history will give to no race a prouder place in their country's history than we shall possess, and no race or condition of people will be prompted by a purer or loftier patriotism than we, in our efforts to make our beloved South the home of a happy, prosperous and contented people.

Dr. Robert Fulton Boyd.

THE subject of this sketch was born on a farm in Giles County, Tennessee, where his early boyhood days were spent. His mother was taken from him before the time for weaning and he never lived with her very much from that till he was nearly grown, and yet he has always been a most devoted son. When the great civil war broke out his mother was carried South and there remained till 1866, when she returned to Giles County and carried her two children, the oldest of which was Dr. Boyd, to Nashville. At the age of eight years he went to live with Dr. Paul F. Eve, one of the greatest surgeons of his day. It was there that our hero first conceived the idea of making a physician of himself. While living with Dr. Eve he attended night school at the old Fisk School, now Fisk University, where he learned to spell and read in McGuffey's First Reader. In 1868 he was put to work on a farm in Giles County. Here he worked till 1871 when he returned to Nashville and began to work at the brick trade. He had not yet learned to write and knew but the elements of reading. His soul was kindled with the hope of an education. His ambition was aroused so in 1872 he hired himself to General James H. Hickman, a real estate agent, to work half the day for something to eat, and he attended school the other half. He kept up this contract with General Hickman for three years, at the end of which he was doing all the outside collections and doing the entire bookkeeping of the office. The General never paid him any money during this time, but when he found that the Doctor meant to quit he offered him $20, $30 and $50 per month to stay and do the same work that he had been doing for his meals. But our hero had

DR. ROBERT FULTON BOYD.
Nashville, Tenn.

higher ambition and more lofty aspirations. He left General Hickman in the early summer of 1875 and entered upon the profession of school teaching at College Grove, Williamson County, Tennessee. His soul was in the work and he impressed the people with his earnest, energetic, conscientious spirit. At the close of a most successful term here, he returned to his studies at the Central Tennessee College. In the summer of 1876 he went to Giles County and began teaching. Here he gradually rose from the country schools to the principalship of the male school of 170 boys in Pulaski. In 1878 and 1879 he was principal of the female department of the public schools in Pulaski. In 1880 he entered Meharry Medical Department of the Central Tennessee College, where he graduated with the first honors of his class in 1882. After graduating the Doctor went to New Albany, Mississippi, where he took the principalship of a high school and practiced medicine till the fall of '82, when he returned to Nashville and was made adjunct professor of chemistry in his *Alma Mater*. He entered upon his work at Meharry and at the same time he entered the College Department of the Central Tennessee College from which he graduated with honors in May 1886. From 1884 to 1888 he was professor of physiology in Meharry. He graduated from the Dental Department of this college in 1887. In 1888 and 1889 he was professor of anatomy and physiology in Meharry. In the summer of 1890 he took a post course in the Post-Graduate School of Medicine at Chicago, and in the summer of 1892 he took a special course in the same school on the diseases of women and children. While in Chicago he did work in all of the big hospitals there under some of the greatest men of the profession. While connected with the Central Tennessee College as a student he taught in the various departments of the school, and was during the whole time professor of hygiene and physiology. In June 1887 he entered upon the practice of his profession in Nashville, Tennessee. He did not ask nor expect the better classes who were able to employ experienced and well known physicians to patronize him; but he went into the alleys, old cellars, dilapidated stables and unhygienic sections of the city. Under his treatment nearly every case got well and the incurables were greatly benefitted. His success was unparalelled. In all difficult cases he freely sought the consultation and advice of the physicians and surgeons of high standing.

His work has steadily grown in quantity and quality till it is second in importance to that of no physician in the city. Really he does more work than any other physician in Nashville. He goes to the homes of high and low. He goes in the parlors and lowest tenement houses. Whether there is money in the visit or not he goes. He boasts that he has never denied any person his professional services. He is a blessing to the people of Nashville and they realize it. The people there know him well, love him, trust him and honor him, as is demonstrated by the fact that in 1891, they nominated and ran him on the Republican ticket for the General Assembly. In 1892, when both the Democratic and Republican Executive Committees refused to allow colored men to have a say in nominating candidates for Mayor and City Council, the colored citizens met in convention and put out a full city ticket, at the head of which for Mayor was Dr. Boyd. A great many whites were in sympathy with the colored people and voted for this ticket. Colored voters rallied around the ticket to a man, and by so doing forever wiped out the color line in Nashville politics. In May, 1891, his *alma mater* conferred upon him the degree of A.M. For the years 1889 and '90, he was professor of physiology and hygiene. For the years 1890 to 1893 he was professor of physiology, hygiene and clinical medicine. Since 1893 he has been professor of the diseases of women and clinical medicine. He is at the head of the college hospital and gives two hours free to the sick and indigent poor every Wednesday, Friday and Saturday during the college year. Hundreds attend his free clinic and are helped, benefitted and cured of all kinds of maladies. While the Doctor does a larger charity and benevolent practice, yet he does a good paying practice. He has made money right along and invested it wisely. He owns several pieces of good property among which is a magnificent three-story double brick on a corner opposite the Duncan House, one of the largest and most popular hotels in the city.

His office, library and instruments will compare favorably with those of our most wealthy physicians and surgeons. His horses and vehicles are of the best. Dr. Boyd is a typical example of what a young man can be in spite of the greatest oppositions. He is a hard worker and uses all of his power to elevate the race and bless mankind. He is at present one of the Tennessee commissioners for the Southern States and International Exposition at Atlanta, Ga.

Residence of Dr. R. F. Boyd, Nashville, Tenn.

THE MORTALITY OF THE COLORED PEOPLE AND HOW TO REDUCE IT.

[Read before the Tennessee State Convention of Colored Teachers, held at Nashville, Tenn., June 11-14, 1895.]

A GREAT deal has been said and written about the great mortality of the colored people in the South, especially in the large cities. The statistics are alarming, so much so that the less thoughtful are expecting the race to become extinct. And why not, since the actual figures show that we die three and four times as fast as we are born in large cities of the South? What is the cause and how can it be diminished? There is no longer any doubt in the minds of physicians and the well-informed laity as to the cause of disease and the real possibility of reducing the mortality of a community and thereby prolong life. Under hygienic rules and regulations the health can be improved and the cause of disease entirely removed. The profession formerly understood and defined hygiene as the art of preserving the health; but under modern investigation it is made to increase as well as to preserve the health. The term applies to the place as well as to the people who live in it. We now go further than this, for we include under hygiene the examination of the conditions which affect generation, development, growth and decay of individuals, nations and races. On its scientific side it is co-extensive with biology, the science of life. It includes both sociology and physiology and whatever can cause or help to cause discomfort, pain, sickness, death, vice or crime. And whatever has a tendency to avert, destroy or diminish such causes are matters of interest to all who are interested in our subject. The old belief that disease and death are due to a special providence or the vengeance of an offended deity still lingers in the minds of many with regard to the great epidemics; but to the more intelligent cause and effect do not thus seem. Some would attribute all disease to vice For this there is an apparent reason, but a deep investigation will convince us of their mistake. Vice and disease are close, their relations are very close, yet each has its separate origin; and in each the public is equally interested. Every city and well-organized community are being awakened from their stolid indifference of centuries to a sense of the importance of hygiene; and well they might for all the powers moral, intellectual and physical depend upon a proper knowledge and an obedience to the laws of hygiene—the fundamental principle of all efforts to improve and preserve the health. For man is an organized being just as subject to organic laws as the inanimate bodies which surround him are subject to mechanical and chemical laws, and we as little escape the consequences of neglect or violation of those natural laws which effect organic life through the air we breathe, the food we eat, the clothes we wear, the exercise we take and the circumstances surrounding our habitation, as a stone projected from the hand or a shot from the mouth of a cannon can place itself beyond the bounds of gravitation.

A proposition well established by an extensive observation of facts is that a human, supposing him to be soundly constituted at first, will continue in good health till he reaches old age, provided certain conditions are observed, strict hygienic rules, and no injurious accident shall befall. At what age he will die we cannot say. There has been much speculation as to the natural term of man's life. Physiologists have fixed it at a hundred years, which is nearly in accordance with the law indicated by Florens. He states that the period of the life of an animal is five times that required to develop perfectly the skeleton. At present the actual duration of life is less than half this time. But there is satisfactory evidence that it can be increased in civilized countries under hygienic rules and regulations. The ancient estimate of the duration of life is expressed in David's declaration that "the days of man are three-score years and ten, and if by reason of strength they be four-score years, yet is there strength, labor and sorrow."

Kolb, a careful and reliable statistician of our times says that the maximum age reached by man has not changed in many centuries, but the number of persons who now survive infancy, and those who reach ripe old age under hygienic laws and regulations has decidedly increased, and this opinion is sustained and concurred in by Mr. Lewis, the secretary of the chamber of life insurance of New York City. He points out while civilization largely interferes with the laws of evolution by survivorship, it aids by encouraging the waste which occurs in its absence. He says under natural selection when variation in capacity arises, thousands of them are wasted. While we have no record of the duration of life in Ancient Greece and Rome, it is quite possible that it was greater than in Western Europe during the middle ages which formed a period of retrocession from a sanitary view. The early Jews and the ancient Romans were clean in their person and dwellings, they undoubtedly had a much smaller degree of mortality than the people at the time when dirt became the odor of sanctity. It is impossible for me to speak truth certainly of the vote of mortality of the ancients because statistics are not at our command. But I can and do speak of the good results of modern hygienic rules and sanitary regulations. When properly observed, they increase the longevity of life, decrease the mortality and bring greater health, comfort and happiness to the individual and the community at large. Then if we would preserve for ourselves and the community in which we live what is justly esteemed the greatest earthly blessing, good health, and live out the naturally appointed time, we must observe ten essential rules:

1. A constant supply of pure air.
2. Cleanliness of the person and of the surroundings.
3. A sufficiency of nourishing food properly taken.
4. A sufficiency of exercise to the various organs and the system.
5. The proper amount of rest and sleep.
6. Right temperature.
7. Proper clothing.
8. Sufficiency of cheerful and innocent enjoyment.
9. Exemption from harassing cares.
10. The proper habitation.

If individuals and communities will conform strictly to these rules all avoidable diseases would be completely annihilated and epidemics would be unknown. The physicians would then be employed to prevent rather than to cure. On the other hand wherever hygienic and sanitary science is not enforced, filth, decaying and putrifying matters are sure to accumulate. These are the suitable material for the propagation, generation and development of the disease germs, bacteria micrococci, micro-organism spores, microzomes, etc., which are the cause of all communicable, contagious and epidemic diseases. These germs all have the power of self-propagation in unhygienic surroundings in warm climates such as we have in Southern cities.

A population under the influence of filth, poorly housed in crowded dwellings or low, damp localities, where no rules regulate the habits of eating, drinking, sleeping and exercise, the mortality is sure to be great. Under these conditions infectious diseases spread, become epidemic and stalk through the land carrying death and destruction. I need not tell you that the greater part of the sickness and mortality of the human race are due to these causes, due to the epidemics, and yet these diseases are all avoidable. They can be stamped out by personal efforts. We have a thorough knowledge of how to prevent most of the diseases that enter the body through the respiratory, digestive, cutaneous, circulatory, nervous and genito-urinary system, and yet they are frequent and their effect is great. Now if what I have stated is true, and it is, not only do health and longevity depend upon laws which we can understand and successfully operate, but man has in his power to modify to a great extent the circumstances in which he lives, with a view to the promotion of his wellbeing and preservation. Everybody knows that the draining of a marsh pond banishes malaria, a change from city to the country reinvigorates, and those who live in the high, well-drained portion of a city have the smallest degree of mortality; and that the greater comforts possessed by the rich and affluent secure them longer life than the poor. To diminish the mortality of our race will depend both upon our individual efforts, as well as upon the public measures of the legally constituted authorities. We must begin in the homes. The dwellings of our people must be improved. The old dilapidated stables in the narrow filthy alleys are not fit for human habitation. The low, damp, dark basements and cellars often beneath the level of the ground with insufficiency of both light and air are occupied by our people. The cluster of homes built in the bottoms and low places, the closely pent up, back to back, so built as to cut off and prevent free ventilation, with only one entrance to each and a privy in the centre, the dirty neglected portions of the cities where heaps of rubbish, animal and vegetable matter, are allowed to decay and send their poisonous odors from house to house are the habitations of colored people. And to add to the woful condition of things, these uninhabitable quarters are over crowded. I don't think I miss it far when I say that one third of the colored people in our Southern cities live in just such dwellings as I have here described, while most of the white population live in well built houses in the healthy portions of the cities. Then is there any surprise that there should be a great disproportion in the mortality of the two races? Do you wonder that the colored people die so fast? Suppose we add to the disgraceful inhumane dwellings of our people the quality of food they eat, you will have more light on the mortality of the race. As you know our people are the working classes in the South; they go to the markets Saturday nights and buy the spoiled meats and vegetables on which the flies and smaller insects have preyed all day. In these vegetables are the seed of indigestion disorders and death. The vegetables and meats which are left over and not sold in the market and grocery houses are put in wagons and driven to the colored settlements where they are sold cheap for cash. Do you wonder that the death rate of the colored people is so great? If the white people were similarly situated would their death rate be as it is to-day? Compare the statistics of all the large cities of the North and of Europe and you will find that under similar circumstances this same disproportion exists between the upper and lower classes where the dwellings and food have the same difference. But this same difference exists nowhere else in the world as it does here in our own Southland. In most of the Southern cities it is impossible for a colored man to rent a first-class uptown building, no matter how much money he has, and in many places not even a respectable dwelling can be rented. But the low, dark, damp, confined, ill-ventilated cellars, basements and alley houses are rented to colored people for as much as good comfortable quarters ought to bring. I assert without fear of a successful contradiction that any other race of people situated as the colored people are in the South would be exterminated in twenty years.

In his last annual report Dr. N. G. Tucker, the efficient health officer of Nashville, states that the entire number of white people who died during the year 1893 was 786, and of colored people 839. He says in his report, "As usual the death rate among the colored people exceeds that of the white. If we were to consider alone the death rate of our white population the exhibit would be an exceedingly favorable one for our city." The good doctor gives facts; but he does not tell the city why the death rate of the colored people is so great, nor does he give a remedy for it. Of course the sanitary measures which he recommends are for the good of all; but the key that will unlock the mystery of high death rate among the colored people is to better their condition, improve their habitation, enact and enforce laws against allowing people to sleep in the basements, cellars, old stables, alley houses and pent up cluster houses in low malarial sections of our Southern cities.

Make the penalty against landlords so heavy that they will not rent such places for dwellings. Regulate the kind of tenement houses to be rented and the number of persons who shall sleep in one room. Enforce the laws against selling tainted meats and decaying vegetables to the poor. Break up these late church meetings in poorly ventilated houses. Prohibit the collection of large numbers of persons in the dens where dancing and whisky drinking are indulged in till the wee hours of morning and the mystery will be solved. By the proper legislation and enforcement of laws we will have prevention. The whole system of medicine is now turning upon prevention rather than the cure of disease. The time has come when physicians must be employed to prevent as well as to cure. If this is done there will be less sickness, and epidemics will be a thing of the past. Then sanitary science under strict hygienic observance will reach perfection. The rude, careless and gross habits of living will be corrected and a system of perfect drainage and pure ventilation will be inaugurated. The pure air and a good water supply will be furnished to every public and private house. Then, only pure and unadulterated foods will be allowed in our markets and grocery houses. Every hotel, private and public boarding house will furnish properly prepared foods, and universal cleanliness will be the law, and the death rate among our people would reach its minimum.

To reduce the mortality of the race we must begin with the new born. The death rate of colored infants in the cities and towns is alarming. More than half of the children born in the cities die before the third year, and about one half of the remainder die before the twelfth year. Of course the circumstances and condition of the parents affect the children and greatly increase their mortality, but still a greater part of it comes from the ignorance of those who handle the mothers and their infants. The ignorant grannies and meddling old women are very largely responsible for the death rate of colored children. None but trained nurses and educated mid-wives under the direction of a physician should handle mothers and their infants.

The infant mortality will be reduced at least one half when our people learn that the care of a good, well-informed, conscientious physician is necessary from generation and development through the entire stage of adolescence, not so much to look after the sick but to prevent disease.

Another most potent remedy for diminishing the mortality of the colored people in the large cities of the South is the establishment of hospitals in which the members of the churches and various societies can be treated and have the constant care of trained nurses. The churches and societies with the benevolently disposed people could easily support a hospital in every city. The hospitals would afford an opening for our young women to become trained nurses, and whether they give their services to the public or use their training in the schools, they would be a blessing to the race and the country in which we live. The good physicians everywhere would lend their aid and give their services to these hospitals. Meharry Medical College would furnish interns whose services would be given free of charge, and the good people everywhere help. The mortality of the colored people must be diminished. Let us all turn our attention to this particular work of urging upon the people better homes, better food, better clothing and better habits of living. Let us urge upon law makers to pass such laws as will help us in our efforts and the call upon the legally-constituted authorities to enforce them. If we will all do our duty a change will soon come, and we will prove to the world that under proper hygienic laws the colored people will die no faster than other peoples; but, on the other hand, where all things are equal, they will live longer.

The Colored Man in Medicine.

[Delivered by L. T. Burbridge, M.D., at New Iberia, La., January 1, 1895, at Emancipation exercises.]

HAD I been called upon to select a subject upon which to address you on this occasion, I doubt my ability to select one more appropriate to my thoughts and feelings, and more suitable to this audience and this occasion than the one given me by its promoters, viz.: The Colored Man in Medicine. Although I am as yet but a young disciple of the healing art, I believe in common with most young practitioners who have had ample leisure to reflect upon the hopes and possibilities of the medical profession so far as the colored man is concerned there is for him a bright and promising future. I, therefore, thank you for the privilege of addressing you on this subject and on such an auspicious occasion, an occasion (if you will allow me to say) when the heart of every true and loyal colored man should turn in thankfulness to God for his great deliverance from the greatest curse that ever afflicted any Christianized people. Thank God we to-day are living under entirely different circumstances to those existing previous to the time this day is intended to commemorate. Under the blessings of freedom we enjoy a purer air, a more lofty existence than before, and the sunlight of peace, prosperity and intellectual growth is shedding softened rays upon our pathway, lighting up the darker places and beckoning us on to a future as bright and promising as any ever enjoyed by any other people. May it shine more and more unto the pefect day.

Having been so recently released from bondage, burdened with all the ignorance and superstition which that state implies, it would appear that the colored man had had short time in which to prepare himself for the learned professions. Not so however. With his characteristic power of imitation, and his readiness to adapt himself to the study of scientific medicine with the same zeal and earnestness he had manifested in working his old master's crops, naturally quick of perception and kind and sympathetic in disposition, he made rapid strides in the most difficult of sciences, and the medical history of the last few years furnishes ample testimony to his success.

Had I statistics at my command I could furnish some interesting figures of the growth and progress of the colored man in medicine. It is sufficient to say, however, that thirty years ago, there were few if any Negro M.D.'s to be found, while to-day there is scarcely a Southern town and a large proportion of the Northern towns and cities that cannot boast of one or more colored physicians, regular graduates of authorized Medical Colleges. While this is true we are compelled to admit that there is a field for many more. It is estimated that there is one white physician to every 300 of his people, while there is only one colored doctor to every 20,000 of his people. This furnishes an idea of our need, for we feel assured that when the colored physicians become more numerous so as not to be a rare object then he will be more respected by all classes of people. Then too we feel proud to state that the practice of the colored doctor is by no means confined solely to his own race. For even here in the historic old State of Louisiana, whose fertile vales have often echoed to the cry of the oppressed, the Negro physician enjoys in many instances a small, but growing white patronage. This in itself is a confession of a recognition of skill and ability, wrung as it were from the lips of the oppressor. And what has been the reception of the Negro physician from his white professional brother? Has he been laughed at, and scoffed upon as being unworthy of any consideration as a scientific man? By no means is this true. While we admit that in all cases he has not been received with open arms due, more perhaps, to petty prejudices and jealousies than any doubt of his medical skill, still on the whole he has received many marks of respect and appreciation, and many kindnesses in the loan of books and instruments from his white professional contemporaries, for which he has been duly grateful. And in many instances the white physicians have not hesitated to avail themselves in consultation over grave cases of his sound common sense and superior medical and surgical skill. The outlook, I say then, is hopeful yet the path of the Negro doctor is by no means strewn with flowers. Isolated, as many of them are, from a daily intercourse with colored men of their own profession and despairing of any assistance from the opposite race, often their only recourse is their books and journals. Under such circumstances the Negro physician sometimes finds himself confronted with a deep and seemingly impassible gulf over which it seems impossible to leap and around which he can see no way. Turning back is not to be thought of, go ahead he must. Then it is that his self-reliance and manhood, if he has any, show themselves. If he stops to reflect he will remember that others have passed the same way, and why should he not do likewise? So summoning all his skill and strength for the effort he makes the leap, lands safely on the other side and has won. I will cite an instance: A surgical operation of importance is to be performed, and the case falls into the hands of the colored doctor. He knows that there is little hope of any professional assistance from the neighboring physicians and his future reputation and success depend, perhaps, upon the issues of the case. The responsibility is a grave one but does he hesitate? Not for long, but he resolutely goes to work, determined to do or die, with no help but that afforded by untrained bystanders; and he usually achieves success. These are not the only difficulties that confront a Negro doctor, but he meets serious drawbacks in the lack of race pride, and confidence which some of his people manifest toward him. It seems that many of our good people have not as yet learned to appreciate the merits of the doctors of their own race. There are those who not only fail to give their own patronage, but take every reasonable opportunity of throwing obstacles in the way of their progress. This, I am glad to say, is rather the exception than the rule, still it is an exception that occurs entirely too often for the comfort of the doctors, and for the welfare of the race he represents. The advent of the colored man into medicine worked an era of better sanitary protection, and better medical attention generally for his people than they had ever enjoyed before, because of the competition it excited. It would appear then that the colored physician instead of arousing their animosity, should be an object of their confidence and respect. The colored physician does not ask patronage on the score of color, and on the other hand he does not want to be denied work on that account. He does not ask that allowances be made for his deficiencies because he is a Negro, and on the other hand he does not want to be denied the privileges that skill and ability should demand for any medical man whether he be white or black. A recognition of skill and competency is all that he asks regardless of color. In other words he wants to be treated as a man—one who has fully prepared himself to do the work as thoroughly and skillfully as any other man of whatever nationality. The Negro physician realizes the fact that this is his only hope for successfully overcoming the many discouraging features of his work, and with this fact in view he has ever bent diligently to the accomplishment of the task set before him. One has not to go far to judge of his success. Here in your own thriving town you have a specimen of a diligent, hard-working, aspiring Negro physician, Dr. Jefferson, who has been with you now about two years, deserves much credit for the success with which his efforts have met in this community. This, I judge, he has won not from the fact that he is a colored physician, but from the manifest skill and ability with which he has undertaken, and accomplished difficult work. So it is that in spite of opposition, in spite of discouragements, in spite of the numerous obstacles which arise to impede his progress, the Negro doctor is steadily moving onward.

In November last the colored doctors of Florida, and adjacent states, met and formed a Colored Medical Association. At this meeting papers were read and discussed that would have done credit to any medical association of this country, and the daily papers in commenting upon this association spoke of its action as being highly creditable to the colored medical profession, and to the Negro race at large. Is not this encouraging, and does it not bid us to look hopefully forward to the future?

The advantages offered to the colored man for a medical education are good. Meharry, New Orleans and Shaw Medical Colleges, in the South are doing good work, and in the North but few if any doors are closed against the colored aspirant; while England, France and Germany all extend to him a welcoming hand. And if as yet we have not a Treve, we have a Newman, if we have not a Koch we have a Stewart, and if we have not a Sims we have a Boyd. These are among the pioneers of the Negro medical profession, and where they leave off their posterity will take up and carry on the work so well begun. I repeat that the colored medical profession is yet in its infancy. If in thirty years they have accomplished so much what may we not hope for a century? When we reflect that our white professional brother has not one, but many centuries back of him, does not that encourage us to look for brighter things for the Negro physician? May we not hope that the day will come when the Tulane and Vanderbilt Medical Colleges will open their doors to all regardless of color, where the white and black doctors of the South will travel side by side in the same railway coach, when there will be no white or black medical associations, but all be united in one band of harmonious fellow workers with but one object, and that the relief of suffering humanity? We smile at the thought, but history has repeatedly chronicled greater and more wonderful revolutions than these, and so will it again. Then with a firm reliance on self, and an unwavering trust in God, the great harmonizer and peace-maker, we press manfully onward in our struggle for truth and right, believing that in the fullness of time all things will end well.

> "Let us then be up and doing,
> With a heart for every fate;
> Still achieving, still pursuing,
> Learn to labor and to wait."

A Valuable Remedy for Diptheria and Throat Diseases.

A FEW years ago, when diptheria was raging in England, a gentleman accompanied the celebrated Dr. Field on his rounds to witness the so-called "wonderful cures" which he performed, while the patients of others were dropping on all sides. The remedy to be so rapid must be simple. All he took with him was powder of sulphur and a quill, and with these he cured every case without exception. He put a teaspoonful of flour of sulphur into a wineglass of water, and stirred it with his finger, instead of a spoon, as the sulphur does not readily mix with water. When the sulphur was well mixed he gave it as a gargle, and in ten minutes the patient was out of danger. Sulphur kills every species of fungus in man, beast and plant in a few minutes. Instead of spitting out the gargle he recommended the swallowing of it. In extreme cases when he had been called in just in the nick of time when the fungus was too nearly closed to allow the gargling, he blew the sulphur through the quill into the throat, and after the fungus had shrunk to allow it, then the gargling. He never lost a patient from diptheria. If a patient cannot gargle, take a live coal, put it on a shovel, and sprinkle a teaspoon full or two of sulphur at a time upon it, let the sufferer inhale it, holding the head over it, and the fungus will die. If plentifully used the whole room may be filled almost to suffocation; the patient can walk about in it, inhaling the fumes with doors and windows shut. The mode of fumigating a room with sulphur has often cured most violent attacks of cold in the head, chest, etc., at any time, and is recommended in cases of consumption and asthma.

VIRGINIA'S FIRST WOMAN PHYSICIAN.

SARAH G. JONES, M.D., the first woman to be licensed to practice medicine in Virginia, is a daughter of George W. Boyd, the leading colored contractor and builder of Richmond. She was born in Albermarle County, Va., and educated in the public schools of Richmond, being graduated in 1883. She then taught in the schools of this city for five years. In 1888 Miss Boyd was married to M. B. Jones, who, at that time, was also a teacher, but now is G. W. A. Secretary of the True Reformers. Mrs. Jones entered Howard Medical College, Washington, D. C., in 1890, and was graduated this year with the degree of M.D. She appeared before the State Medical Examining Board with eighty-four others and received a certificate, which entitles her to secure a license to practice her profession. Mrs. Jones received over 90 per cent on the examination in surgery. Out of the class of eighty-five, twenty-one white graduates, representing several colleges, failed to pass. Dr. Jones and her husband are representatives of the best society of colored people in the State, and are well-to-do-people. When a school teacher she was known as one of the brightest young colored women in the city. She will practice among her race.—*Noted Negro Women.*

THOMAS A. CURTIS was born at Marion, Perry County, Ala., November 30, 1862. His parents were slaves, but by earnest toil and study his father became State Senator of Alabama. His son, Thomas, inherited his father's love for knowledge, and therefore took advantage of every opportunity to develop his mind. He graduated from the State Normal School at Marion, 1881, and begun teaching in his native State. He afterwards went to Texas where he taught for five years. Abandoning the profession of teaching, he entered Meharry Dental College from which he graduated in 1889 with honors, being the best practical dentist of his class. For this excellency he received a gold medal. His success as the first colored dentist of Alabama was marvelous. During the first year of his labor as dentist he earned more than $2,000, and every succeeding year finds him making improvement both in proficiency of his profession and increase of his practice.

DR. T. A. CURTIS,
Montgomery, Ala.

THE NEGRO IN DENTISTRY.

BY THOMAS A. CURTIS, D.D.S.

HERODOTUS, the father of history, who traveled in Egypt the fifth century B.C., devoted one of his books to the description of the manners, customs, art and science of the Egyptians. Herodotus, speaking of the ancient Colchis, whose inhabitants were originally Egyptians and were colonized when Sesostris was King of Egypt, said: "I believe that the ancient Colchi to be a colony of Egypt because like them they have black skins and frizzled hair." Volney says, in noting these remarks of Herodotus, "It showed that the ancient Egyptians were real Negroes of the same species of all the natives of Africa." Diodorus, another ancient historian, informs us that the Ethiopians considered these Egyptians as one of their colonies.

Egypt, the mother of science and art, claims dentistry as her elder daughter. She was the first nation of the world to adopt dentistry as a branch of medicine. It is not known how far the specialist of that day had advanced in this art; Herodotus, however, five hundred years B.C., noticed that medicine was divided into branches, among which was dentistry. Evidence in abundance is found to prove that the ancient Egyptians understood the art of filling teeth with gold and the manufacture and setting of artificial teeth. Museums contain mummies from Thebes with gold filled teeth, artificial teeth of sycamore wood set in gold; therefore it is evident that the Negroes are the originators of the art of dentistry. He is now beginning to re-enter the dental profession, and may do for its perfection what his ancient ancestors did for its infancy. But little progress was made in the practice of dentistry until the last century. During this period it has outstripped every other branch of medicine, and now stands before the world as a specialty equal in importance to any branch of surgery, in fact it may justly claim what medicine cannot, to have risen from an art to the dignity of a science.

Prior to 1776 there was not a practicing dentist in this country.

All operations were performed by the general practician or surgeon. The key, that instrument which came near debasing the profession, was the only instrument in use. Dr. Woffendale, of London, arrived in New York in 1776. Although he was the only man in the entire country devoting his time to dentistry, the public so little appreciated his services that he was obliged to return to England in 1787, being unable to support himself. In 1783 Dr. Jas. Gardetta came to this country and settled in New York. He afterwards removed to Philadelphia and continued there as a successful practician for forty-five years.

Dr. Hyden commenced the practice of dentistry in Baltimore in 1804. He was a man of great energy and ability. It was he who first realized the importance of a higher standard for the profession. He induced a number of gentlemen to join him in petitioning the Legislature of Maryland to establish a dental college. From this time on dentistry has made rapid strides, until it now numbers among its practicians some of the most scientific and enlightened men of this country. From a mere itinerant existance it has risen to a position equal to any branch of medicine, and is decidedly the most remunerative of all.

Dentistry now opens to view a broad, lucrative and inviting field for the aspiring and educated Negro youth. The opportunities it furnishes have not been grasped in the past as readily as I hope the possibilities will warrant in the future. Our young men have drifted into a stream which has flown steadily into the medical profession. A very few have stopped to ask the all-important question, "Am I better fitted by nature for the practice of dentistry than for the practice of medicine?"

Prior to 1862 we hear nothing of the Negro in the dental profession, but at the close of the war he is remarked as being established as a successful practician of dentistry, born and matured, as it were, in a day. When the surprised public had time to ask the question, "Who are these men?" on investigation, they were found to be the former office boys of their masters, who picked up the fundamental principles of dentistry, and now emancipated, practiced it with confidence and ability. The State of Georgia appears to take the lead in producing these noted pioneers, among whom are the Dr. Badger Brothers, of Atlanta, and Dr. Zeque, of Augusta. All of these gentlemen won distinction and wealth in their professions, had as their patients some of the best white families of Atlanta and Augusta. I have examined with a degree of surprise and satisfaction some of their gold fillings, which at the time, was more than twenty-five years old. Artistic and durable, their work stands a monument to their ability and profession. Many of these old pioneers have passed away, but I am proud to have had the pleasure of saying to Dr. Badger, of Atlanta, that it was from his success that I caught the inspiration to adopt dentistry as my life's work.

The late Dr. Wm. J. Simmons, of Kentucky, a noted Baptist divine, entered the office of Dr. DeLangie, a dentist in Bordentown, N. J., he learned rapidly and was soon able to do good work. Though often rebuffed by the white people, he operated on some of the best white families in the city. But he was unwilling to remain in the profession without the thorough knowledge of dentistry, such as only could be given in a dental college, and on being refused admission to a dental college in Phildaelphia, he therefore abandoned the profession.

Dr. Smith, of Little Rock, Ark., also one of these early pioneers, has won wealth and fame in the dental profession. He is one of the wealthiest Negroes in Little Rock. The dentists of to-day are too numerous to mention. There are now about one hundred Negroes practicing dentistry in the United States, graduated from dental colleges. Some of the most prominent are as follows:

Dr. Grant, of the Harvard Dental Faculty, has acquired great distinction as a practician and professor of dentistry, having lectured before the Harvard Dental School for a number of years. His practice is said to net him ten thousand dollars a year.

Dr. C. E. Bently, of Chicago, Ills., is one of the foremost young men in the profession irrespective of color. He has several times been honored with positions in the Dental Associations of Chicago, and is now one of the assistant editors of the leading dental journal of the West.

Dr. J. R. Porter, of Atlanta, Ga., is a practical dentist, a gentleman, affable, refined and cultured. He graduated from Meharry in 1889, and was valedictorian of his class. His success in Atlanta is assured. Day by day he is building monuments of gold and silver that will attest his worth and ability.

Dr. Fields, of Memphis, Tenn., and Dr. Ferrill, of Houston, Texas, enjoy the confidence and respect of all who know them. They are the leading young men in the dental profession in their respective States. There are other young men as prominent and successful in the practice of dentistry as the ones I have already mentioned. In fact I have yet to hear of a single young man who properly prepared himself for his work who has made a failure.

As an inducement to young men to enter the profession of dentistry in this country, we cite as a fact that the Americans have the worst teeth of any people on earth. The reason for this is we change the proportion of the various food stuffs we eat more than any people on earth. What nature has stored up in food to build up hard tissue we constantly eliminate, consequently we do not take the proper material into our system that would be carried back atom by atom to take the place of this tissue metamorphises. What is true of the white people under the same circumstances is true of the Negro. There seems to be a prevailing, but erroneous, opinion that Negroes possess better teeth than the white people. There might have been a time when this statement was correct, but since the Negro has adopted all the civilized modes of living like the Caucasian his teeth are no better than his, if as good. The advantage the Negro has over the white people as to predisposing causes he looses in exciting causes, carelessness and wanton neglect.

In conclusion; we do not evolutionize by the advancement in civilization made by other people as much as we advance and become civilized to the extent we are able to evolutionize ourselves. This evolution is nowhere more noticeable than in the practice of dentistry by the Negroes, the establishment of schools of dentistry, the graduating of young men from these schools to take care and preserve our teeth, mark an epoch in the history of our civilization which only future generations will be fully able to comprehend and appreciate.

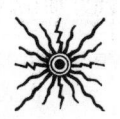

6

Shall Our Women Extract Teeth?

BY DR. D. P. REED, IN "NEW YORK AGE."

THE time has long since passed when the availability and fitness of woman for the practice of dentistry can be questioned; and whatever may have been the differences of opinion as to her qualifications, both physical and mental, for this work, when measured by the standard of male requirements, the fact remains that in dentistry, as in all other branches of the "healing art," woman has found and successfully occupied a field of usefulness in which the sum total of those distinctively feminine qualities, which go to make up an ideal womanhood, have been invaluable.

Why should not a woman, if qualified, practice dentistry as well as medicine? Dentistry is only a specialty in medicine, and it takes nerve to practice either with success. But remember that dentistry requires coolness and steadiness of nerves. A frail, nervous woman has no business in this profession. Good health is especially requisite for dentists, because they must do most of their work standing, inhale foul and unhealthy breaths, be indoors most of their time; and when all this is added to their business cares, they must have a good constitution not to succumb to these depressing influences. I am told by a practicing woman dentist, who is a graduate of a reputable college of dentistry, that the question her patients usually ask is, "Can you pull teeth?" Her answer is, "Why, yes; pulling teeth is only an art!" I saw her attempt to extract a tooth one day, and it certainly required more strength than art. Very few dentists can extract teeth properly, and for this reason dentists are now specializing, performing only such operations as the cases require.

There are about seventy-five women dentists in this country, and of this number about twelve are practicing in Philadelphia, which seems to be their centre. There they have organized a society, and at their first meeting about half of the women dentists from all parts of the United States attended. Notwithstanding the fact that only a few colleges will graduate them, they are rapidly coming to the front. Our New York College has several times refused, to my personal knowledge, to admit the fair sex; and it has been only since the Philadelphia Dental College has been graduating them. I had the pleasure of graduating with a woman dentist, and during our college days we spent many a pleasant hour together over our cadavers. She was an American and full of genius. We have about four practicing in this city and they are doing comparatively well. There is Mrs. Lydia C. Clare on Eighth Avenue taking care of her husband's practice. There is one now on Madison Avenue and one on Third Avenue. The first woman dentist to open an office in this city was Mrs. Dr. Olla Neyman, the daughter of Madame Clara Neyman, the writer and lecturer. With these women already in the field demonstrating the capacity of their sex in this profession, there is no reason why some of our able, enterprising and energetic young women should not take up and successfully practice the science of dentistry. I hope these remarks will come under the eye of some watchful, capable young woman and stimulate her to make the effort. As a rule it certainly hurts a sensitive woman to inflict pain, although eventually, she becomes used to it and maintains her sympathetic nature through it all. Thus this very sympathy would attract to her the sensitive and nervous of both sexes; and men as well as women and children would rather submit a troublesome and aching tooth to the gentle ministrations of a woman, than to the harsher manipulations of a sterner and less sympathetic man. It is difficult for the average individual to associate the idea of profound learning and sciencific attainments with the fair countenance and unassuming grace of a girl graduate, even when the bright, intellectual eyes look up at him and he has the ocular demonstration that she is skillful even to the tips of the dainty fingers that can quiet a throbbing nerve, plug a fulsome cavity or use the forceps, if necessary, with a dexterity equal to some of our old D.D.S.'s.

DR. IDA GRAY, DENTIST.

AT the writing of this sketch, Miss Gray is among the leading Afro-American dentists. She resides in Cincinnati, Ohio, and is highly respected by all classes. She was educated at Gaines High School. From there she entered the University of Michigan, graduating from the dental department in 1890. After the completion of her course, she returned to her home in Cincinnati where she opened an office on Ninth Street, and commenced the practice of her profession. The success of Dr. Gray only demonstrates what can be accomplished by an Afro-American lady when they manifest the necessary pluck and energy. In the past few years Miss Gray has built up a lucrative practice, her patients being about equally divided between white and colored. Miss Gray is a very accomplished lady, and is spoken of in the highest terms of the press without regard to nationality.

Prof. Booker T. Washington.

[Principal of the Tuskegee, Alabama, Institute—How and Where the Great Educator Grew to Distinction.]

MR. WASHINGTON, of Tuskegee, Ala., was born a slave at Hale's Ford, Va., April, 1857. He belonged to a family by the name of Burrows. Very soon after the war he went with his mother, Jane Ferguson, his stepfather and the remainder of his family to Malden, W. Va., to live. Here he worked in the salt furnaces the greater part of each year and went to school during three or four months. Mr. Washington usually secured some one to teach him at night when not permitted to attend school in the day. After working in the mines and furnaces for a considerable time, he secured employment at the house of Mrs. Viola Ruffner, a lady of New England birth and training, and who, though very exacting regard-

PROF. BOOKER T. WASHINGTON,
Tuskegee, Ala.

ing all matters of work, was very kind and showed her interest in the education of young Washington in a number of ways. In 1871, in some way, Washington heard of the Hampton Institute in Virginia. He at once made up his mind to enter that institution. With his own small earnings, amounting to $6 per month, and with what his family were kind enough to give him, he found himself in Richmond, Va., but friendless, shelterless and homeless. Casting about, however, he soon discovered a hole under a sidewalk that offered a night's sleep. As luck would have it, when he awoke next morning he found he was near a vessel that was unloading pig iron, and application was at once made to the captain for work, which was given. Mr. Washington worked here until he had enough money to pay his way to Hampton Institute, which place he reached with a surplus of fifty cents. He remained at Hampton three years, working his way through, and graduated with one of the honors of his class. After graduating and teaching in West Virginia, his old home, for a while, and spending a year in study at Wayland Seminary, Washington, D. C., Mr. Washington was invited to return to Hampton as a teacher. In this capacity he remained at Hampton two years, till 1881, when application was made to Gen. S. C. Armstrong by citizens of Tuskegee, Ala., for some one to start an institution at Tuskegee on the plan of Hampton.

Mr. Washington was at once recommended for the position. Upon reaching Tuskegee he found neither land nor buildings, nothing but the promise of the State to pay $2,000 annually toward the expenses of the school. The school was started in an old church and shanty with thirty students and a teacher. The history of the school and its present condition are already known to the readers of this book, and to the world for that matter. It is enough to say that the institution with its 1,900 acres of land, its 28 or more large buildings, with its 1,000 or more teachers and pupils, its wealth in live stock and its valuation of over $250,000, is a prodigy of development. Principal Washington has met with unusual success in making the acquaintance and securing the confidence of prominent and wealthy people throughout the country. This is attested by the fact that he succeeds in raising from $50,000 to $60,000 each year with which to carry on the school work. Several individuals give from $3,000 to $10,000 each annually toward the support of the school. Mr. Washington's services are in constant demand to speak at associations, clubs and prominent churches. The speech that brought him first into prominence was before the National Education Association, Madison, Wisconsin, in 1884. Soon after he was invited to address the Boston Unitarian Club, the most intelligent and wealthy club in the world, he being the first Afro-American to address the club. He has spoken at Plymouth Church (formerly Henry Ward Beecher's); Trinity Church, Boston, (formerly Phillips Brooks') and many other of the most prominent churches in the country; also before the Political Science Club, of Cornell University; the Congregational Club and the Twentieth Century Club, of Boston. The "Outlook," one of the greatest Christian journals in this country, published in '93 the cut of Prof. Washington, along with those of the presidents of twenty-eight of America's leading colleges. Mr. Washington is regarded as one of the leading men of the country and is held in high esteem in Massachusetts, as was shown by his being made the guest of honor at the governor's table recently. Mr. Washington is among the foremost men of this country and time.

Mind and Matter.

[An address delivered by Booker T. Washington, Principal Tuskegee (Ala.) Normal and Industrial Institute, before the Alabama State Teachers' Association, Selma, Ala., June 5, 1895.]

MR. PRESIDENT, LADIES AND GENTLEMEN:

THE question comes before me to-night with a greater force than ever, it seems to me, To what extent is our education reaching, penetrating the heart of the masses of people by whom we are surrounded; to what extent is our education affecting the heart, affecting the hand, affecting the head, the whole man, of the masses by whom we are surrounded in such counties as Bullock, Lowndes, Wilcox, Dallas and Montgomery? Now I understand that there are favored ones in all parts of the State, but an education that does not, sooner or later, lift up the masses, has its weak points. The question arises to what extent is the education that we are getting in our universities, academies, high schools, common schools, reaching the heart of the masses of these people, and to what extent are we able to appreciate an improvement in the condition of the masses by reason of the education we are getting from day to day?

There was an incident which happened sometime ago up in the State of Kentucky, which aptly illustrates what I am speaking of. There was a man who had spent a good many hundred dollars in educating his son known as Solomon. This man and his wife, both of whom were very ignorant so far as books are concerned, began sending Solomon to school when quite young, keeping him in school four and five months each year. During vacations Solomon would earn two and three dollars a week, which he gave to his father and mother regularly. When he grew older, Solomon was sent to college where he remained seven or eight years at the expense of his father and mother. Finally Solomon received his diploma and returned to his old home. It was not very long before the old folks began to note a change in Solomon's appearance and especially in his disposition to work. There was a kind of restlessness about him. The old people began to notice that he cared little for home, that he didn't go out into the field each day and help his old father as he used to do before going to college, and that at the end of each week Solomon didn't bring in the usual two or three dollars. They noticed that he did nothing but walk around the streets with his hands in his pockets, and that as one Saturday night drew near, Solomon got nearer the old man, and asked him for fifty cents with which to buy a silk necktie. The old man scratched his head, but said nothing. And Solomon continued to walk about the streets with his hands in his pockets and stand on the corners. When the next Saturday night came around, Solomon asked his father to give him four dollars with which to buy a new pair of shoes. The old man had never heard of a pair of shoes costing more than two dollars, and started to speak out, but kept his tongue and gave Solomon the four dollars. These requests and the great changes in Solomon began to make the old man think about Solomon and his college education. Finally there appeared in the town, a man from Massachusetts. Solomon's father one day went to this man, whose acquaintance he happened to make, and said, "I want to speak with you about my son Solomon. He has been to college and has a good education. I am sure of that; but my friend, for God's sake take Solomon aside and tell him what to do with that education."

Now my friends, wont you agree with me that there are a good many Solomons getting scattered all through the South? Aren't there entirely too many of our people whose heads are full, but who don't know how to use it?

This Massachusetts man took Solomon aside and said to him, "Solomon, what did you study in college?" "Chemistry, sir." "Well, that's good, but what are you going to do with that chemistry?" "I don't know, sir," replied Solomon. "Well Solomon, your father is a farmer; you take your chemistry and go out into that field and show him how to enrich his soil. What else did you study at college?" "Geometry, sir." "Well Solomon, isn't it possible for you to go out there with your father and show him how to check off that land, how to run his corn rows straight instead of crooked?" "That is true, I had never thought of that," said Solomon. Then Solomon began to think, and by reason of that good, sound and timely advice, joined his old father and began to apply his education; and to-day, my friends, in the whole State of Kentucky, I venture to say, you cannot find a more intelligently conducted farm than Solomon's. (Applause.)

Now my friends, I believe there is no difficulty, however great, out of which we cannot find our way. The story is told that at one time, two unfortunate frogs fell into a jar of milk over night. After kicking for several hours, endeavoring to get out, one of the frogs said to the other, "It's no use kicking, I'm going to give up and sink to the bottom. The sooner it's over the better." Not so with the second frog, who kept on kicking until morning when the milk turned to butter, and he once more found himself on *terra firma*. We must all get out of our difficulties by kicking.

We are born, so far as our educational career is concerned, in time to take advantage of all the mistakes the white man has made during the last two thousand years, and the question is, simply, Are we going take advantage of these mistakes he has made, or are we going over the same rough ground and learn by the same hard experience what the white man is just realizing? (Applause.) I for one, am in favor of taking advantage of these mistakes, and making the most of them. If you have watched the trend of education for the past fifty years, you have noticed that it has tended in one direction, namely, the cementing of mind and matter. It has tended in the direction of making mind a part of matter. In this city to-day there is extended to the poorest and most humble child the opportunity of receiving a better education than was given the child of the President of the Union fifty years ago. Fifty years ago the little boy of four or five years went to school and was taught to count abstractly, one, two, three, etc.; to-day he goes into the school room and counts, one apple, two definite apples that he can lay his hand on. Fifty years ago this little boy learned to read by pronouncing abstract and often meaningless words; to-day he reads of a dog, not some dog far off in the distance which he cannot see and feel, but one that really exists and upon which he can lay his hand. Fifty years ago he studied about chemistry, he sat up in a school or lecture room, and was told about chemistry, and the chemical experiments which were made; to-day, instead of studying about chemistry, the student feels, handles and comes in immediate contact with the matter about which he studies. He performs with his own hands the experiments which, fifty years ago, were lectured about.

Now my friends this brings me to the question that I have especially in view to-night; it is what we are wont to call industrial education, the application of mind to matter, and to the conquering of the forces of nature. A few days ago I visited a certain institution where mechanical drawing is taught. I went into the room where a class in this study were reciting. I noticed on the blackboard, this problem: "Draw out, design and create a plan for dairy." The teacher told me that none of his students had ever seen the kind of building he had in mind, yet he wanted them to draw from their own resources and create a dairy.

What is education? By education the mind is strengthened, whether through the study of the classics, or through mechanical drawing, or through the carpenter shop. No matter how he gets it, a man is educated whose mind is so strengthened that he has complete control of the organization and use of his mind. And so this teacher told his students to create a dairy. My friends, is n't that education? Compare an education like that with merely having a boy sit down and memorize something that happened a thousand years ago.

Now, my friends, I never plead for less education. I believe in the highest development of the mind. I believe with the poet—

> "Had I the power to reach the pole
> Or grasp the ocean with a span,
> I'd still be measured by my soul,
> The mind's the measure of the man."

But we must remember that I am pleading for the use of the mind, for the use of education, no matter whether it is little or much education, no matter whether it is secured in this way or that way, I am pleading for the use of education.

We had just as well inculcate this in our pupils once for all, that the world cares very little about what a man or woman knows; it is what the man or woman is able to do that the world cares about. An educated man standing on the corners of the street with his hands in his pockets is of no more value to the world than an ignorant man doing the same thing. In almost every community in the South and throughout the North they have what is known as "smart men," men of education and culture. You go into any city and it will not be very long before the news reaches your ears that there is a very smart man in that community. I saw one of these smart men some time ago. I had heard a great deal about him, and asked some one who he was. "O that's Mr. Soandso, and I tell you he's a smart man," "What does he do?" I asked. "O he is n't doing any thing in particular just now; he's just a smart man, that's all." (Laughter.) "Can he build any houses?" "O no, he never builds any houses." "Drow the plans for any? Does he farm, raise hogs?" "Oh, my, no! He does n't do anything like that, he would n't be caught raising hogs for any thing. He's just a smart man, but just now he is n't engaged in any particular line of work."

Now, my friends, when we speak usually of hand-craft, the average man gets the idea that it is something to teach a man to work. When you speak of industrial education, he is immediately prejudiced. He will say, "My son or my daughter knows how to work already." My friends, never was there a greater mistake made than this. I do not mean to say that the Negro does n't work. Whether you find him in the Mississippi bottoms, on the sugar plantations of Louisiana, on the rice swamps of North Carolina, or the cotton fields of Alabama, the Negro works hard from morning till night. And he works at a tremendous disadvantage, and he does everything in the most costly manner. I will tell you what industrial education means: It means teaching a man how *not* to work. That is what industrial education means. It teaches a man how to harness the forces of nature and make them do his work instead of working out his brains and strength, accomplishing very little good.

Sometime ago, while traveling through the State of Indiana, I saw a man engaged in planting corn. Instead of following a plow he was seated on a large machine called a cultivator. Hitched to this were two fine horses. The man was not only sitting down, but was holding a large umbrella over him, and all the strength he had to expend was in holding the horses back to prevent their working themselves to death. This machine plowed up the ground, laid off the furrows, dropped and covered the corn. Besides, instead of planting one row at a time, two rows of corn were planted. On another occasion I saw a farmer plant corn in Alabama. Instead of being perched upon a cultivator, he had an old plow that was loosely tacked together, and about four inches wide. Hitched to this plow was an old mule that traveled about a mile an hour. Instead of riding this fellow was following this plow, barefooted, and carrying with him a long hickory pole which he occasionally laid on the back of the weary-looking mule. Nearly every time he reached the end of the furrow, he would have to stop and repair the plow, and very often the harness, which was composed partly of rags and partly of leather, and too, the mule had only one eye. In addition to ploughing the ground, he had to go over it with the same old one-eyed mule, and then another man came along to drop the corn and then another to cover it. He was what you call one of these "one-gallused" farmers, and he very often found it necessary to stop and repair his suspenders in order to keep his pantaloons in position. Now here was this farmer in Alabama competing with this Indiana farmer? (Laughter.) This man in Indiana had learned how to apply his education to agriculture. And still people tell me that the black man does n't need industrial education. What I mean by industrial education is getting the black boy to the point where he can sit upon an instrument of that sort that the Indiana man used, and raise more corn than the Indiana farmer can raise. (Applause.)

While education brings with it certain privileges, it brings with it also certain responsibilities and certain opportunities. Here it brings an opportunity to compete for the American dollar, and there is nothing that has so little sentiment, so little prejudice in it. We are going to be mortgaged in Alabama, Georgia, Mississippi and all over the South, we are going to continue buying corn from the Indiana farmers until we can get our boys to raise corn just as fast and just as cheaply as the man in Indiana.

At Tuskegee we have in operation what is known as the Aladdin Oven, a machine or vessel for the purpose of teaching a woman how to cook a meal and take a nap at the same time. Would n't you like to cook that way? I claim that industrial education is meant to teach a person how not to work, how to make the forces of nature work for him; and in this vessel a woman can cook a piece of tough beef by putting a lamp under it, and by morning she will find it ready for the table, tender and nicely cooked. This is industrial education.

I was in a dairy a few days ago where I saw men making butter, and in only a few minutes after the milk came from the cow, it was put into a separator, out of which I saw the milk come out of one little tube and the cream out of another. This cream was then transferred to another vessel, a churn, I believe it was, and a man began to turn a crank for a while, and in a very few minutes from that I saw laid off in nice square blocks, some of the finest butter I ever saw. This man hardly touched the butter with his hands. The man who made this butter has had a college education, has studied chemistry. That is the way he applied his education. That is industrial education.

To be a little more practical. There are some things which we have got to learn to do. If we are going to hold our own in this Southland, right about us, we have got to learn, in the first place, to dignify labor, and in the second place to put brains into labor. Now is it common sense to take a girl and teach her to analyze Mars, bound Jupiter and at the same time neglect to teach her? Now I don't say it is wrong, but is it common sense to teach a girl to do that, and at the same time neglect to teach her the composition of the corn bread that she is compelled to eat three times a day? (Laughter.) Is that common sense?

It used to be true throughout the North, as it is now throughout the South, that a great many colored men made their living by white-washing. The old colored man came along with his pole and white-wash bucket, and would occasionally get a fence to white wash, and less frequently, some one would let him in their parlor to white wash the walls. He would not only white wash the walls but would also touch up the pictures, curtains and carpet. (Laughter.) When he was done the whole thing would be pretty well white washed. That sort of thing went on, and when anyone wanted any white washing done they always sent for Uncle Joe, and so for many years Uncle Joe was the chief white-wash monopolist. But soon the white man began to think. The white boy went to college, to the school of technology, and learned chemistry, geometry and physics, and came out and applied his knowledge of these branches to mixing materials, figuring and decorating. He went into the house which old Uncle Joe used to white wash and took his job away from him, and wherever that white man has gone Uncle Joe can never go again. But you don't call that young white man a white washer; you call him a house decorator. He has taken that once common occupation, raised it up, put brains into it.

You know it used to be true that every large and paying barber shop in Boston, New York, Philadelphia and other large northern cities, was in the hands of colored men. Go into either of these cities to-day and you will not find a single paying barber shop controlled by colored men. When the colored man had a monopoly of this business, he went on in the same old way day after day without thinking and educating himself, without planning how to enlarge his business and advance the work. The whiteman saw his opportunity and opened a barber shop in which he put a newly made chair, a nice carpet and hung some pictures on the walls, and then he published a journal relating to the interests of the trade. He had a desk put in the shop at which he sat and kept his accounts. Thus he dignified that labor. But you don't call that man a barber; you call him a tonsorial artist, but he has got the black man's job just the same. (Laughter.)

I think I do not exaggerate when I say that three-fourths of the colored families in the cities of the South are supported by washing clothes. Recently I had an investigation made into the condition of twenty-seven families in the city of Montgomery, and there was not a single one that did not support itself in part by washing. We have had a monopoly of that, but, if you will notice closely, you will see that it is passing away. The white boy leaves school to-day with a knowledge of physics or mechanics. He sets up a steam laundry. He introduces a machine that washes two thousand shirts a day by electricity, and at a much less cost than many washwomen can do it. Now how long are we going to sit still and let this thing go on? The fact is, we have neglected too long to put our brains into these common occupations of life.

We are a great race of consumers, but we produce very little. We consume steam cars, but produce none; hats, but produce none. Suppose a law was passed preventing colored people from wearing hats made by white men; how many of us would go bare-headed? (Laughter.) Did you ever see a colored man who manufactured toothpicks? Of course you have seen plenty of men manufacture one perhaps for his own use out of a piece of dry goods box. You con't afford to do that, can you? The idea of an educated colored man manufacturing toothpicks! He has got to teach or preach. I was up in the State of Maine a few months ago, and found there men who were many times millionaires, and I asked, in one case, how they got their start. I was told that a certain man, one of these rich men, would go home at night after his day's work on the farm was done, and with a jackknife which he had bought whittled out several dozen toothpicks, and finally he was able to buy another jackknife which he gave his wife, and she whittled. Both would sit around the family fireside and whittle toothpicks, and they kept on in that way until they were able to buy a small piece of machinery, and after a while added another piece of machinery, then applied steam. Thus that man got to be a millionaire by making these little things that we chew up and spit out and think nothing of.

You have perhaps heard the story told by Henry W. Grady of a burial that took place in Pickens County, Georgia. It is said that the grave was dug through a solid bed of marble, but the marble head stone came from Vermont. The burial took place in the midst of a pine forest, but the coffin in which the dead man was buried came from Cincinnati. An iron mountain overlooked that grave, but the picks and shovels used in digging it came from Pittsburgh, Pa. The wagon that hauled the dead man's body came from South Bend Indiana, yet there was an immense hickory grove near by. The shoes that the dead man wore came from Boston, his pants and coat from Chicago, his shirt from Troy, N. Y., and the cheap white cravat came from Philadelphia, and the old one-eyed mule that drew the corpse was bought years ago in the State of Tennessee, and the only thing that Pickens County produced for that burial was the hole in the ground, and the dead man, and had it been possible these would have been imported also. (Laughter.) I fear that as a race, we are pretty much in the same fix as those people in Pickens County.

But I am talking about a practical thing, whether or not it is a practical thing for the teachers who know something of agriculture to take their knowledge and go into such counties as Lowndes and Wilcox where the schools are lasting but three months during the year and get the patrons to let you have their children for a half day each day and with their help raise enough cotton and corn to extend your school term four and five months, instead of the usual three months. If our young men and women who are taught agriculture cannot use it in extending the school term it does seem to me that that education is, to a large extent, useless. And the old colored people on these plantations are beginning to think about this thing. I was at the Georgia State Teachers' Association last year, and some one read a table of statistics relative to the colored people's educational progress, and it was stated that they were not giving so much attention to college education now as formerly. I do not say that this is true, but if it is, I think I know the cause. The old colored farmer worked hard some years ago, saved every cent that he could get hold of, sacrificed in order that his son might remain in college. But he noticed that as soon as John got his college education he was not satisfied to come and live with mother and father and help them, but wanted to go back to Nashville or Atlanta just as soon as possible.

Since then John hasn't gone home any more. After awhile another son in that family wants to go to college; he wants to go to the same college that his brother John attended. He lets this boy go, but he thinks of John and his college education, of how much money he has spent on John, and that he has not seen John since he got his diploma. Very soon the time comes for the third boy to want to go off to college; but the old man refuses point blank.

Now, what you want to do is to take that old man's boy in Wilcox county and so educate him that he will take his knowledge of chemistry and gemoetry, etc., and go back and show his old father and mother how, by reason of his education, by reason of his increased intelligence, on the same acre of land where only ten bushels of corn were formerly raised, to raise forty bushels on the same acre. Do that, and every man in the State of Alabama who has a son will be willing to sacrifice in order that his son may go to college.

Now, somebody is going to say, "You are too utilitarian in your plea, you overlook the moral and religious." No, I don't. I know that I tell you that we must have a certain amount of industrial and material foundation on which to rest our moral and religious life. The most moral and religious people to-day are to be found in New England. It is easy for a man to be a Christian when he has a hundred thousand dollars in the bank.

To come out flat-footed, as the old man said, the trouble with us is we are hungry. I don't mean to say that you people here in Selma are hungry, but in the broader acceptation of the term—shelter, clothing, provisions for a rainy day, we are a hungry people; and I know some of these ministers will agree with me. The hardest thing that the minister has to do is to make a good Christian out of a hungry man. You can't make a good Christian out of a hungry man; I don't care how much he gets up and shouts in church, if, after he goes home from church at night and finds nothing there, he is tempted (and very often succeeds) to find something before morning.

This is human nature the world over, and I don't say that it is confined to the black man.

As a race you know we are very emotional. The white man can beat us thinking, but when it comes to feeling the white man isn't in it. We can feel more in five minutes than the white man can in a day. The colored man spends much time in preparing to live in the next world. Analyze the average colored preacher's sermon, and you will find that three-fourths of it is devoted to an imaginary description of heaven. It tells about white mansions above, while the members of his congregation live in log cabins; about wearing golden slippers, when more than half his audience are barefooted. He talks about living on milk and honey in the next world, but when he goes to take dinner with one of his sisters he is given cornbread and peas. (Laughter.) I was on a plantation some time ago and heard a preacher preach, and the whole burden of his sermon was, "You get religion and give up the world." Now, I am not speaking irreverently; I have no patience with that sort of thing. I happened to know the people in that community, and I knew that there were not two persons in the whole community who owned land, hogs, cattle and who were not mortgaged. I said to this preacher: "My friend, what have these people to give of the world; what is it you want them to give up?" That is not the kind of doctrine to preach. The people want to be taught to get hold of the world, and mix in with their land, cotton and corn a good bank account, and when they get that, they have a religion that you can bank on seven days in the week.

There is nothing that is going to be so effective in removing whatever friction that exists between the two races in this country as the idea that I have been trying to enforce, the idea of letting the colored man's education tend in the direction of producing something tangible, something that somebody can feel and see. When I went into the town of Tuskegee, fourteen years ago, there were some white people who wouldn't look at me. I went on for awhile. After a while these same white people wanted some bricks and they came to us to get them. That relation has gone on, so that now we have no warmer friends anywhere than in Tuskegee. When we began the manufacture of buggies they came to us. They came to our printing office to have their printing done, and to-day the main Democratic paper of Tuskegee is printed in our office. I don't say we edit it, we only print it.

You will find that the friction will pass just in proportion as the black man gets something the white man wants. Nobody cares anything for a man that hasn't something that somebody else wants. A white man doesn't care anything about another white man unless he has something, property, influence or perhaps a daughter, and that something brings the two individuals together and makes friends and neighbors of them; and the same thing is true of races. I remember that when I first went to Tuskegee there were some poor white people who were always talking about driving that nigger school teacher away from town. I would meet one of these old fellows and try to impress my importance upon him, but it didn't work. I knew a little about Latin, Geometry and Physics, but what did they care? After a time we began to put up a large brick building. The building brought them and they became our best friends.

And so we have gone on putting up building after building until now we have 37 on the school grounds, the larger part of them being built wholly by the labor of the students. Our property is valued at $215,000. The annual expense of carrying on the school is about $75,000 or about $250 for every day the school is in session. We have some 250 head of live stock of various kinds, three steam boilers, and thirty-five or forty buggies, wagons, carts, etc. In all the school owns nearly 1,800 acres of land, 600 of which are under cultivation. There are twenty-two industries including the following: Carpentry, wheelwrighting, blacksmithing, tinning, foundry and machine work, shoe making, harness making, dressmaking, millinery work, stock raising, horticulture, dairying, brick making, brick masonry, plastering, printing, cooking, laundering, agriculture, mattress making, agricultural and mechanical drawing, tailoring, painting and saw milling. These industries involve a thorough course in mechanical and architectural drawing. Since the organization of the school over a half million dollars have been collected and expended in building up the work. Students have worked out during the past year $41,000. The whole property as well as the control of the institution is in the hands of a board of trustees. There is no mortgage on any of the property.

We try to surround students in Tuskegee with an air of thrift and business, so that the spirit of industry gets deep into one's blood and bones, as well as to make the institution an object-lesson as to the capability of the Negro and of Negro civilization. There are over 800 students, representing seventeen States and one Territory. Sixty-six instructors, all colored, are employed. The average

age of the students is eighteen and one half years, none being admitted under fourteen.

I have no patience with that class of people who say that the Negro cannot find use for his education after he has obtained it. There are opportunities all about us which we are not using. How many educated horticulturists among the colored people are there in this country? How many educated agriculturists and landscape gardeners are there? Not only are horticulturists needed, but mechanical and civil engineers, architects, brickmakers, trained nurses, educated cooks. If our educated young men and women will turn their attention more and more to the physical, they will find themselves more and more in demand.

CASSEDY INDUSTRIAL HALL.

My friends, there is an unexplainable influence about a black man's living in a brick house that you cannot understand. When the black man can make his education felt in producing a brick house or something that somebody wants to get hold of nothing causes friction to pass away so soon. Suppose someone would go into the city of Birmingham and make the assertion that the Germans as a race are lazy, shiftless, good-for-noting class of people. Will any heated argument be necessary to prove that he didn't know what he was talking about? No. Some one would say, "Do you see that large block of brick buildings over there? It is owned by a German. Do you see that large cotton mill? That is owned by a German." And there the argument will end. When Thomas doubted whether Christ had arisen from the dead, he did not enter into a long argument with him; he said, "Thomas, do you see where the nails entered my hands and feet?" That was the most convincing, the most tangible argument that could have been produced.

We had just as well acknowledge that after the war we made some great mistakes. We began at the top when we should have begun at the bottom. We spent time and money trying to go to Congress that could have better been spent in becoming the leading real estate dealer in our town. We spent time in making political stump speeches that could have better been spent in operating the finest dairy or truck farm in the country. We spent all this time uselessly instead of laying a material foundation upon which we could have stood and demanded our political rights.

Now in conclusion, my friends, there are a good many rights withheld from us, and wrongfully too, yet we must not spend too much time in giving attention to our grievances and neglect the many opportunities that are about us. We are denied the opportunity in many Southern cities of riding in a first-class car, even after we have paid for first-class fare, but in Dallas County, and all through the State, I tell you of an opportunity that is not denied us. We have the opportunity of living 365 days in the year in the neatest, most attractive and comfortable house in Dallas County, and nobody objects to that. The average colored man has the opportunity of being denied accommodation in a first-class hotel about twice in a year, yet at the same time he has the opportunity all through Alabama, of living and sleeping in the neatest and cleanest room to be found, and no law will say he cannot do it. The average colored man is denied the privilege of sitting on a jury about once in two years, but there is no law to prevent our young men and women who are being educated from owing and operating the finest dairy farm from which butter that is eaten by every man who does sit on the jury is raised. What I mean to say is that he who holds the dollars, brains and intelligence will, in the long run, hold the offices.

We expect too often to get things that God did not mean for us to have in certain ways. At one time an old colored man was very anxious to get a turkey, and he prayed and prayed for the Lord to send him a turkey. The turkey did not come, and finally the old man changed his prayer somewhat, and said, "O Lord, send dis nigger to a turkey," and he got it that night. (Laughter.) God means for us to get many things in about that same way, that is by working for them rather than by depending merely on the power of mouth.

At one time a ship was lost at sea for many days, when it hove in sight of a friendly vessel. The signal of the distressed vessel was at once hoisted, which read, "We want water," "we die of thirst." The answering signal read, "Cast down your bucket where you are," but a second time the distressed vessel signaled, "We want water, water," and a second time the other vessel answered "Cast down your bucket where you are." A third and fourth time the distressed vessel signaled "We want water, water," "we die of thirst," and as many times was answered "Cast down your bucket where you are." At last the command was obeyed, the bucket was cast down where the vessel stood and it came up full of fresh, sparkling water from the Amazon river. My friends we are failing to *cast down our buckets* for the help that is right about us, and spend too much time in signaling for help that is *far off*. Let us cast down our buckets here in our own sunny South, cast them down in *agriculture*, in *truck gardening, dairying, poultry raising, hog raising, laundrying, cooking, sewing, mechanical* and professional life, and the help that we think is far off will come and we will soon grow independent and useful.

TUSKEGEE NORMAL AND INDUSTRIAL INSTITUTE— THIRTEENTH ANNUAL REPORT.

TO THE TRUSTEES OF THE TUSKEGEE NORMAL AND INDUSTRIAL INSTITUTE, TUSKEGEE, ALABAMA.

GENTLEMEN :

THIS report marks the closing of the thirteenth year of the history of this Institution. Beginning July 4, 1881, without a dollar except an annual appropriation of $2,000 from the State for tuition, during the thirteen years there has come into our treasury $511,955.42 in cash from all sources. Of this amount $73,000 has come from the State; $5,162.50 from the Peabody Fund; $15,500 from the John F. Slater Fund; $51,450.91 from the students toward their expenses. The remainder, $413.842.01 has come in the form of gifts from individuals, organizations, concerts and the county of Macon. During the thirteen years the students have done labor for the Institution to the value of $203,612.52.

Beginning in a small church and shanty with no property, the property of the Institution, including land, buildings, live stock, outfit and apparatus, is now valued at $215,000, and there is no mortgage on any of it. In all the school owns 1,810 acres of land. Counting large and small there are thirty-one buildings used for class work, industrial training and dormitory purposes. There are 256 head of live stock, consisting of horses, mules, cows, calves, hogs, etc. The first enrollment consisted of thirty pupils and one teacher. The enrollment for the present year is 809 students and 66 instructors. Including the present class 166 have graduated and are doing excellent work as teachers in the class room and as industrial teachers in other schools, farmers, mechanics, housekeepers, etc. Besides at least 400 under-graduates are doing excellent work in the lines just mentioned. The demand for our graduates is usually larger than we can supply. There are no loafers to be found among those who graduate at Tuskegee.

Since May 31, 1893, the close of our last financial year, to May 31,

1894, the income of the shool from all sources has been $73,107. Of this amount two-fifths have gone into the permanent plant, and three-fifths into the current expenses of the school; $7,911.28 has been paid in cash by the students toward their own expenses; $3,000 from the State, and the remainder has come from generous individuals and organizations. Students have done work to the value of $41,893.20 for this year. The average salary paid the teachers is $395.58 per year.

In connection with the growth of the Institution, it is encouraging to note the following: During last year the John F. Slater Fund Trustee Board increased its appropriation to the school for the present year from $2,000 to $4,000. During the month of February, Dr. J. L. M. Curry, Chairman of the Educational Committee of the Slater Fund, in company with Dr. D. C. Gilman, the President of the Slater Trust, visited and thoroughly inspected the work of the school; and as a result of the visit and report, the Board has just notified us of its decision to increase the appropriation for the coming year to something over $5,000.

PHELPS HALL.

Phelps Hall, the beautiful and commodious building given by Miss Olivia E. P. Stokes, of New York City, for Bible study, has been completed and furnished at a cost of about $12,000—the whole expense being borne by Miss Stokes.

A lady who wishes to be known simply as an "Elderly Northern Friend," has given $2,000 toward a permanent fund of $10,000 to endow the Nurse-Training Department. $1,000 of this is invested in the Macon County Bank at 6 per cent interest.

Following is an explanatory letter from the donor of this fund:—

To the Trustees of the Tuskegee Normal and Industrial Institute:

"Enclosed please find one thousand ($1,000) dollars toward the ten thousand ($10,000) dollars needed for the establishment of Permanent Fund for the Nurse-Training Department of the Tuskegee Normal and Industrial Institute; this Fund to be designated as the Lafayette Fund.

"One-half of the annual interest on the above one thousand ($1,000) dollars, and, also, on whatever sums may be added to this Lafayette Fund from time to time by the present donor, or by other donor or donors, or by accrued interest, is not to be expended, but to be added to the principal, until the needed amount of ten thousand ($10,000) dollars accrues.

"Meanwhile, the remaining one-half of the annual interest is to be used annually for the benefit of the Nurse-Training Department of the Tuskegee Normal and Industrial Institute.

"After the required sum of ten thousand ($10,000) dollars has accrued, then the entire interest thereof shall be used annually to defray the expenses of the Nurse-Training Department of the Tuskegee Normal and Industrial Institute.

"Or, at the discretion of the trustees of said Tuskegee Normal and Industrial Institute, part of the annual interest of this said Lafayette Fund of ten thousand ($10,000) dollars, may be used for hospital needs of said Institute.

"May 12th, 1893."

Mrs. Mary E. Berry, formerly of Macon County, Ala., but now residing in New York City, has given the Institution a deed to a plantation ten miles from Tuskegee, that contains four hundred acres of land; has on it several buildings, including one brick building with nine rooms. The estate with improvements is valued at $10,000.

The Fund of $2,000, given some time ago by Miss Olivia E. P. Stokes, for investment—the interest to be used in helping students having the Christian Ministry in view—is invested as follows:

$1,200 temporarily invested in the supply farm, "Marshall" Farm; $800 lent to A. A. Torbert, for building.

A gentleman and his wife, residing in Boston, who do not care to have their names made public, have established the "Dizer Fund," the object of which is described in the following letter:

To the Trustees of the Tuskegee Normal and Industrial Institute, Tuskegee, Alabama:

I hereby donate to the Trustees of the Tuskegee Normal and Industrial Institute, Tuskegee, Ala., ($1,500) one thousand five hundred dollars, to be known as the "Dizer Fund," and to be used by them in the following manner:

As fast as practicable, I desire the trustees to lend the above-named amount to colored people in sums of $50.00 to $300.00, in a way to enable them to secure comfortable homes. In all cases where loans are made, I desire that the Tuskegee graduates or students be given the preference. The loans are to be secured by mortgage on the real estate, and the rate of interest charged is to be 8 per cent. per annum. It is further my wish that the trustees so lend the money as to cause to be built in as many different communities as possible, at least one model Christian home. The annual income from the Dizer Fund is to be used by the Trustees of the Tuskegee Normal and Industrial Institute in any manner that they deem best for the benefit of the Institution, and if at any time, in the judgment of the trustees, the good of the Institution requires it, they are at liberty to use the Dizer Fund for the immediate wants of the Institution, instead of in the manner specified in the foregoing."

At present this fund has been loaned to graduates and others on the conditions named, and it is accomplishing great good. It is eagerly sought after by graduates, and there are many applicants now waiting to secure a loan.

Mr. Henry L. Stearns, of College Hill, Mass., has established a scholarship in memory of his father, Maj. George L. Stearns, by the gift of one thousand dollars, which has been invested at 6 per cent. interest.

A few years ago Rev. Frederick Frothingham, of Milton, Mass., who has been interested in this Institution almost from its beginning, left by will $20,000 to the American Unitarian Association, of Boston, the income of which was to be used for all time to promote education among the colored people. The American Unitarian Association, at a meeting last fall, voted unanimously to give the income from the Frothingham Fund to this Institution; $10,000 left the Institution some time ago by the bequest of Mr. Horace Smith, of Springfield, Mass., was paid by the executors during the month of March.

Mr. A. H. Parker, of Brooklyn, N. Y., has recently given us a second mortgage for $1,000. The money, when collected, is to be used in erecting on the school grounds, a Model Home, to be occupied by the girls of the Senior Class. The mortgage is at present in the hands of Mr. Parker as a matter of convenience for collecting the interest and principal.

Three new cottages for teachers' residences have been built on the school grounds during the past year. In connection with the literary work, there are at present 23 industries in operation, which are as follows: Carpentry, painting, architectural and mechanical drawing, brick-making, brick-masonry, saw mill work, plastering, wheelwrighting, harness-making, farming, shoe-making, tinning, printing, mattress-making, nurse-training, dress-making and sewing, stock-raising, blacksmithing, laundrying, tailoring, house-keeping and cooking.

There has never been a year in the history of the school when so much improvement has been made in the teaching of the industries. Most of the industrial work now has as its foundation a thorough course in mechanical and architectural drawing. The article to be manufactured in the shop is first drawn by the student and then manufactured in the shop. Every student now receives three-fourths of an hour each day bearing upon the principles and theory of his trade or industry in addition to the practical work. This has greatly increased the interest of the students in the industrial work as well as added to the value of the industrial work. One of the greatest needs in the industrial work is more teaching force, so that the head of the department can have more time for planning, research and study. The colored people throughout the world are beginning to demand industrial education in a way that they have never done before. All of our industrial departments have been full, and many students refused for lack of room.

A large number of other schools and individuals are applying to this institution for information that will assist them in starting or improving an industrial department, and this furnishes another reason why everything at Tuskegee should be done in the best manner. In a word, an increasing number of institutions are using us as their model.

The Bible Training School, founded by Miss Olivia E. P. Stokes, of New York, about eighteen months ago, is meeting with very satisfactory success. The enrollment for the present year is forty-three, consisting mainly of ministers or those intending to be ministers. Perhaps the most interesting and unique feature of the Bible Training School is the fact that theology in the usual sense is not taught, and the question of denomination is wholly ignored. The students, as a rule, are about equally divided between Baptists and Methodists, but other denominations are also represented.

The teaching as far as possible is also confined to the simple truths of the English Bible. Special stress is laid upon having the students receive practical training in applied religion, especially in its relations to the industrial and moral needs of the masses of the colored people in the "Black Belt." The simple presentation of the abstract truths of the Bible from the pulpit is not all that the masses of the colored people need. Not much religion can exist in a one-room cabin and in an empty stomach. The prospects now are that the attendance in this department will be greatly increased next year.

This institution perhaps never did a wiser or more helpful thing than when it inaugurated what is known all over the country as the "Tuskegee Negro Conference," which has now held three meetings, the objects of which have been the bringing together for quiet conference, not the politicians, but the representatives of the hardworking farmers, mechanics, teachers and ministers, to find out the actual condition of the race industrially, educationally, morally and religiously, and to suggest remedies for present evils. The conference devotes itself, not to the discussion of wrongs perpetrated upon the race, but to the race's opportunities to better their condition. The good these conferences are doing is very apparent.

Some of the most urgent needs of the school at present are closer attention to the improvement in matters that concern the nicer and smaller details of the work in every respect; also during the coming school year much attention should be given to making the literary and normal work more thorough and effective.

A building to contain sleeping rooms for young men and recitation rooms are badly needed; also a chapel that can be used for large gatherings. Greater efforts should be put forth in the future in securing an endowment fund upon which the school can rely in a large measure for its income.   BOOKER T. WASHINGTON,

May 30, 1894. *Principal.*

MISS LUCY LANEY.

AMONG the colored female educators of the South, the subject of our sketch stands pre-eminently first. In speaking of her, Rev. George C. Rowe, of Charleston, S. C., says: "Miss Laney is a graduate of Atlanta University, and has taught school for a number of years in various places in Georgia. She left Savannah in 1886 where she was receiving a salary of $400 per year, and went to Augusta for the purpose of establishing an industrial boarding school, without the promise of aid from anyone. She rented a large house, became responsible for the support of teachers and the boarding department and began work. The first year her school enrolled 140 pupils; the second, 250, and it has steadily increased in numbers, power, and influence." This school is under the auspices of the Presbyterian Church, but is open to all who will comply with the rules and regulations. A few years ago a benevolent Northern lady gave her $10,000 with which a site was purchased in a desirable locality and a handsome five-story brick building was erected, and four years after it was founded Miss Laney transferred her school to this handsome edifice. We are not surprised at the success with which Miss Laney is meeting since she has associated with her such competent assistants as Miss M. C. Jackson, Miss Irene Smallwood, and Mrs. Mary R. Phelps. Miss Laney is a model for her numerous pupils in everything that the word implies. The "Palmetto Poet," Dr. George C. Rowe, puts it this way:

> Not on the height of Bunker Hill
> Nor Concord's battle ground,
> Nor on the field of Vicksburg, will
> Our heroine be found.
>
> Not in the annals of the wars
> That history records;
> Not in sayings 'neath the stripes and stars
> Shall we hear her thrilling words!
>
> But where the ranks of the coming men
> And women may be found,
> With books and slates and ready pen,
> Lo, there is her battle ground!

Not where the din and conflict reach—
    Nor hidious bugle toot,
But where the patient teachers teach
    Ideas how to shoot!

To reach the top her mind was bent;
    Patience and faith her rule;
To-day she sits as President
    Of Haines Industrial School!

Among the women of our race
    We know of few, if any,
Who fill a nobler, worthier place—
    Thou earnest Lucy Laney.

Haines Normal and Industrial Institute.

A VERY significant mission school in the South is that one located at Augusta, Georgia, and known as the Haines Normal and Industrial Institute. It is the life and effort of a young Negro woman, Miss Lucy C. Laney, who when very young conceived the idea of founding a school for the uplifting of Negro women. The idea was too noble to perish. Upon her own responsibility the school was founded in 1886 in rented buildings. Four years afterward the work was transferred to a handsome, spacious, five-story brick building.

HAINES NORMAL AND INDUSTRIAL INSTITUTE.

In that building, together with a smaller wooden building, are taught sewing, printing, and laundry work. The first story of the brick building contains a very large engine used for heating the different recitation rooms and the building in general. The second story consists of a very large assembly room, reception room, dining room, kitchen, music room, and two recitation rooms. The third story has six recitation rooms, one music room, library, cloak room and Miss Laney's office. The fourth and fifth stories are rooms neatly furnished and sufficient to accommodate about sixty young ladies, aside from the two bath rooms and reception room. There are small cottages used as dormitories for the young men.

There are two departments of this school, viz.: A normal and college preparatory. The normal prepares the students for teachers and to fill the many openings for our young people. The college preparatory course fits those wishing a higher education to enter college. Sometimes the young men leaving Haines and going to Princeton, Harvard and Lincoln Universities, etc., on examination make the junior college course, so thorough is the training given in this Institution.

We feel that we would do Haines an injustice not to mention the special training class for teachers presided over by Miss M. C. Jackson, the assistant principal of Haines. Those wishing a thorough knowledge of "theory and practice" and all or most of the new methods of teaching the young idea how to "shoot," will find themselves greatly benefitted by becoming members of Miss Jackson's training class. There is also a class for training nurses for the sick. How important it is to know how to care for the sick; many die because of ignorant nurses. I would that all Institutions had departments for training nurses. Some of the young women after having finished a course in the training class, nurse in private families for very good salaries, others attend in hospitals as matrons, etc.

One of the recent features of the Haines school is the establishment of the Kindergarten department, which is so ably presided over by Miss Irene Smallwood, a graduate of the Kindergarten Training School in Buffalo, New York. In this school little children from three to six years old are taken and put through a thorough and practical drill in many things which train the intellect, direct the imagination, and tend to make the little ones skilled in the use of their hands. They sew, learn to call things by their names, learn to distinguish colors, and in a hundred things do they receive a training that is indispensable to them when they enter the school room proper.

Haines' School is under the auspices of the Northern Presbyterian Board, with Miss L. C. Laney as its principal. The average enrollment of the school has been about four hundred. This is the only Presbyterian mission school in the State of Georgia, and for that reason it is a very interesting part of the Presbyterian Church.

MRS. MARY R. PHELPS.
Augusta, Ga.

MARY R. PHELPS.

MRS. MARY R. PHELPS is the daughter of Hilliard and Adeline Rice. She was born in Union County, South Carolina. She could read when but four years old, at the age of five she entered the public school. She had a wonderful memory, could recite from memory every dialogue, every piece of poetry, and every page of importance in her school books. When only thirteen years old she was asked to take charge of a large school. With her parents' consent she accepted, was examined and received a teacher's certificate and taught the fall and winter term of said school. Her parents noting her improvement and aptness, notwithstanding her limited advantages, determined to have her educated. They sent her to Benedict Institute, Columbia, S. C., where she remained one term, making one hundred in her examinations. During that vacation she taught as usual, and the term of 1881-2 she entered Scotia Seminary, Concord, N. C., where she completed both courses, graduating from the higher course in 1885. While attending Scotia she was noted for her high style of writing, and for her worthiness received a two years' scholarship in Scotia Seminary. After graduating she was principal of the public schools at Glenn Springs, S. C., three years.

In 1890 she resigned at Glenn Springs to accept a position in the Graded School, of Rome, Ga., where she taught a part of two terms. For the term of 1890-91 she was elected Assistant Principal of the Eddy School, Milledgeville, Ga. On the 25th of October, 1891, she was married to John L. Phelps, of Milledgeville, Ga., at her home, Helena, S. C. In 1893 she was elected Assistant Principal of Cleveland Academy, Helena, S. C., and resigned before the term closed to accept a position in Haines Institute, Augusta, Ga. Aside from these named schools she has taught school in Newberry, Chester, Union, Lexington, Laurens, and Spartanburg, Counties, South Carolina, and Gordon County, Georgia. She has taught more than a thousand children from the age of thirteen to the present. Mrs. Phelps is also a great Sunday school worker. She spends her vacations in the rural districts teaching the country boy and girl, and on Sunday you will find her gathering the children into the Sunday school. If the community has none she will organize a Sunday school. The women in the country look forward with eagerness to her coming, for she assists in whatever they do, especially in dressmaking. She has written articles for several papers, and some of her friends have urged her to write, but she holds to what she feels is her peculiar calling, that is, the schoolroom.

"The Responsibility of Women as Teachers."

BY MRS. MARY RICE PHELPS.

I HAVE a nature somewhat poetic, and might try to please you with simile, metaphor or trope, but the simplest way of saying things is best. To show you the importance of our subject, we would smite you with the wand of imagination and lead you through "Eden" of old to behold man as he languished, surrounded with all the beauties of nature, in a garden of variegated grandeur, till one more perfect came to bless his home in Paradise. Or we might wander with you through ancient days, in the dark ages of the world's history, and there, among the musty volumes of other ages, the dusty archives of long forgotten generations, read of woman's worth from one parchment, and on another behold the world's wretchedness while she is excluded from society. She was bound by fetters of corruption to endure that which was degrading in itself. Yet we find a sense of pure principle and noble purpose found wherever she is found.

In the dawn of the Christian era she threw off the manacle which society had placed upon her, and rose, step by step, from one degree of usefulness to another, filling almost every honorable position, till she comes forth as man's equal and companion. We wish to speak briefly of her responsibilities and the preparation necessary to meet them, trusting that we may say something or suggest some thought that will help the young women of our race to place more value upon opportunities, and to more thoroughly and thoughtfully prepare themselves for the great work of moulding a more perfect negro race. There are manifold reasons to pause on the threshold of womanhood and ask ourselves: "What is the responsibility of women?" If we ask this question it is because it is grave; because society asks it; because we have a responsibility. This in itself is significant.

The first and most important question with every woman should be: "What did God mean for me to do? Am I preparing myself to meet the demands of my people? Am I equiping myself with the elements that make a true woman?" She who seeks to make herself what God intends her to be is sure of success. Woman's responsibility as teacher is great, grand and awful. Great and grand because of the material used; the thoughtfulness and discretion with which she must labor to make a success. The combined influences, the steadfast purposes, patience and several dispositions that constitute the true man and woman must be so simplified and so developed as to appear so desirable that they will in time become a part of those taught. The responsibility is awful because of the results that will follow. Have you ever thought what a fearful thing it is to shape a character for future usefulness, and instil right principles in an immortal soul?

The field is vast; more than eight millions of negroes in America; the majority to be taught loyalty to one another, and what it is to be true men and women; for the time may not be far distant when they will be called to fill positions of trust. Who can tell what event will begin a new epoch in the history of our country? Who can tell when the balance of power will be equally weighed among American citizens, and the sons of Ham will be a power? We have everything to hope for, though we sometimes murmur and think that stern Justice takes his nap unusually long. So long, until we have cried in our inmost souls, "How long, O Lord, how long?" But this is deviating from our subject.

To what extent does woman teach, and where does her tutorage begin? Every woman is a teacher, whether she be worthy or unworthy; whether educated or ignorant. In the home circle, and around the fireside, her teaching begins with the first dawn of intelligence. This is her inalienable right, the charter given by the Almighty hand. It is she who first points out those paths which are so full of pleasantness and peace, and directs the innocent minds to a heavenly Father. She makes her own life a daily example (we speak of the true woman) of all that is pure and ennobling. She it is who teaches those qualities that are so essential to any race or tribe of beings, morality, the cornerstone in the building up of any race; Christianity, the thread that must make the warp and woof of a prosperous people;

economy, one of the foundation stones that cannot be dispensed with.

It is woman's responsibility to teach the coming generations to live inside of their means, and to reserve extra pennies for rainy days (they will be sure to come), and secure a home for old age. How many are paid large salaries, "live high," unmindful of the future, and end their existence in the almshouse?

The time is fast approaching, so near that we can hear his footstep in the distance, when nobody will care for that class of persons who are content to live in poverty. Such have neglected opportunities, misused means and wasted time. They are content to know little, and possess less, a universal sentiment, because it is a universal experience. Woman's responsibility is great, and its importance vast, when we analyze it. She alone has the power to set at naught the monster, "ignorance," uproot "base desire," break down the barrier, prejudice, and bury the race problem under the black pall of oblivion, beyond the possibility of a resurrection. Why should they fill positions as public teachers? Why, because our educated men are needed for so many avocations that the work of teaching is left almost wholly to women.

True we have little or no part in the political arena, but that gives time for preparation and thought. Seeing the awful blunders that politicians now make will but give a clearer insight to them when it is theirs to act and to do. While they may be debarred from the ballot-box, and we cannot even offer them a clerkship after having worked manfully to acquire an education, we know of other fields. We need jewelers, machinists, engineers, lawyers, merchants, physicians and an educated ministry. We need leaders, not only in politics, but in the pulpits, in the pews and everywhere.

Thirty years have passed since we were liberated from a condition of servitude and extreme degradation to enjoy the rights and privileges as citizens of America. We have waited and looked for a leader these thirty years with such anxiety as did our ancestors two hundred and fifty years ago for the glorious light of freedom. It came. So will a leader. Woman's work in the world is great and multifarious. It is a work which she alone can do. We do not mean to compare her with a man, but compare woman with woman. Judge of what I can do by what I have done; of what women can do by what they have done. She can inspire when man fails. 'Tis hers to uplift, purify and adorn. What great cause of the world has brought about the desired result without woman's help? She did not bring down the lightning and connect electricity with thought, that different countries could talk to each other; but what did not the Reformation owe to the clear, womanly insight of Catherine Von Bora? Does not American independence owe much to the courage and steadfast resolution of the women of the Revolution?

She did not soar on telescopic wings and poise on ethereal pinions amid the fiery planets of the blue canopy to make a catalogue of the stars and discover the laws that govern them, and "unlock their complicated movements;" but we find her shaping character and moulding the minds that sway the government of our country. What does not missions owe to the Christian women of our country? It holds true that

> "Warriors and statesmen have their meed of praise;
> And what they suffer men record;
> But the long sacrifice of woman's day
> Passes without a thought, a word of praise."

'Tis woman's responsibility to teach the young men what it is to be true men; what it is to be a loyal man; "a man" in every sense of the word. To teach the young woman to be womanly; that it is honorable to work; that fashionable and frivolous women who live only in self-indulgence and to have a "good time" are a dead weight upon their parents and a blot in society. In the age of chivalry and knighthood the laws of human nature were expressed when the crowning of the victor was assigned to woman's hand. As on the knightly fields, so it is on the great battle-fields of life, contestants and combatants are animated and encouraged by woman's approval and cheering words. If you fail, young women, to use this power, you fail positively, not negatively; so fail that you will drag down instead of elevating. This power is yours, and you cannot change it. It belongs to you as women.

Catherine de Medici urged and Protestantism died in France. The women of Rome became dissolute, and the Romans were conquered by the barbarians from the North. Esther pleads, and a doomed nation is rescued. Abigail intercedes, and her household is spared. She teaches the king to think of the folly of rashness. Young women, if you are weak, wicked and worldly, men will follow you as if you were pure. They will seek you, learn of your wicked ways and follow you, even to destruction and death. Knowing these things, equip yourselves with all that make a true and noble woman.

If you have never been a factor in the upbuilding of your race, count up the cost and begin to do your part. If you have never thought of race pride, think now. Not only think, but act well your part. Without the ennobling power of the woman we can never be a great and noble race. If young men aspire to reach the highest pinnacles of fame, they rise but to fall lower, unless the women are pure and will demand respect. Learn to resent insults, young women. Learn to respect and defend the women of our race, young men.

I would that I had a thousand tongues, and every tongue a thousand voices, and every voice a thousand echoes that could reach from America to the utmost parts of Africa, and I would speak in loudest tone, with animating voice to every negro woman, and bid her take up woman's responsibility, come together and begin to act, begin to do, and exert her power in the right direction, and the world will feel it. Not as it would feel an earthquake shock, but as the globe feels that grand cohesive power which cements its heterogeneous masses and binds them in one harmonious band.

REV. GEORGE WYLIE CLINTON, A.M.

EDITOR OF THE "STAR OF ZION," THE OFFICIAL ORGAN OF THE AFRICAN METHODIST EPISCOPAL ZION CHURCH.

THE subject of this sketch was born in Lancaster County, South Carolina, March 28, 1859. His father having died when he was but two years old, he was brought up in the home of his grandparents, with whom he and his mother lived until he was sixteen years old. He received the training of the common schools of Lancaster County and entered the senior class of the preparatory department of the South Carolina University, an institution which has sent out some of the first men of the South, in both the civil and the ecclesiastical spheres. He remained in the South Carolina University until he had completed his sophomore year in the classical department. This was the year 1876, when Wade Hampton was elected by the Democratic party Governor of South Carolina, and as a consequence colored students were compelled to withdraw from the university. His education being thus suddenly broken off, he returned home, assisted his mother and grandmother in harvesting the crop of that year, and then began his career as a teacher in the public schools of his native State. It may be observed here that young Clinton was very much devoted to his mother, and that this devotion was largely the natural result of the pious training which she had given him. The death of his father when he was so young necessarily brought him more fully under the care and training of his mother and more constantly into her association. Without any disparagement to fathers, may not such a situation, together with the fact that the boy must more largely rely on himself, explain the advancement and success of many a young man?

REV. GEORGE WYLIE CLINTON, D.D.,
Salisbury, N. C.

While at home young Clinton was appointed to the position of clerk in the office of C. P. Pelham, Auditor of Lancaster County, and remained in this position till called to larger fields as a teacher of his race. One incident in connection with his experience in this office deserves special mention, because of its suggestion of the guidance of the unseen hand of Providence. In connection with his other duties he began the study of law in the office of two leading Democratic lawyers of Lancaster, and, as it was recommended by Blackstone, he undertook a close and earnest reading of the Bible. His interest in the Bible soon outgrew his interest in Blackstone and Kent; and, having believed on Him who saves to the uttermost, he abandoned law as a profession and was licensed to preach on February 14, 1879. This was the turning point in his life. He continued preaching and teaching until November, 1891, when he joined the South Carolina Conference of the A. M. E. Zion Church, and forsook all and followed Him.

From this time on Rev. Mr. Clinton's history is a part of the history of his church in South Carolina and in the nation as a preacher and religious teacher with both tongue and pen. His first appointment as an itinerant preacher was near Chester, S. C. He resided in the town and in order to complete his college course connected himself with Brainard Institute, a high grade institution located there. This was another characteristic and significant step. He must complete the foundation upon which he proposed to build the education of a lifetime.

While studying in this institution he so commended himself as an earnest and successful student that he was given by Rev. Samuel Loomis, A.M., the principal, a position as teacher which afforded some remuneration and at the same time permitted him to carry out his resolution to complete his college course. He graduated with high rank, and entered more regularly upon the work of the intinerant ministry in his conference. He continued in this capacity seven years when he was transferred by Bishop S. T. Jones, D.D., to the Allegheny Conference to take the difficult appointment of John Wesley Church, Pittsburgh, Pa., perhaps the most important appointment west of New York. In this appointment he followed one of the most experienced and successful men in the entire connection and one who, it was thought, had carried "John Wesley" to its high-water mark. But our subject made a new mark for her, and gave her a record and standing which alike astonished and delighted the membership and the chief pastors under whom he labored.

The proof of the success of his management of this church was given in the manner in which it entertained the great General Conference of 1892. This appointment may be considered to mark the end of the first stage of Rev. Mr Clinton's career as a rising young divine of his church.

Before proceeding to review the second stage of his career, it would be proper to remark that during almost the entire period of Rev. Mr. Clinton's itinerancy in the South Carolina Conference he was without question the leading man of the conference, confessedly the standard by which the best material of the conference was gauged. He was a sort of standing secretary of the conference and perpetual compiler and publisher of the minutes. This distinction was due in no sense to an inclination to favoritism on the part of the conference. He won it by his merit as an accurate, painstaking, scholarly worker, and nobody thought of anything else than that this business of the conference was in his hands. When he was transferred he was conference steward or connectional treasurer of the conference, showing that his colleagues saw in him not only scholarship but sound business methods and unwavering integrity. These characteristics of Rev. Mr. Clinton had already opened up to him the columns of the leading papers of his State, like the Charleston *News and Courier*, the Charleston *Sun*, the *Century*, the *Union Times*, and the Landcaster *Ledger*, and all the colored journals sought him.

His contributions to these periodicals always furnished evidence of thought, literary taste and scholarship. Editor Clinton's popularity in his conference and his influence in his State were the means by which the writer first came to a knowledge of his usefulness and prospects.

Returning now to the beginning of the second stage of his career, we find him the accomplished, eloquent and popular pastor of John Wesley Church, Pittsburgh, Pa. From this time on South Carolina can claim him only in common with other portions of the great church of which he has now become a leading figure. Even before he left South Carolina, as a representative of his conference in the General Conferences at New York and New Bern, N. C., his merits were acknowledged by the general church in his being chosen assistant secretary at both these conferences; and at the latter he was also created one of the commissioners of the A. M. E. Zion Church to confer with similar representatives of the C. M. E. Church on Organic Union. But along with his appointment to Pittsburgh, the church urges consideration of him as a suitable man to succeed Hon. John C. Dancey as editor of the church organ, the *Star of Zion*.

Rev. Mr. Clinton had long ago demonstrated his right to such consideration by his luminous contributions to the papers above referred to as well as to the *Star of Zion*, and in Pittsburgh as editor of the *Afro-American Spokesman*, to which position he was chosen by the colored ministers of Western Pennsylvania of all denominations, he proved beyond a doubt that he had talent and calling in that direction. But he gives further and conclusive demonstration of his fitness for the position that was evidently looming up for him by projecting, founding and runnning the *A. M. E. Zion Church Quarterly*. This effort showed not only his genius for organization but his ability to manage successfully a large and important literary venture. He ran the *Quarterly* on his own resources for two years and then turned it over to the General Conference in Pittsburgh without a cent of cost to the connection. The *Quarterly* is now one of the established institutions of the church, and if Editor Clinton had originated and established no other great enterprise this would be sufficient to give him perpetual fame in the church. But brilliant and creditable as is this effort of his it is only the door by which he enters into larger avenues of usefulness to his church and his race. At the General Conference in Pittsburgh in 1892, he was elected by a good majority to the place of editor of the *Star of Zion*, his church organ. He was by this choice elevated to one of the most responsible and distinguished positions in his church—a position of honor and one matched only by the Presidency of Livingston College in its requirements for scholarship, broad culture and sound judgment as a good business man and high executive officer of the connection.

Editor Clinton's genius to originate is powerfully evidenced also by the following fact: In February 1893 while attending the Florida Conference, he conceived the idea, and planned its execution, which has culminated in the Varrick Memorial Hall and Publishing House of the A. M. E. Zion Church in Charlotte, N. C. He presented his plan to the Board of Bishops in its semi-annual session in Birmingham in March, 1893, and the fruit thereof will be the connection's great plant at Charlotte, N. C., which in its development will undoubtedly become an honor to the mind that conceived as well as to the church which carries it to success.

By way of incident, but a very significant incident, it may be remarked that it was Editor Clinton who proposed the organization of our Sunday School Union and who headed the committee that formulated the plan for carrying out the organization. Editor Clinton has been progressive not only in the sense that contemplates personal advancement, but he has also manifested a noteworthy philanthropy and public spirit. As an evidence of his philanthropic spirit it may be related that he has assisted seven students through Livingston College, some of whom have gone forward to advanced scholarship and have already achieved considerable success in the professional walks of life. His public spirit was signally illustrated by the brave and courageous part which he took in the famous Flemon-Yeddell case. His earnest and untiring efforts to secure to Flemon justice and his perilous trip to Western South Carolina during the trial were no small part of the means which brought about the acquittal of Flemon.

No sketch of Editor Clinton would be complete that did not include some reference to his relation as husband and to the influence of his wife on his young manhood. At the early age of twenty-one he married Miss E. J. Peay, of Rock Hill, S. C., who was also a student at Brainard Institute, the *alma mater* of her husband. This was a most happy union and it is but just to say that Mrs. Clinton was a large factor in the rapid progress and advancement of her husband. The writer was an eye witness of the halo of grace and gentle inspiration which her presence cast around the home of which she was the center. But alas! As the bud fadeth in the time of its sweetest fragrance her soul eluded the grasp of time and was transplanted to the great beyond where it fadeth not for evermore.

The memory of the General Conference of 1892 becomes poignant only in the vididness of this other precious memory, but its poignancy becomes soothing when we remember what sister Clinton illustrated in her life and won in her death. But the picture must be changed for the final view. Editor Clinton's life has been hallowed in her taking away and his consecration is only increased. He is moving on to brighter goals of success. He is now bending all his energies toward making "The Star of Zion" thoroughly worthy of the great organization which it represents. He is a fair specimen of Zion's coming men, and is making a conspicuous record not only for himself but for his church. One of the proofs in point is the invitation extended to him by Principal Washington, of Tuskegee (Ala.) Institute, to deliver a series of lectures on the Bible in his institution. He is thus chosen as the representative of his church, to do this service calling for theological learning and a wide acquaintance with letters. It will be according to his custom to fill this engagement with credit to himself and profit to his hearers. He is characterized by a lucidness of speech and a forcefulness of utterance which mark for him a towering place among the leaders of his church as a preacher and public speaker, and his logical and earnest style together with his sterling integrity guarantees to him no decline in his ascent of the higher heights of Zion.

HON. H. C. SMITH.

[For eleven years editor and proprietor of the "Cleveland Gazette," and a member of the Ohio Legislature.]

BY PROF. W. S. SCARBOROUGH.

THE well known subject of this sketch was born in Clarksburg, West Virginia, on the 28th of January, 1863. He was taken to Cleveland, his present home, in 1865. Here he attended the schools of the city from an early age, finishing in 1882. During the next year he devoted his entire time to the study of band and orchestral music. In this he also reached distinction. The same desire to rise above mediocrity and thereby demand respect for himself and race because of his fitness and thorough preparation for the work of life, took possession of him here as in his earlier life. He lost no time, but continued to plod upward. The result is, that as a young man of scholarly attainments, of comprehensive views, as a journalist and musician—especially a cornetist—he stands to-day *facile princeps* among the first colored citizens in the State of Ohio.

In addition to his editorial duties, for years Mr. Smith was leader and musical director of the famous Excelsior Cornet Band, of Cleveland, Ohio. His compositions have found ready sale, especially his song and chorus, "Be True, Bright Eyes," now known throughout the country.

In August, 1883, H. C. Smith, with three other gentlemen, launched the *Cleveland* (Ohio) *Gazette* upon the sea of journalism. Since that time, however, he has become sole owner and proprietor. This paper has proved a success, and is now by far the best colored paper published in the State of Ohio, and is one among the best edited by colored journalists in the United States. It is vigorous in tone, fearless in its defense of right, an uncompromising enemy of prejudice in all its forms, a strong advocate of equal rights to all men without distinction, and a staunch Republican in politics, with principle rather than expediency as its basis.

Mr. Smith has always wielded a fearless and able pen for right and truth. He has fought squarely in behalf of his race, demanding for it recognition wherever denied. No other proof of this is needed

HON. H. C. SMITH.
Cleveland, Ohio.

than the *Gazette* itself. The Hon. Frederick Douglass wrote: "In the midst of hurried preparations for a long tour in Europe, I snatch my pen and spend a few moments to tell you how completely I sympathize with your political attitude." Then, again, he adds: "I do exhort your readers to stand by you in your effort to lead the colored citizens of Ohio to wise political action."

Though at times Mr. Smith has been severely criticised, he has never varied from what he considered his duty. He believes that the Republican party conserves the best interests of the Negro, and thereupon he becomes its able and active defender. His articles are read with both pleasure and profit, to which fact is largely due the increased and increasing circulation of the *Gazette*.

The Republican governors of Ohio are indebted to Mr. Smith about as much as to any one journalist, colored or white, in the State. The colored members of the Ohio Assembly have always had a strong supporter in the editor of the *Gazette*. A few years ago he was appointed a Deputy State Oil Inspector, at Cleveland (the first Afro-American in the North so recognized) and held the position four years, until the election of a Democratic governor (Campbell). This appointment not only fittingly recognized the race, but the individual in the choice of one in every way qualified for the position and especially deserving of the appointment. The bond required was $5,000. This he soon secured in the persons of three of the oldest and most respected colored citizens of Cleveland. Mr. Smith is what we might call a self-made man, as it is through his own indefatigable efforts that he has reached his present position in life.

He is the author of several pieces of music for the guitar, in addition to compositions for the voice and piano. His various public utterances rank him as an active, wide-awake observer of passing events. Broad in his views he is withal charitable, zealous and conscientious. He is, perhaps, the first colored member of a white press association in the North, and is one of the youngest of our leading editors.

H. C. Smith is one of the young men of whom we all may feel proud and from whom we may justly expect an ever increasing career of honor and usefulness. His election to the Ohio Legislature at the election held November 7, 1893, by a majority of over 8,000 over his Democratic opponent (white) in a county (Cuyahoga) which polls over 40,000 Republiacn votes (about 2,000 being those of Afro-Americans), is indeed a fitting recognition of Mr. Smith's ability and worth as a man.

In order to secure the nomination, he had to contest with a very popular white Republican who had served in the preceding assembly. Nominations are made in Cuyahoga County under what is termed "the popular vote plan." That is, Republicans go to the polls on the day of the primaries and vote direct to nominate as all voters do to elect on election day. The same care is taken by the Board of Elections with the vote of the primaries as with the election day vote. The following from the Indianapolis (Ind.) *Freeman*, is pertinent.

"When the voters of 'Old Cuyahoga,' in Ohio, were casting about for a representative to send to the legislature, the *Freeman* shied its castor in the ring for Editor Smith, of the *Gazette*, as a proper and fit person to be selected for the honor. Mr. Smith received the nomination and was triumphantly elected, and his record as he has made it up to this time has amply vindicated the choice and judgment of his constituents. Mr. Smith has quickly and easily taken first place among the three Afro-American representatives selected by the voters of the Buckeye State to assist in making laws, and is in fact one of the few marked and growing young members who have succeeded in making themselves noticed and esteemed for the merit and value of their work. A few days since the colored citizens of Oberlin held a mass meeting, at which the following resolution was reported and adopted:

Resolved, That we do most heartily commend Hon. H. C. Smith, our representative in the Ohio Legislature, for the manly stand he has taken in behalf of equal rights for all citizens of Ohio.   THOMAS JENNY, *Chairman.*
GEO. W. M. LUCAS, *Secretary.*

His bill against lynching, drawn upon lines suggested by Judge Albion W. Tourgee, attracted even more attention than the Civil Rights bill he had passed. Mr. Smith did good work for his white constituents also, which they thoroughly appreciate. His term expires November 7, 1895. It is customary to elect members for a second term who make a good record. There is no doubt of his renomination and re-election should he desire it. Two of Cuyahoga's eight legislators are Afro-Americans. Our lives are measured by what we accomplish and not by "paltry years of existence."

Shall I Take a Paper?

AT this season of the year, when publishers are making special offers to the reading public, we are all debating the mental fare with which we shall spread our table in 1895. We ought to have first a good church paper thoroughly representative of our denomination.

The Methodist ought to have the *South-Western Advocate*, published at New Orleans; the African Methodist ought to have the *Christian Recorder*, published at Philadelphia; the Congregationalist ought to have *The Congregationalist*, published at Boston, or the *The Advance*, published at Chicago; and so on for the Baptists, Episcopalians,

Evangelists and other denominations among us. Each home ought to have its church paper. Next to that stands some good clean helpful race journal. Get one, in the columns of which the editors are seeking to help the race up, and not working to pull it down. When you subscribe for a race journal get one in which the editors display not pessimistic, but optimistic views of the race.

It will be well to remember that it takes brains to edit a newspaper, and men who have not been trained to think are hardly men to be entrusted with the perilous task of giving direction to public opinion. The editorial chair requires more than that culture gotten from the reading of newspapers. The editor who is sending out week by week his paper into the world ought to be able to grapple with the problems of the day and think them through. There is too much guessing on the grave social problems of the day by editors. Riots and mobs are the result of false teaching, both on the part of the hot-headed anarchists and incompetent editors who are not anachists. In selecting your race journal for the next year find one whose editorial columns show moderation, and one which is not always squared off with a chip on its shoulder daring someone to knock it off. The paper which busies itself with fighting its contemporaries cannot be of very much help to you. When you raise the question about taking a race journal remember there are two reasons especially to be remembered why you should. The first is a duty you owe to yourself to keep up with the movements among your own people. Second, you owe it to the race to support laudable enterprises which look to the betterment of the race. Let us remember, too, that the press, the pulpit and the platform have been the great liberators of the nations. In this land of ours we need the influence of all of these to plead our cause up and down the length of our land. Put some good race weekly on your list for 1895.—*Cleveland* (Ohio) *Gazette*.

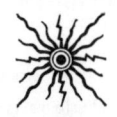

NEWSPAPERS

The following is a list of newspapers and magazines edited and published by and for Afro-Americans. Alphabetically arranged by States:

ALABAMA.

1	Birmingham	Harrison's Pet	Weekly.
2	"	Wide Awake	"
3	"	Southern Broadaxe	"
4	Eutaw	Weekly Blade	"
5	Huntsville	Huntsville Gazette	"
6	"	Huntsville Journal	"
7	"	Southern Freeman	"
8	"	The Independent	"
9	Lovan	The Eagle	"
10	Mobile	Southern Watchman	"
11	"	Ferret Journal	"
12	"	Weekly Sentinel	"
13	"	West Alabama Advocate	"
14	Montgomery	The Argus	"
15	"	Baptist Leader	"
16	"	Odd Fellow's Journal	Monthly.
17	Opelika	The People's Choice	Weekly.
18	Selma	Student's Voice	"
19	Tuskegee	The Tuskegee Student	Monthly.

ARKANSAS.

20	Fort Smith	The Post	Weekly.
21	Helena	Helena Progress	"
22	Little Rock	Arkansas Dispatch	"
23	"	Baptist Vanguard	"
24	Osceola	Afro-American Leader	"
25	Pine Bluff	The Echo	"

CALIFORNIA.

26	Los Angeles	The Vindicator	"
27	" "	The Eagle	"

28	Los Angeles	The Hustler	Weekly.
29	" "	Weekly Examiner	"
30	San Francisco	The Elevator	"
31	" "	Western Outlook	"

COLORADO.

32	Colorado Springs	Western Enterprise	"
33	Denver	Exponent	"
34	"	Denver Statesman	"
35	Pueblo	Pueblo Times	"

CONNECTICUT.

36	New Haven	Zion's Trumpet	"

DELAWARE.

37	Wilmington	Twilight	"

DISTRICT OF COLUMBIA.

38	Washington	The Bee	"
39	"	The Colored American	"
40	"	The Globe	Daily.
41	"	The Pilot	Weekly.
42	"	Woman's Tribune	"
43	"	National Baptist Messenger	Quarterly.
44	"	The Zion Methodist	Weekly.

FLORIDA.

45	Gainesville	Florida Sentinel	"
46	Live Oak	Florida Baptist	"
47	Jacksonville	Southern Courier	"
48	"	The Daily American	Daily.
49	"	The Advocate	Weekly.
50	Winter Park	Winter Park Advocate	"

GEORGIA.

51	Athens	The Clipper	"
52	Albany	The Dispatch	"
53	Americus	People's Messenger	"
54	Atlanta	The People's Advocate	"
55	"	Voice of Missions	Monthly.
56	"	The Georgia Speaker	"
57	"	Spellman Messenger	"
58	"	Hope Spellman Seminary	"
59	"	Atlanta Times	Weekly.
60	"	Southern Appeal	"
61	Augusta	Georgia Baptist	"
62	"	Augusta Sentinel	"
63	"	Methodist Union	"
64	"	The Haines Journal	Monthly.
65	Blakely	The Mouthpiece	Weekly.
66	Brunswick	The Gleaner	"

67	Cartersville	The Negro Educational Journal	Monthly.
68	Dalton	Dalton Argus	Weekly.
69	Eastman	Negro Exponent	"
70	Rome	Baptist Banner	"
71	"	People's Journal	"
72	"	The Woman's World	Semi-Monthly
73	Savannah	Labor Union	Weekly.
74	"	Recorder	"
75	"	Tribune	"
76	Valdosta	Black and White	"

ILLINOIS.

77	Chicago	A. M. E. Record	"
78	"	Appeal	"
79	"	Bee	"
80	"	Brotherhood	"
81	"	Chicago Legal News	"
82	"	Chicago Standard	"
83	"	Chicago Clipper	"
84	"	Church Organ	"
85	"	Conservator	"
86	"	Christian Science	Monthly.
87	"	Free Speech	Weekly.
88	Peoria	The Negro Problem	"
89	Springfield	State Capital	"

INDIANA.

90	Indianapolis	The Freeman	"
91	"	The World	"
92	Terre Haute	Afro-American Journal	"

INDIAN TERRITORY.

93	Lee Creek Nation	Weekly Sun	"

IOWA.

94	Des Moines	The Avalanche	"
95	"	The Bystander	"

KANSAS.

96	Atchison	The Blade	"
97	Coffeeville	Afro-American Advocate	"
98	"	Kansas Blackman	"
99	Kansas City	American Citizen	"
100	Leavenworth	Leavenworth Herald	"
101	Parsons	Weekly Blade	"
102	Topeka	The Call	"
103	"	State Ledger	"
104	Witchita	National Baptist World	"

KENTUCKY.

105	Hopkinsville	Indicator	Weekly.
106	Henderson	Gleaner.	"
107	Lexington	The Standard	"
108	Louisville	American Baptist	"
109	"	National Baptist Messenger	Quarterly.
110	"	Ohio Falls	Weekly.
111	"	Zion's Banner	"

LOUISIANA.

112	New Orleans	The Crescent	Monthly.
113	" "	Journal of the Lodge	Weekly.
114	" "	Christian Herald	"
115	" "	Crusader	Daily.
116	" "	People's Reporter	Monthly.
117	" "	South Western Christian Advocate	Weekly.
118	" "	The Ferret	"
119	" "	The Monitor	"

MARYLAND.

120	Baltimore	Afro-American	Weekly.
121	"	Church Advocate	"
122	"	Prohibition Advocate	"
123	"	The Colored Harvester	"
124	Elkton	The Dawn	Monthly.
125	Marlborough	The Crusader	Weekly.

MAINE.

126	Augusta	The Wide World	Weekly.

MASSACHUSETTS.

127	Boston	The Courant	"
128	"	Watchman	"
129	"	Advocate	"
130	"	Woman's Era	"
131	"	Woman's Journal	Monthly.
132	"	Woman's Column	"
133	"	Boston Banner	Weekly.
134	"	The Republican	"

MICHIGAN.

135	Detroit	American Catholic	"
136	"	Detroit Plaindealer	"
137	"	National Independent	"
138	"	The Beacon Light	"

MINNESOTA.

139	St. Paul	The Appeal	"

MISSISSIPPI.

140	Columbus	New Light	Semi-Monthly
141	"	Baptist Reflector	Weekly.
142	Jackson	People's Defender	"
143	"	The Jackson Light	Monthly.
144	"	The Messenger	Semi-Monthly
145	Meridian	Fair Play	Weekly.
146	Natchez	The Brotherhood	"
147	"	The Reporter	Monthly.
148	Senatobia	The Baptist Herald	Weekly.
149	Shaw	The News	"

MISSOURI.

150	Hamilton	Baptist Standard	"
151	Kansas City	Future State	"
152	" "	Gate City Press	"
153	" "	The American Citizen	"
154	" "	Kansas City Messenger	"
155	Independence	The International	Monthly.
156	Moberly	Christian Recorder	Weekly.
157	"	Western Optic	"
158	Pine Bluff	The Echo	"
259	Sedalia	Sedalia International	Monthly.
160	"	Afro-American	Weekly.
161	St. Louis	St. Louis Advocate	"
162	"	Missionary Record	Monthly.

NEBRASKA.

163	Omaha	Progress	Weekly.
164	"	Enterprise	"
165	"	Afro-American Sentinel	"

NEW JERSEY.

166	Newark	New Jersey Trumpet	"

NEW YORK.

167	New York	The Echo	"
168	"	The Age	"
169	"	The Examiner	"
170	"	Union Times	"
171	"	National Temperance Advocate	"
172	"	Home Mission	Monthly.
173	Brooklyn	National Monitor	Weekly.
174	Buffalo	The Basis	"

NORTH CAROLINA.

175	Charlotte	Afro-American Press	"
176	"	The Messenger	"
177	"	Baptist Pilot	Monthly.
178	Raleigh	The Gazette	Weekly.
179	"	North Carolina Sun	"

180	Readsville	Baptist Headlight	Weekly.
181	Salisbury	Star of Zion	"
182	"	Livingston	Monthly.
183	Winston	The Student	"
184	Wilmington	A. M. E. Zion	Quarterly.
185	"	The Afro-American Presbyterian	Weekly.

OHIO.

186	Albany	The Diadem	"
187	Cleveland	The Gazette	"
188	"	Ringwood Journal of Fashion	Monthly.
189	"	Voice of the People	Weekly.
190	Cincinnati	American Catholic Tribune	Monthly.
191	"	Journal and Messenger	Weekly.
192	"	The Race Problem	"
193	"	Old Hughes	Monthly.
194	Ringwood	American Journal	"
195	Springfield	The Beacon	Weekly.
196	Toledo	Afro-American Standard	"

OKLAHOMA.

197	Langston City	The Herald	"

PENNSYLVANIA.

198	Philadelphia	The Christian Banner	"
199	"	Astonisher	"
200	"	The Speck	"
201	"	The Christian Recorder	"
202	"	Independent Advocate	"
203	"	Masonic Herald	"
204	"	Weekly Tribune	"
205	"	Standard Echo	"
206	"	A. M. E. Church Review	Quarterly.
207	Pittsburg	The Spokesman	Weekly.
208	"	The Broadaxe	"

RHODE ISLAND.

209	Providence	New England Torch Light	"
210	"	The Sun	"

SOUTH CAROLINA.

211	Aikin Court House	Little Observer	Semi-Monthly
212	Beaufort	New South	Weekly.
213	Bennettsville	Pee Dee Educator	Semi-Monthly
214	Brunson	Hampton County Elevator	Weekly.
215	Charleston	Enquirer	"
216	"	Messenger	"
217	Chester	South Carolina Herald	"
218	Columbia	People's Recorder	"
219	Florence	Baptist Herald	Semi-Monthly
220	Valcluse	South Carolina Tribune	Weekly.

TENNESSEE.

221	Athens	Watchman	Weekly.
222	Clarksville	Montgomery Pilot	"
223	Columbia	Headlight	Semi-Monthly
224	Fayetteville	Colored Presbyterian (Cumberland)	Weekly.
225	Jackson	Christian Index	"
226	Knoxville	The Herald	"
227	"	Negro World	"
228	"	Weekly Gleaner	"
229	Lebanon	The Gleaner	"
230	Memphis	Head and Hand	Monthly.
231	"	Afro-American	Weekly.
232	"	The Baptist Messenger	"
233	"	The Christian Herald	"
234	"	The Living Way	"
235	"	The Watchman	"
236	Nashville	The Citizen	"
237	"	Fisk Herald	monthly.
238	"	Central Tennessee College Record	"
239	"	Tennessee Baptist	Weekly.
240	"	The Bugle Blast	"
241	"	Immaculate Headlight	———
242	"	Hope	Monthly.
243	"	The Bulletin	Weekly.

TEXAS.

244	Austin	Herald	"
245	Beaumont	Beaumont Leader	"
246	"	Weekly Advertiser	"
247	Corsicana	The Reflector	"
248	Dallas	Missionary Reporter	———
249	"	Southern Mercury	Weekly.
250	"	The Baptist Star	"
251	Fort Worth	The Item	"
252	"	The Organizer	"
253	Galveston	Freeman's Journal	"
254	"	Galveston Witness	"
255	Houston	The Texas Freeman	"
256	Hearn	The Hearn Academy	Monthly.
257	Kaufman	Kaufman Pilot	Weekly.
258	Navasota	The Echo	"
259	Prairie View	State Normal	Monthly.
260	San Antonio	The Texas Globe	Weekly.
261	" "	The Blade	"
262	Leguin	The New Test	"
263	Waco	The Searchlight	"

UTAH.

264	Sult Lake City	Western Recorder	"
265	" "	Womens' Exponent	"

VIRGINIA.

266	Alexandria	Zion's Leader	Weekly.
267	"	The Christian Clipper	"
268	Boydton	Midland Express	"
269	South Boston	The Boston Banner	"
270	Berkley	Atlantic Baptist	"
271	Cappahosic	Clancester Letter	"
272	Danville	The Methodist	"
273	Graham	Headlight	"
274	Lawrenceville	Southern Messenger	Semi-Monthly.
275	Lynchburg	Counselor Herald	Weekly.
276	"	The Laborer	"
277	Manchester	Manchester Weekly	"
278	Newport News	The Caret	Monthly.
279	Norfolk	The Speaker	Weekly.
280	"	The Rambler	"
281	"	Recorder	"
282	Petersburg	The Herald	"
283	"	The Recorder	"
284	"	Petersburg Lancet	"
285	"	V. N. and C. T. Gazette	"
286	"	National Pilot	Quarterly.
287	Port Royal	The Press	Weekly.
288	Richmond	The Planet	"
289	"	Southern News	"
290	"	Woman's Weekly—Virginia Reporter	"
291	"	Young Men's Friend	Monthly.
292	"	The Times	Weekly.
293	"	The State	"
294	"	The Weekly Cyclone	"
295	"	The Performer	"
296	"	Religious Herald	"
297	Roanoke	Roanoke Daily Press	Daily.
298	Suffolk	Christian Visitor	Monthly.
299	Vanna Grove	Henrico News	Weekly.

WEST VIRGINIA.

300	Martinsburg	Pioneer Press	"
301	Montgomery	The Baptist Pioneer	"
302	Parkersburg	The Freeman	"

WISCONSIN.

303	Milwaukee	Northwestern Recorder	"

WASHINGTON.

304	Seattle	The Seattle Republican	"

MRS. M. A. McCURDY,

EDITOR OF THE "WOMAN'S WORLD."

IN 1852, when all England and many persons in the United States were greatly enthused and cited to action in defense of the Negroes of this country, who were being crushed and demoralized by the cruel hand of slavery as portrayed by Mrs. Harriet Beecher Stowe in her famous book known as *Uncle Tom's Cabin*, there was born to Alexander and Martha Harris, on the 10th day of August, 1852, in the little village of Carthage, Ind., a girl child who was destined to become an instrument in the hands of God for the defense of her people and the cause of temperance. I refer to the lady whose name graces the head of this article, which is a biographic sketch of her life. Mrs. M. A. McCurdy acquired the rudiments of an education in the mixed schools of Rush County, but deprived of the privilege of attending any other college, by the death of her father, nevertheless she was so determined to fit herself for usefulness that she sought diligently for knowledge obtained from books that prepared her for teaching a county school near her home, long ere she was nineteen years old. Soon after the close of her school she was wedded to J. A. Mason, and for more than eight years filled with profit and precision the worthy position of wife and mother, never failing in the meantime to embrace opportunities presented wherein she could glean knowledge necessary to fit her for the promotion of causes that honor God and elevate humanity.

During the course of time mentioned the all-wise Giver of good gifts and one who doeth all things right took to heaven her four jewels and suffered her to become deprived of her husband. Thus left to herself she became more anxious to do something to elevate humanity, and accordingly became identified with other ladies of Richmond, Ind., in the temperance cause.

In the year 1884 she became first the secretary, and in a few weeks the editress of the only temperance paper at that time in the city. Through the columns of the paper she became widely known as a staunch advocate of the temperance cause, and was the first person

D   MRS. M. A. MCCURDY,
Rome, Ga.

to sound the alarm of prohibition. At a public meeting held by the white people of that city, being of a philanthropic and missionary disposition, a desire to go South where the greatest good could be done for her race, seized hold of her, and through the kindness of Rev. J. M. Townsend, Bishop H. M. Turner and wife offered her a home. Therefore, on the 26th of January, 1886, she landed in Atlanta, Ga., the Gate City of the South, and became a member of the good Bishop's family, and when that learned divine caused to appear on the 25th of September, 1886, the neat journal, known as the *Southern Recorder*, she became its efficient secretary and served as editor *pro tem* of the same for at least half the time that it was the property of Bishop Turner, and was therefore styled the mother of the *Recorder* by many of its supporters. The good Bishop enjoyed frequent hearty laughs over many things said in other papers concerning the wise sayings in his paper that were thought to be his but were things said by Mrs. M. A. Mason, the secretary.

She is neither a poet nor a fiction writer, but is indeed a ready writer upon subjects of solid and philanthropic character, as has been seen or proven by her utterances in papers South and West. During her four years' stay in Atlanta, Ga., she built up a fine mission in it, St. James A. M. E. Church, of that city. She served as superintendent of the Sunday school in the above church for three years; visited the chain gang in the interest of the temperance cause; acted as secretary of local and county W. C. T. U., and did so much other Christian work, that when Rev. C. McCurdy, of Rome, Ga., did on the 16th of July, 1890, take her unto himself as wife there were many hearts made sad in the Gate City of the South.

SKETCH OF HER LIFE AND LABOR IN ROME, GA.

BY REV. A. B. ALLEN.

Her coming to Rome has proven to be a great blessing to all the people in many ways. Socially, she has contributed no little to society. She has entered the homes of the people and has been the means of inspiration as well as the means to incite them to greater excellence in morals and religion. She has never had in mind this thought, that virtue and intelligence are the greatest interests of a community including all others, and worth all others, and the noblest agency is that by which they are advanced. She is ever active in fostering the truths which are calculated to fit the people into whom she plants them, for the greatest usefulness to God and man. In this she has been eminently successful. She visits daily damp and dark cellars where the people are found in squalor and destitution, and like the good Samaritan she comforts the sorrowing, pours oil upon the wounds of the wounded, feeds the hungry, clothes the naked, and like a messenger from the celestial world points the lost and straying to Jesus, the world's Redeemer and heaven. No home is too humble for her to enter, no person too base for her to labor to save.

INDUSTRIAL WORK.

The industrial work which has been done by her has been a blessing to the people throughout this city with its fifteen thousand inhabitants. An organization known as the "Rome Branch of the Needle Work Guild of America," was organized two years ago, in which time it has grown to an immense proportion. Three hundred and three garments have been made and distributed indiscriminately throughout this city and vicinity, also to orphans' homes of Atlanta, Ga.

SECRETARY OF STATE.

She is now serving as Corresponding Secretary of State of the Woman's Christian Temperance Union for the State of Georgia, performing the arduous and difficult work with apparent ease, and certainly she gives the highest satisfaction. Her eminent fitness and ability to do the work make her one of the foremost women of the State, if not the foremost in the State. She has served as editress of the temperance column in the *National Presbyterian*. In this position she is apt to teach the reading public and thereby leaving upon them the impress or her noble spirit. One has only to read her articles to become a total abstainer. The truths which she has sent forth have at all times been sharper than any two-edged sword. Certainly if the people knew the good that has been accomplished by her they would be convinced more than at any age that "the pen is mightier than the sword." She is a cogent writer; always forceful and impressive whether writing or speaking. Her productions must always live because they will be read with interest by all the peoplle, whether erudite or otherwise.

Superintendent of the Juvenile Work of the Knox Presbytery of the Presbyterian Church.

In this department of the great church which has for many years sought to secure the good of man and the glory of God, this great woman is actively engaged in leading the child out while his mind is pliant and susceptible and preparing him for his life work. She is beyond any reasonable doubt better qualified for so great a cause than any of whom it has been my privilege to meet. Her intellectual culture, her religious stamina and her interest in the youth of our land give her the essential merits which the importance of the case demands.

Superintendent of Presswork for State W. C. T. U. No. 2.

All who know anything about this work know how difficult it is to do this work accurately. Yet the subject of this sketch has done this work most acceptably and creditably. Her broad experience upon all lines of work makes her useful almost to a limitless degree.

President of Missionary Work in the Presbyterian Church.

In the first place she is loyal to her church. The pastor has ever in her a faithful ally; the church an unceasing and untiring worker; the Christian Endeavor and Sunday school, a loving, wise and diligent teacher, one who is in every way possessed with the sublime capability of pushing forward the cause which she so earnestly advocates. The work has been enhanced greatly by her effort. Indeed there is doubt in my mind as to whether anyone has been able to do so much work for God and the whole people as she has done.

Editress of the "Woman's World."

This is a paper devoted to the intellectual, moral and spiritual interest of the people. It has met with marked success as it has gone forth, laden with rich things to bless and uplift and strengthen the minds of the people in their home, like autumn leaves to enrich our earth. It has been wisely and ably managed. The editress is an ardent and firm advocate of woman's suffrage. Seeing she is president of the local W. C. T. U., she believes if women had the right of franchise the infernal liquor traffic would be banished from the land so as never to return to blot the pages of the history of our fair country. In either of these departments of work she has not only made herself known and felt in this city but throughout the State and in all of the important cities. She is the beginner of reforms in society; as such she is deservedly popular, esteemed and honored by all. During last Christmas the Mayor of this city had all of the barrooms and drunkeries of this city closed. It is known by many that such an achievement in the history of this city was never accomplished before. It was due to the strong Christian influence of this noble woman. She is an uncompromising foe of this liquor demon and is bent upon his utter destruction. The paper she edits is arrayed against him, her speeches, her articles and her prayers. The difficulty with which she has sustained and kept the W. C. T. U. in this place, where drunkeries meet the gaze of the eye, is in many respects remarkable and bespeaks volumes for her, and must finally result in the downfall of the monster and the final triumph of her tears, prayers, faith and work. She unconsciously throws herself into all she says and does. She is putting spirit into the age, old and young; she labors upon immortal nature; she is laying the foundation of unperishable excellence and happiness. Her work will outlive empires and the stars.

DUTY OF THE STATE TO THE NEGRO.

BY MRS. M. A. M'CURDY.

"Whate'er thy race or speech, thou art the same,
Before thy eyes duty, a constant flame,
Shines always steadfast with unchanging light
Through dark days and through bright."

WHEN the Negro was brought to America as a slave and thus held for more than two hundred years, he was robbed of all privileges allotted to mankind to compete morally, intellectually and politically with other races, and as a natural consequence, his five senses became dormant to an alarming extent, and thus made him a subservient creature with but a faint hope of ever being relieved and allowed to exercise his faculties in common with other men. Time upon fleet wings rolled on, the Negro ever submissive and obedient to his earthly master, trustful, prayerful and always confiding in his Heavenly Father, did so ingratiate himself to many, as to cause them to conceive the idea of liberating the slave and then place him on equality to a limited extent with other races of this country. This being done, more than 4,000,000 souls found themselves in great need of improvement from a moral, intellectual and financial standpoint, and accordingly sought the aid of friends, who came from the North and other points to their rescue, and have assisted very largely in placing the Negro on the road of intellectual success by the public school system, the erection of colleges and other institutions of learning, that have benefited him quite materially. But all that does not suffice to make him the peer of others in character, morals and political requisites. True, churches can be seen with their spires pointing upward in every village, town and city throughout the United States, owned by the Negro, but they do not serve to save the great number of souls in the higyways and hedges who are starving for the want of that Heavenly Manna that is in the hands of the Anglo-Saxon and Afro-Americans, who employ them to serve in the capacity of servants and come in contact with them as they go about their daily avocations; neither do the churches serve to right the political wrongs. Duty in that respect has not shown itself, it seems to have taken leave of its "strong aid, champion conscience," consequently thousands of human beings are now writhing in the agonies of sinfulness in their forlorn and poverty-stricken homes, while the penitentiaries and other prisonhouses of the land, poorhouses, insane asylums and the few reformatory schools known are oftener crowded than otherwise by those who have been neglected at a time in their lives when they could have been approached and saved from sin and utter distruction of mind and morals, and thus escaped the pangs of deranged senses, the excrutiating pains and scorching fevers that prey upon the vitals of physical wrecks, the horrors of dungeons and cells in prisons, untimely graves and the judgment of an avenging God who says that none but righteous shall see his face and live with him in glory. Then more and more manifestly appears the Duty of the State to the Negro from a political standpoint. True the right of equal franchise is said to have been given to the Negro (males) in a very short time after his emancipation, and we doubt not but that his emancipators fully intended that he should take an unmolested part in the acts of life that make up the mighty drama, and in that way prove himself to be the equal of other races in thought, word and deed, and thus assist mightily in supporting the constitution of the United States, and die, if it need be, in defense of the flag of this great republic; but in many instances he has been deprived of a free exercise of his franchisement by office seekers and profligates, who ever take advantage of the ignorant by the use of money, whisky and other things as bribes, and have thereby caused men to cast votes for nominees and thus insured the election of many who otherwise would have been defeated by men more worthy of the position than they. Then again many have been cheated out of a free exercise of their franchisement by wicked men who seek to scare and drive men into subjection by the use of weapons of war. This and many other things have been allowed to come to pass, because of the fact that those who are in power and are acknowledged upright men have failed to do their duty toward the Negro from a strict sense of the word. The Negro forgets, it seems, that "men who sell themselves are slaves" and the buyers prove to be (beyond disputation) dishonest and unprincipled.

The ignorant need to ever remember that they are always at the mercy of the unprincipled and allow the knowledge of the fact to serve as an incentive for high endeavors that will enlighten the mind, purify the morals and thus prepare them for usefulness and excellency in the political field of battle; notwithstanding all that and the possibility of great changes being made in the future by individual exertion in particular instances and locality, we realize that there is need to plead with those who are in power, to throw the law's strong arm of protection around the Negro. Do their whole duty in the premises and thereby give the Negro a chance to enjoy his freedom as other men. We realize that the Constitution of the United States is beautifully constructed and its diction perfect in every part, yet there is a lack of conformity to the spirit of the law practiced by many who profess to be one of its supporters, and it is the Negro who suffers most from the result of the non-conformity. Then we dare to insist upon the State doing its duty to the Negro (males), and in the meantime forget not the thousands of women who are pleading to-day for equal franchise. Yes, women who are worthy of much consideration; women who would prove most valuable to the State on account of their executive ability, their culture, learning and wisdom, the four great somethings that assist mightily in bringing to pass those things that make for the good of all concerned. Then, there are women who can expound the law of the State in a precise manner and are therefore fully equipped for service in that capacity in this progressive age, while in the performance of your duty to the Negro (males). Emancipate the Anglo-Saxon and the Afro-

American women who are wearing a yoke of oppression, the equal of that which did hold the slave in bondage for more than two hundred years. Do this and cause such changes to take place as will result in the annihilation of many evils. With all that we remember that there are many moral and intellectual Anglo-Saxons and Afro-Americans who fail to remember that "man does not live for himself alone," and that the sphere of "duty is infinite;" but they go steadily on acquiring knowledge, amassing wealth, striving to save self, seeking honor and fame, and ever pushing aside the inebriate, the poor, the weak and sinful whom they could save in many instances by a kind look, a gentle stroke of the hand, a sixpence or more added to pleasant words, serving to remind them of God and his blessed commands. They (the moral and intellectual) seem to forget that the creatures whom they push aside carry with them the "hidden spring of force" and "creative power" to a large extent "the flower," "the germ," "the potency of life" that has never been cultivated, but could be quickened, caused to grow and to so expand, that there would be no occasion of our reminding the State of its duty to the Negro; but we would be able to exclaim in part as did Wordsworth of duty:

> " Stern law giver! yet thou dost wear
> The Godhead's most benignant grace;
> Nor know I anything so fair
> As is the smile upon thy face;
> Flowers laugh before thee on their beds,
> And fragrance in thy footing treads;
> Thou dost preserve the stars from wrong,
> And the most ancient heavens are through thee fresh and strong."

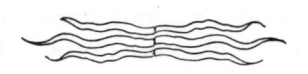

Opportunities and Responsibilities of Colored Women.

[Delivered before the Ladies' Auxiliary of the Whittier Association, of Memphis.]

BY MRS. FANNIE BARRIER WILLIAMS, OF CHICAGO.

MY heart has been so warmed by the generous kindness of welcome extended to me continuously since my arrival in your city that I shall always be happy to add my testimony to those who have been delighted by Southern hospitality. When some of your good women honored me with an invitation to visit Memphis and speak as best I might in behalf of our women who yearn for a larger freedom of development, I was not sure of my fitness to speak acceptably in a part of our country to which I am so much of a stranger, but your generous cordiality has given me such confidence of heart that I feel at home and in sympathetic touch with women who can do me more good by their soulfulness and suggestions of duty than I can return by any words of advice or inspiration. My own sense of happy surprise in this my first experience of Southern hospitality and eagerness of welcome suggests what we all need, who are respectively on the opposite sides of that imaginary line dividing the North and South is a more perfect understanding of our relationship to each other.

It is said of that genial easayist, Charles Lamb, that when he was asked on one occasion why he hated a certain person he answered, "I don't know him, that is why I hate him." The point of this story aptly suggests that a more perfect knowledge of each other will remove mistrust, hatred and conflict. This radiant Southland, so fair and full of the brightness and abundance of nature and promising, as I want to believe, all the excellencies of social order and human happiness, and yonder North, so buoyant and powerful, with its mighty sweep of commerce, vast intelligence and resources, need a closer union of sympathies and interests in order that national progress may be broad enough and intense enough to helpfully reach, protect and inspire every man, woman and child under the flag of the republic.

We of a peculiar race with our faces ever turned toward the Western star of hope and advancement especially need the help that comes from knowing each other better. We who live in the North need to understand better than we do the many peculiar advantages and disadvantages, promises and discouragements that belong to those of us whose homes are under Southern skies. We will think more and better of you and become more respectful in our interest in all that concerns you when we understand more clearly that in spite of the many agonies of the past and the many distressing limitations of the present the progress of the Negro race along the highest levels and in the most surprising instances has been right here in the South. That nearly all the money earned, accumulated and saved by the Negro race since emancipation has been accumulated and saved by our Southern men and women.

MRS. FANNIE BARRIER WILLIAMS.
Chicago, Ill.

That our men of real wealth are nearly all Southern men; that most of the men and women who have risen to public importance are of Southern birth and education, and that it is easier for our boys to learn a trade and successfully follow it in the South than it is in the North. I say when we of the North know and appreciate all this our sense of race pride will increase and we will be able to place a higher estimate upon the possibilities of our race. Men and women who can so proudly signalize their freedom and under conditions discouraging in the extreme by so many evidences of real worth are an inspiration to all mankind. On the other hand we of the North who have much freedom and little work, but who are in touch with all the forces of intelligence, morality and the regenerating spirit of reform that are fast making for the better weal of our republic, are not understood by our Southern kinsmen in a way that makes for race unity and progress. The young men and women who have been educated in those great free institutions of the North should be the great leaders and teachers of our generation. They are needed as the messengers of newer gospels of love and hope and inspiration. They should be encouraged and welcomed to this ample South where there are so many inspirations to high duties. These young men and women ought to be made to feel that here in the South where their talents are needed so much the highest premium is placed upon brains, character and industry.

But without further comment on this line, I want to say that I come here in the spirit of good will. I want if possible to bring her a message of hope and inspiration to higher resolves. I gladly come at the bidding of your committee, not to attempt a discussion of the race problem. If I can say anything that is helpful it is not to suggest problems and difficulties, but to suggest duties and responsibilities that our women must begin to feel and exercise if we would become a part of the forces that are working everywhere about us for the things that deeply concern the kingdom of womankind. Nothing in the whole realm of questions that effect home, religion, education, industry and all phases of sociology command more interest than the growing power of woman. Interest in woman and her possibilities is so widespread and intense that whatever she does or says or proposes receives more public attention and comment than any other theme of current history.

Does this absorbing interest in woman and her progress, does this advancing power of woman in all the important determinations of American life concern and affect colored women in any important way? Does the progressiveness of womankind in all things suggest to us any opportunities, duties or hopes that have failed thus far to influence us? Can we say that we are preparing ourselves sufficiently to use and exercise the privileges and responsibilities of that larger and more inclusive citizenship toward which other women are progressing, and for which they are fitting themselves by all kinds of experience? Is it too much to say that no class of women in the world have such rare opportunities for signalizing their worth as the colored women of America?

If it can be a good fortune for women to come into possession of freedom when the heart of civilization is open and responsive to all the complaints, wants and demands of womankind; if it can help to make women strong in sympathy, in unselfishness and in the love of humanity to live in the midst of countless opportunities for heroic devotion, for self-sacrifice, and for the invention of ways and means to help a whole race of people to reclaim itself from the debasement of servitude, then our women are many times blessed. The thing for us to consider is what we can do to become a conscious part of all the agencies at work for the elevation of those of our women who are in, but not a part of, our civilization. Alas! to most of us this question suggests only discouragement and hopeless problems. Our philosophers and leaders have talked so much and confusingly about the vast difficulties in the way of Negro advancement in America that we too have been more or less unfitted to see and do the simplest duties incumbent upon us.

There has been so much looking toward Providence and so little exercise of our senses and confidence in ourselves that most of us have become useless and stupidly indifferent to the inspirations of the hour. Surely we need no oracle to tell us what to do to be better than we are. A whole race of women whose only heritage has been ignorance and isolation needs no philosophers to lead them to a higher state. Their needs are elementary, and the duties of Christian women in their behalf are near, direct and easy of comprehension. If the colored women who are sufficiently intelligent and warm-hearted to share in the responsibilities of helping where help is needed, could be aroused from their do-nothing, unsympathetic and discouraged condition, and could be conscious of their opportunities for accomplishing good deeds, there would at once come the dawning of a new and better era for the American Negro. We would then understand that the question is not what we ought to demand; but what can we do, not what are our rights, but how can we best deserve them, not so much how to condemn prejudice, but how to remove its cause. The hour is not for the lamentations of Rachel, but for the hopes, courage and duty becoming women who are called by large opportunities to noble work. If we would have the public interested in us and our needs, we must become interesting, and we will become interesting just as soon as we begin to help ourselves to the utmost extent of our opportunities.

One of our first duties is to inform ourselves as to what has been done, is being done, and what needs to be further done to help ourselves. It should never be said that colored women know less about the status of colored women than is known by women of another race. Nearly all the great churches of this country and scores of undenominational societies have for the past thirty years been carrying on missionary work that aims to reach every phase of the general condition of the colored people of this country.

The reports and literature of these churches and societies are full of encouraging and sugsestive information. The facts and figures to be gleaned from this source form a most interesting history of the mental, religious and material development of the colored people since 1865. You will find in this annual library of interesting information a message, an invitation, an appeal and challenge to every woman's heart. These reports of work done, and to be done, are procurable without cost by any one interested enough to ask for them. I can but wonder how many of us avail ourselves of this opportunity to learn the lessons of our advancement and further needs.

The one thing that should appeal most strongly to our hearts is the need of a better and purer home life among our people in many parts of the South. I scarcely need tell you that our most embarrassing heritage from slavery was a homelessness and a lack of home ties. All the sanctities of marriage, the precious instincts of motherhood, the spirit of family alliance, and the upbuilding of home as an institution of the human heart were all ruthlessly ignored and fiercely prohibited by the requirements of slavery. Colored people in bondage were only as men, women and children, and not as fathers, mothers, sons and daughters, brothers and sisters. Family relationships and home sentiments were thus no part of the preparation of colored people for freedom and citizenship. It is not agreeable to refer to these things, but they are mentioned merely to suggest to you how urgent and immensely important it is that we should be actively and helpfully interested in those poor women of the rural South who in darkness and without guides are struggling to build homes and rear families. When we properly appreciate the fact that there can be no real advancement of the colored race without homes that are purified by all the influences of Christian virtues, it will seem strange that no large, earnest, direct and organized effort has been made to teach men and women the blessed meaning of home.

Preachers have been too busy with their churches and collections, and teachers too much harassed by lack of facilties, and politicians too much burdened with the affairs of state and the want of offices to think about the feminine consideration of good homes. Money, thought, prayer, and men and women are all freely and nobly given in the upbuilding of schools and churches, but no expenditures to teach the lesson of home making. Colored women can scarcely escape the conclusion that this work has been left for them and its importance and their responsibilities should arouse and stir them as nothing else can do. Let us not be confused and embarrassed by the thought that what needs to be done is too difficult or far away. There should be no limitations of time and space when man needs the helping sympathy of man. If our hearts are strong for good works, ways and means will readily appear for the exercise of our talents, our love, and our heroism.

The first thing that should interest us, is the fact that thousands of colored families in the South are still living in one-room cabins. Though the South is filled with our professors, ministers, and smart politicians, yet few have attempted to teach these people the difference between a slave cabin and a Christian home.

Booker T. Washington, who has done more for practical education of the colored people in all things than any other one man in America, tells us that the one-room cabin is the very root of all social evils in the South. It also appears that this indiscriminate huddling together of a whole family, large or small, in one room, is due more to ignorance of a better way than to poverty. The reform so earnestly needed in the mode of living in a large part of the South should not be left to a few chance individuals who are struggling to effect it.

Colored women in every part of this country, who know what good homes mean to the well-being of the colored race, should come together in organization to study the situation, and earnestly put in motion every possible agency for reform. Such organization would learn at once, to their surprise and shame, how many things they could do that are not being done. They will learn that those who need our hearts, hands, and advice, are not suffering so much for want of equal rights, and political rights, and some easy escape from prejudice, as they are for the simplest necessities that make for decency, order, and the sanctities of home making. Thousands of our women in the South are eager to learn some of the primary lessons of houshold sanitation, moral guides, mental stimulants, and the purifying environments for the children of their hearts yet; these yearnings are heeded not by those who can help and comfort them.

Bright and promising children by the thousands all over the South are without clothing to attend either school or church, yet a dozen zealous colored women, in any small town of the beautiful North, or the larger towns of the South, could obtain and supply, almost without cost to themselves, clothing enough to clothe the mothers and children of a whole community.

Thousands upon thousands of colored children in the South are out of school for want of schoolbooks, yet there are millions of second-hand books in all houses that are lost and wasted every year because no one asks for them to be sent where they are needed for the mental salvation of a whole generation of children. Thousands of capable young men and women, who are eager for enlightenment and culture, are without books, papers, and pictures, yet good literature and art of all kinds are prodigally wasted under our very feet, because there seems to be neither sense nor sympathy enough to know where to send them as rays of light into dark places. In short, there are a thousand sources of plenty and helpfulness for our fellow men and women, if we would but organize agencies to command and use them.

It is easily possible to establish direct lines of communication between the crying need of every crude and impoverished home, and every philantrophic impulse of our hearts. This is no dream woven in fancy thread. The near possibility and reality of it all lie in the heart and brain of colored women.

What I have thus suggested has already been accomplished, to a limited extent, by certain white women, whose vigilance and zeal in our cause should be an inspiration to us.

Some of these women have happily assumed the responsibility of looking after the home interests of certain districts in the South. At regular intervals they send boxes of clothing, books, pictures, and home furnishings, medicines and other comforts, into many households of the darkest South.

There are very few colored women, who, from time to time, add to their gifts of necessities their personal visitations with messages of sympathy, and deeds of blessed service. The brightness and joy of a new life follow everywhere in the wake of such practical beneficience.

One of the young lady graduates of the Provident Hospital and Training School for nurses, in Chicago, went down to one of the Carolinas with her heart and hands open to good work in behalf of friendless and benighted women and children, and her letters to Northern friends are a startling revelation of the neglected opportunities for the helpful service of colored women. Such is the testimony of all women who have gone among our more unfortunate sisters in a like spirit of love.

Heaven grant that our souls may be possessed by a consuming desire, by a restless anxiety, and a noble enthusiasm to see and discharge our responsibilities and duties to the Macedonian cry of our sisters in misery.

In order to equip ourselves with knowledge, sympathy, and earnestness for this work, we need the soul-strengthening influences of organization. Women unorganized in the presence of the heart-stirring opportunities are narrow, weak, suspicious, and sentimental. Women organized for high purposes, discover their strength for large usefulness, and encircle all humanity with the blessedness of their sympathy. Organized womanhood to-day, the world over, is the spirit of reform incarnate. It impresses its reforming influence upon every existing evil, and its protecting power of love hovers over every cherished interest of human society. All combined institutions of Church, State, and civic societies do not touch humanity on so many sides as the organized efforts of women.

In reference to the interests that especially concern us as colored women, we can receive much inspiration from the examples afforded by the more favored class of women in reformatory movements. In studying the aims, methods, and results of women's organizations, we will learn that no evil that menaces the purity of home, no lurking or open danger to the saving power of woman in all social aims, and no breath of possible harm to life, health, and culture of children, is without the opposing force of organized women. Art, literature, science, invention, and all other things of heaven and earth are made to pay tribute to the refining requirements of women, and children, and home. Take the cause of temperance as an example of the successful earnestness and practical value.

When woman stood at her hearthstone, with caressing care and fond hopes for her children, and saw the invasion of her home by the dread spirit of intemperance, as she saw all things that were nearest and dearest to her heart menaced and falling beneath the blighting pestilence of drunkenness, she did not falter, or hesitate, or wait for a remedy or protection, but quickly uniting women everywhere in one common cause of resistance, and raising aloft the white banner of home, sobriety, and native land, she has triumphed over Bacchus in more ways than you can dream of. The prayers of women in a million homes, the songs of a million women making melody in the sweet influences of purity, and the steady, vigilant, and unyielding activity of women in behalf of soberness, have conspired to make temperance in all things the whitest sentiment of the century, and the saloon power the greatest indecency of our civilization. Whatever safety you may feel in your household against the destroying power of drink, you are more indebted for it to organized efforts of women than to any other cause. Would that colored women everywhere, and in vast numbers, who have homes to make and protect, could be imbued with this anxious, militant, and resistless spirit of temperance. If temperance could be the cardinal virtue of our race, nothing would be able to resist our advancement toward the enjoyment of all the equalities of freedom and citizenship of this country.

Another fine example of how organization helps women to find work of usefulness in behalf of those who need our helping hand and heart is afforded by those devoted and heroic women of the Salvation Army. The frank and whole-souled sincerity of these women in the cause of a more practical righteousness has put to shame much that passes for religion and goodness in these days of ours. When we see these sisters of a more active mercy, with no shield for their protection save the holy purpose of doing good to others, follow wretched humanity as it slinks away in shame to its hiding haunts of vice, carrying either bread to the starving, a cup of water to the athirst, a blanket to the shivering, a gentle word of sisterly interest, or the uplifting voice of prayer, we can but feel a strong uplift of heart and a desire to be more genuine in our interest in humanity's ills. It is the chivalric spirit of these women, like true soldiers of the cross, extending the gracious influence of the Master into the highways of sinfulness, that our women need to make us eager to put our hearts into human relations, and our hands to good work. The example of these saintly women should say to us, "Be brave in your faith, wait not for duties that are afar off, look not to white women to do that which you can do, be not persuaded that you are too poor, too ignorant, and too humble to be a part of the highest usefulness that lifts up humanity, and remember, that your highest duty is that which is nearest your conscience and capacity."

The outreaching of woman's heart to help woman is also beautifully exemplified by the wide-spread bands of King's Daughters and kindred societies. "In His Name," is the motto of the women and girls of a higher faith. They stand for the gospel of sincerity, and challenge the hearts of Christian men and women to give the impress of their faith to their conduct of life.

These women have united to show by example, in an impressive way that it is not all of religion to pray and sing, and in soft pews listen to the Word. This new mission is to extend the meaning of the Christian religion so that the Church shall stand more for love than doctrine, more for human worth than for church name, and be wider open more hours in the week for humanity's good than the saloon is open for humanity's woe. So that what men and women do rather, than what they say or profess, shall be the standard of religion; and so that to give force and effect in all human conduct to the example of "Him who came to seek and save that which was lost" will be manifest as such in action out of the church as in worship inside its walls. I scarcely need to tell you all that I feel as to how much our women need the influence of such unions as these. If women who are superior to us in all the chances and advantages of life find it necessary to their advancement to be thus watchful, active and interested in so many ways, can we of greater needs and smaller resources and protections expect to advance by doing less than they? The ministers among us, who are unworthy of their calling, are largely responsible for the fact that our church women generally take less interest in the large field of practical religious work outside of their particular churches than any other class of women. Our women in the churches are organized, for the most part, only for one purpose, and that is to raise money for the churches. Thousands of our women never rise higher in their zeal for good works than the groveling aim of money-getting for the Trustees. Their heads and hearts and strength are all exhausted in devising church entertainments that are largely responsible for so much of the deplorable frivolity of our young people. Much of the needed charitable work among our unfortunate is left to white women because we have no time or interest outside the little church.

Thousands of young girls who need moral protection of the church as much on Monday as on Sunday, who need instruction in the sacred responsibilities of womanhood and in all things that make for the moral integrity of women, are deprived of them all because so many of our women are to the stern necessity of money-getting to pay church debts. If our women could be released partially from this one narrow aim, and see the possible church in the neglected fields where the King's Daughters are garnering such rich harvests of good to humanity, our importance as women of worth in moral work would be wonderfully advanced. Our good church women as well as all women need to be saved from narrowness and its consequences, and the way to be saved is to know more of the resources and possibilities of one another. Our interest in each other as women has been too much gossip sort. The eaves-dropping and key-hole sort of knowledge of what is going on at one another's hearth-stones has almost unfitted us for united efforts. There must be an earnest, honest coming together of all our women to learn what are the essential causes of our common distresses and the great need of reform. Do you know that thousands of our bright young women, comely and capable, are without employment partly on account of American prejudice, partly on account of their own timidity, and especially because no effort is made to suggest or show to them the many new fields of employment that they know not of? Do you know that the tendency of our time is to make all work respectable and honorable that is well and honorably done? and that our girls who can do housework better than anything else, should be as much respected for doing it as they would be if making less wages as clerks? Do you know that thousands of our young men are reckless and unworthy of their privileges because they have no inspiration to better things and no rebuke from our young women? Do you know that our ministers would be nobler in all things, in all the best attributes of their calling, if our women were to insist upon it? Do you know that all things that are pure, healthful, and sacred in the relations of husband and wife and child depend primarily upon worthy women? All these things and many more of like nature are suggested to women who come together in a spirit of reform. Surely we have something more than sorrow, complaints, and tears.

Out of the opportunity for womanly achievement we ought to be strong enough to inaugurate a new era of hope and endeavor. If we would but once look out from our own monopoly of race misfortunes along the highways traveled by all races of people, from the caves of security to the prominence of human excellence, we would be inspired by our opportunities. In this connection too much emphasis cannot be laid upon the necessity of more contact with the best type of American womanhood wherever it can be had, and especially in the North of course. The truly good women, and thank God their name is legion, are always open-hearted and eager to help those who need their strength of personality and interest. It is important for us to know that we cannot learn all about ourselves. We have been so much cut off from every refining influence, from every example and inspiration of good and great women, that our progress in all things womanly will be slow and uncertain unless we can win and deserve this helpful association.

We are scarcely willing to admit the fact that our own prejudices and lack of self-assertion are largely responsible for our separation from the women who move the world by their intelligent progressiveness. If we would join these women in good works we should at least meet them half way by ridding ourselves of preconceived notions of their hostility and prejudice against us. It would add much to our strength and dignity of character and to our sense of importance among women if we could understand that white women can be strengthened in their generous impulses and made more exalted in their outlook to help weak and struggling women if they knew more of our condition, capabilities, and aspirations. The cause of women in all things needs the co-operation of all women of all races and colors in order to work out the conditions that all need and devoutly wish for. The larger interests of women that concern all that is vital in our civilization cannot be advanced and realized if the race line and color line and church line must always divide into petty fragments the moral strength of united women. Colored women of culture and force of character can do much to urge this thought upon women of the dominant race. If I may be pardoned a personal reference, I will say that my best reward in meeting and talking to representative white women at all times and places, is that they are so susceptible to the idea that they need us to some extent in the same way that we need them. All statements to them concerning our wrongs and how we suffer under all forms of injustice are received with startling surprise. I have been happily repaid for all my efforts by fewest assurances of many of the best women in the country that they have been converted to right thinking concerning us. We may feel safe in the belief that the women who are strong enough to resist the domination of fashion's nonsense and the snobbery of caste, are ever ready to lay aside their false presumption against us and accept the truth of our cause if we would but put ourselves more in evidence in their efforts to benefit humanity. I especially refer to the North of course when I say that a plucky competition for place and honor, a wide-awake interest in all public questions, a facility for making ourselves for good wherever and whenever it is proper for true and patriotic women to be, on the part of our women, would do much to change public opinion about us and open up new avenues of influence.

Timidity, fear, and self-disparagement are not respected as virtues in this country. Heaven help us to appreciate that the liberties of this country are large, that its opportunities for progress are too great to excuse failures, and that here and now, as elsewhere in humanity's struggle for right, love, intelligence, character, thrift, and pluck are mightier for conquest than all the multiplied forces of injustice, prejudice, and ignorance. I know, of course, that to many of you this hopeful strain will seem to have no application to conditions existing here. It is true that what I have said is more prophetic than real to you. But remember, we must look upward. It is the business of a race to be self-respectful, ambitious, and aspiring for all that is best in human life. I would have these young women just looking out into the broad fields of possibilities, catch glimpses of the highland of our destiny. I would have them confident of the coming condition of race independence, and be strong in the conviction that the evils that now beset them are but the thorn-covered stepping-stones to our eminence in the future; while it may not now be possible for white women and colored women of the South to unite for any common good, yet as I believe in the regenerating forces of education, as I believe in the ultimate reign of justice and good sense, so do I believe that even sooner than you expect, the right sort of women, on both sides of the color line, will suggest a way for this fraternal coming together in a way by which both will preserve their self-respect.

To continue in this strain of self-criticism, I would say farther that our women have not as yet distinguished themselves by any large-hearted sympathy. There is no such thing as human progress without a large ingredient of the love principle in all human affairs; that kind of sympathy that knows no social lines, or race distinctions, or religious differences, but everywhere expands its wings of protection, and extends its warmth of helpfulness, is the kind of sympathy we need for our own advancement.

Dr. Hartzell, of the Methodist Episcopal Society, exhibits among his panoramic views of the condition of the colored people of the South one picture that has always haunted me with a sense of guiltiness for our lack of sympathetic interest in women who are so much in need of it. The picture represents in the door of a Southern cabin, two or three children, the oldest not more than four years of age. This child of four years holds in her lap, and acts the part of nurse to a babe of four months old. The mother of these infant children is forced to be away from home and children from early morning till sundown. The life, care, and custody of this infant is entrusted absolutely to a child scarcely more than an infant herself. Alas! how cheap is life. How dear is a mother's love! An infant crying for a mother, and answered by the tears of an infant nurse, an infant crying out for one touch of tenderness from the great warm heart of humanity about it, but its little sorrows and distresses are neither heeded nor soothed. No such picture is possible where women are sympathetically interested in all the possible wants and misfortunes of women. When that white-souled woman, Margaret Etta Creche, saw the working women in our cities, like the hard-working mother of these children in this picture, compelled to leave her children to the uncertainties of fortune, she founded what is called a day nursery, provided with all possible baby comforts. Thus supplying the caressing cares of mother during the day, while the mother is necessarily absent. These day nurseries for children of working women are everywhere engaging the hearts of women, and are the most cherished of all the charitable institutions of city life.

Surely there ought to be enough intelligence and love in the souls of colored women of the country to enter every home, every schoolhouse, and every church, wherever women and children especially need the supporting arm of woman-kind. It may well be asked, How can we have the love and sympathy of women of another race, when we manifest so little sympathy for one another?

Many of our more fortunate women seem to feel that any active interest in those who need their friendly interest, will identify them with the degradation of slavery. Others, in still greater numbers, act as if the responsibilities of our condition belong to white women, and that it is for them alone to exercise sympathy for colored women in distress. The wrong of this is too plain for argument. In the spirit of Wordsworth:

> "The primal duties shine aloft like stars;
> The charities that soothe and heal and bless
> Are scattered at the feet of man like flowers."

I would also appeal to the hearts of our women for a stronger sense of self-respect. I believe that it is an infallible rule that people are always weak who believe themselves weak. We help to make ourselves unimportant and underestimated by the habit of confessing our inferiority. We are everywhere hampered by the false and cringing notions that certain positions and achievements are beyond our reach. Hundreds of our young men and women graduate with high academic honors from schools and colleges and pass at once into obscurity as much because of their own low sense of self-importance as from the resisting force of popular prejudice. In nearly all American cities in the North there are libraries full of good literature, art galleries with their refining suggestion, the privileges of university extension, lectures and other institutions that minister to high thought and noble sentiment, but in them our young men and women are seldom seen.

This general fault of living below our opportunities is largely the cause of the popular conclusion that our women have no interest in the things that appeal to the intelligence and good taste of other people. Non-use of these high privileges is quite as bad as mis-use of them. Our conscience is not as yet sufficiently alive to the fact that by the sanction of the supremest law of the land, by the highest maxims of morality and equity, liberty in all its completness, equality in its truest signification, and responsibility in its proudest implications are all ours to use and to enjoy to the fullest extent of our ability to appropriate them. I can but feel that in spite of the darkness that enveloped our past life, in spite of harassing hinderances to our present promotion, and in spite of our despair for the future, it is after all a great thing to be an American woman, even though she be colored. As I stood from time to time in the midst of the great Columbian Exposition and saw the unspeakable glories of it all rise like the celestial city out of the souls and energies of men and women who are free and brave, I was transported by the thrill of a new life as to how much it meant to be an American woman, as I felt myself swayed from one exalted emotion to another by this American passion for great achievements, by this American energy of soul making all things possible that to us seem impossible, and by suggestion of the infinite resources and opportunities of this America, and saw how all things that are true and exalting are coming faster and faster within the reach and touch of woman-kind, I was inspired by a new sense of trust and courage against all the odds and hate of opposition. And so, my fellow-women of a common heritage, I cannot bring you any message of despair; my best word for you is to seek by all the agencies of enlightenment about you so to broaden your views of life as to make you see and feel the forces that are making far better conditions; and that what we complain of is but transitory, and what we so devoutly wish for is surely coming by every highway of civilization.

Thirty years ago we alone were in the wilderness of bondage crying aloud for freedom. Our happy release from that condition thrilled men and women everywhere with a most exalted sense of the value and sweetness of liberty. To-day we are not alone in any of our claims, disabilities, wants, and hopes. That large number of wretched women who are stitching their lives out in the sweat shops of our large cities in order to get a crumb of bread for their children, the toiling men and women of the land who groan and smart under the oppressions of wealth, women of all kinds and conditions who are restive under the restraint imposed by senseless customs and unjust laws, in fact all our countrymen who are conscious of being forced to live short of a complete enjoyment of life, liberty, and the pursuit of happiness are with us in our every contention. We as surely have no monopoly of misery as we have no monopoly of fortune; there is somewhere and somehow a compensation for every difficulty we meet and complain of. Our poetry has opened the floodgates of philanthropy, prejudice has multiplied our friends and has tended to sharpen the mettle of our character, and all forms of injustice against us react in terms of justice for us. Indeed our advantages and opportunities are large, exalting, and a part of the very constitution of things.

We are women claiming, yearning, and aspiring for rights at a time when woman's winsome voice of supplication or stern command is heard and heeded above the din and clamor of the times. Would you win the interest and confidence of the world? The answer comes from a thousand sources: Be brave in the consciousness of your own worth, be beautifully graced with all that virtue asks in woman and you shall in time remove from all laws, ways, and customs the darkening blight of woman's prejudice to woman.

THE FUTURE OF THE NEGRO.

BY REV. J. C. EMBRY, D.D.

I WAS forcibly impressed by an editorial in the issue of the *Recorder* of the 14th inst., representing the need of *higher literary work* by the men of our race and times. To illustrate the force of this observation, reference need only be had to the work of two of the leading men amongst us. These have contented themselves with the modest gift of an autobiography, in which they closely "hug the shore" of personal experience and reminiscence. In none of these, in so far as I have been permitted to pursue them, is there the least attempt at a broad outlook upon the times in which they have lived and wrought out their own achievements, no comprehensive sweep or survey of the contemporaneous history out of which their own aspirations took rise. The conditions—moral, religious, civil—of the recent centuries, of which the issues of the present time are but the culmination, receive no comprehensive treatment, nothing save the mere coloring of local influence.

Now when our youth who have been taught, justly, we think, to admire these men and to emulate them, shall have read these compositions, excellent in themselves as literary productions, the question is, What have they learned? Why, only this, that our gifted subject was born in the midst of a slave-holding community at a certain time, and was reduced to the condition of the captive race to which he belonged. And that thenceforth he had a rough time in recovering the liberty that God gave him at his birth. We are not even told how utterly unphilosophical it is, and in morals impossible, that any man can have been born a slave; how that every single case of slavery was a monstrous rape of human rights. The Declaration of Independence teaches both a philosophical and inspired truth, when it says: "It is self-evident that all men are born free." As soon as the new-born babe takes his first inspiration of vital air, he is endowed with the two-fold right of life and liberty. These rights are co-ordinate, and the complement of each other.

They are natural, universal rights that cannot be combatted without violence to the very principles of our common nature. Then there are other subordinate rights, which may be held as conventional or constructive, but they are nevertheless natural, universal, and hence incontestable. They are:

1. The right to live where one is born; that is, within the territorial jurisdiction of his birth. If he has not the right to live there, then where? Any attempt to expel him thence is an act of war.

2. The right of safety, that is, protection for life and limb. Denial of this right is to jeopardize his life, implicate society itself, and forecast its dissolution. All schools of philosophy agree that where human life is less than sacred, there society, in civilized form, must soon dissolve. Now the civilized nature recoils from anarchy, just as physical nature recoils from a vacuum; and it will—it must come to pass that the civil body will sooner or later fight the Anarchists in its own defense until it has completely vanquished them. And this is not a matter of choice; they will have to do so or else give up the civilized order.

3. Along with the right to life and liberty goes also the right of removal from one jurisdiction to another. Wherever the emigrant goes he carries with him these natural rights. This, too, is the united judgment of all enlightened men. Now, in the light of these fundamental truths, feebly outlined, I most confidently affirm that no man can fail of hopefulness as to the future of our race in this land who has broadly studied the problems and the progress of human liberty and civil justice in the world during the last three or four centuries. There has been a constant warfare and many reverses, together with long seasons of gloomy doubt; but the dominant fact in the whole record is, that throughout the long contest, on the forum, in the sacred pulpit, in the hall of legislation, and on countless fields of bloody carnage the struggle has been substantially the same —a struggle for larger liberty for the oppressed multitude—a better chance for the average man. And this further, that in every century—aye, in almost every generation of this mighty conflict, something has been gained for the right. This gain once made has never been lost. These things being so, it is foolish to say that these victories, and this strifeful gain are matters of merely racial application. It is not so. Every inch of ground taken that is based on universal principles has become the property of humanity. They will never be banished from among men, nor effectually overborne while

civilization, or Christianity endures. Now, as the old Romans used to say: "*Quae cum ita sint,*—Since these things are so," and since it is true that the best fruit of this long conflict is to be found here in this Western Hemisphere, I believe the future hope of the Negro race is to be found in the segment of that race providentially lodged on this soil. Say what we may about this or that, these United States have given us the most advanced, the most progressive Negro to be found on the face of the globe. And this is true for the reason that she is giving him the largest all-round opportunities, the highest civil ideals, and the steadiest aims. The troubles we suffer here, in our day, are only a part of the old, old conflict that has raged so long.

> "Must we be carried to the skies
> On flowery beds of ease,
> While others fought to win the prize,
> And sailed through bloody seas?"

No, we cannot be, and will not be, though we may wish to ever so much. "Through conflict to the skies," is as true for dark humanity as for any other variety of men. Had we then not better learn this lesson and cease our shameful grumbling, as if the Almighty had done us some special wrong? God has given us minds to think, hands to work, and hearts to love. Let us subject these God-given powers to the regimen of a severe discipline, and walking with hope to the future, work out a noble destiny for ourselves and our children.—*Christian Recorder.*

NAMES AND AUTHORS OF MORE THAN ONE HUNDRED RACE PUBLICATIONS.

Africa and America, by Rev. Alex. Crummell, D.D.
A History of the Negro Troops in the Rebellion, by George W. Williams, LL.D.
A Red Record, by Ida B. Wells.
Anti-Separate Coach History of Kentucky, by Rev. S. E. Smith.
Are We Africans or Americans? by J. F. Dyson, B.D.
Apology for American Methodism, by Benjamin Tucker Tanner.
Afro-American Women of Distinction, by L. A. Scruggs.
A Voice from the South, by Mrs. A. J. Cooper.

THOUGHTS, DOINGS, AND SAYINGS OF THE RACE.

African Letters, by Bishop Turner.
Africa, the Hope of the Negro, by R. C. O. Benjamin, D.D.
Aunt Linda, by Victoria Earl.
A Brief Historical Sketch of Negro Education in Georgia, by Prof. R. R. Wright.
Black and White, by T. T. Fortune.
Black Phalanx (history of Negro soldiers), by J. T. Wilson.
Book of Sermons, by Rev. J. W. Hood, D.D.
Book of Sermons, by S. T. Jones, D.D.
Church Financiering, by Rev. J. W. Stevenson, M.D.
Christianity, Islam and the Negro Race, by E. W. Blyden, LL.D.
Clarence and Corinne, by Mrs. A. E. Johnson.
Directory of the A. M. E. Zion Church, by Rev. J. Harvey Anderson.
Digest of Christian Theology, by J. C. Embry, D.D.
Doctrines of Christ and the Church, by Rev. R. T. Brown.
Domestic Education, by Bishop Daniel Payne.
Emancipation, by J. T. Wilson.
Earnest Pleas, by W. H. Smith.
Freedom and Citizenship, by Hon. John M. Langston.
From the Virginia Plantation to the National Capitol, by Hon. John M. Langston.
From West Africa to Palestine, by Edward W. Blyden, LL.D.
Future of the American Negro, by Rev. R. C. O. Benjamin, D.D.
Grand United Order of Odd Fellows in America, by C. B. Brooks.
Glimpses of Africa, by Rev. C. S. Smith.
Hairbreadth Escapes from Slavery to Freedom, by Rev. William Troy.
History of the Colored Race in America, by William T. Alexander.
History of the A. M. E. Church, by Rev. D. A. Payne, D.D.
History of the British West Indies, by R. C. O. Benjamin.
History of the Negro Race in America, by George W. Williams.
Hon. Frederick Douglass, by J. M. Gregory.
Iola Leroy; or, Shadows Uplifted, by Mrs. F. E. W. Harper.
Is the Negro Cursed? by Bishop B. T. Tanner.
Living Words, by Alexander.
Life and Labors of Rev. J. W. Early, by Sarah Early.
Life and Times of Frederick Douglass, by Frederick Douglass.
Life of Toussaint L. Overton, by R. C. O. Benjamin.
Liberia's Offering, by E. W. Blyden.

Men of Mark, by William Simmons, D.D.
Memoirs of Poems, by Phillis Wheatley.
My Bondage and my Freedom, by Frederick Douglass.
Methodist Polity, by H. M. Turner.
Negro Civilization in the South, by C. W. Robert (white).
Negro in all Ages, by Henry M. Turner.
Negro Literature, by Bishop Arnett.
Narrative of My Experience in Slavery, by Frederick Douglass.
Nina; or, the Girl Without a Father.
Noted Negro Women, by M. A. Majors.
Not a Man and Yet a Man, by A. A. Whitman.
Official Sermons A. M. E. Church, by D. A. Payne.
Origin of Color, by J. F. Dyson.
Our Father's House, by Rev. J. C. Embry, D.D.
Origin of the Negro Race, by R. C. O. Benjamin.
Oak and Ivy, by Paul L. Dunbar.
Outline of History, by B. T. Tanner.
Pastor's Annual and Financial Report, by Rev. Robert T. Brown, A. M.
Plantation Melodies, by M. W. Taylor.
Plain Theology for Plain People, by Rev. C. O. Booth.
Poems, by Rev. A. A. Whitman.
Political X Roads—Which Way? by J. F. Dyson.
Patriotic Poems, by Rev. George C. Rowe.
Poor Ben, by Mrs. L. N. C. Coleman.
Plantation Melodies, by A. E. P. Albert, D.D.
Recollections of Seventy Years, by Bishop D. A. Payne.
Richard Allen's Place in History, by J. F. Dyson.
Rise and Progress of A. M. E. Zion Church, by Bishop Rush.
Sacred Heart, by B. F. Wheeler, A. M.
School days at Wilberforce, by R. C. Ransom.
School History of the Negro Race in America, by Edward A. Johnson.
Science and Art of Elocution, by Prof. D. B. Williams.
The Afro-American Press and Its Editors, by I. Garland Penn.
The Underground Railroad, by William Still.
The Sons of Ham, by Lewis Pendleton.
The Work of Afro-American Women, by Mrs. N. F. Mossell.
The New South Investigated, by D. A. Straker.
The Negro Baptist Pulpit, by Rev. E. M. Brawley.

The Hazely Family, by Mrs. A. E. Johnson.
The Rape of Florida, by A. A. Whitman.
The Official Manual and History of the Grand United Order of Odd Fellows in America, by Charles B. Wilson.
The Semi-Centenary of the A. M. E. Church, by D. A. Payne, D.D.
The Centennial Budget, by Bishop Arnett.
The Poetical Works of J. E. Gordon.
The Rising Sun, by William Wells Brown.
The Negro's Origin, by B. T. Tanner.
The Negro (African and American), by Bishop Tanner.
The Negro in All Ages, by Bishop H. M. Turner.
The Future of Africa, by Alex. Crummell.
The Negro in the Rebellion, by William Wells Brown.
The Southland, by Rev. R. C. O. Benjamin.
The Boy Doctor, by Rev. R. C. O. Benjamin.
The Model Homestead, by G. L. Blackwell.
The Aim of Life, by Rev. George C. Rowe.
Twenty-two Years of Freedom, by J. T. Wilson.
The Negro Evangelist, by Dr. Albert.
Theological Lectures, by Benjamin T. Tanner.
Thoughts in Verse, by Rev. George Clinton Rowe, pastor Plymouth Congregational Church, Charleston, S. C.
Universal Reign of Jesus, by Rev. A. E. P. Albert, D.D.
Voice of a New Race, by J. T. Wilson.

"THE POWER OF THE PRESS."

BY MRS. N. F. MOSSELL.

EVERY few months we find amateur literary associations discussing the question of the comparative power of the press and the pulpit. It used to be a standing subject for discussion and amusement, but the laugh, in the opinion of the religious world, has completely died out. That the press is entrenching on the power of the pulpit is growing more evident daily. People are coming to prefer to sit by their own cozy firesides and read sermons at their leisure to traveling in inclement weather to the house of worship;

and the poor feel they are thus on a level with the rich; or, at least, are not pained by the contrast in their conditions as they often are when assembled in the house of God.

What world of meaning in the phrase, "The Power of the Press!" Our colored men are realizing its latent force. Through this medium they are rapidly pushing their way, strengthening race pride, and making their wants and oppressions known. Every corporation or large business house now has its own journals advertising its goods, and delighting its patrons with its literary feast. The press is a sleeping lion which men are just awaking into life. We should estimate rightly the great obligation that is upon us to use this immense power rightly. We, of all people, can ill afford to make blunders. We must teach wisely and lead aright that the generation to come may bless us as we bless those who have passed before us. Our press association is well organized, and we should be able at its meetings to give each other wise counsel. The study of other journals from every point of view has its benefits; their circulation and where they circulate; the editorials, the news letters, the personals; every department; reading articles on journalism; noting our own experiences from day to day; and getting the advice of those who have grown gray, and perhaps lost fortunes in the cause. We should study the field from which our support must come. One New York publisher knows every county in every State, and the literary caliber of its inhabitants, and is therefore able to put each book he has for sale on the market at the best advantage to himself and the author. How many of our editors have thus studied the colored constituency of the various States?

We must watch the signs of the times and show business tact. I am forcibly reminded that the white race, even the ignorant portion, possess this faculty largely beyond our own people, even the intelligent ones among us. A white man knowing it was a season for Negro revivals, furnished himself with a goodly-sized bundle of spiritual hymns, and went shouting them up and down the streets, and the colored people flocked to him with their pennies. Not a single white face did I see among them but that of the singer who was gathering in the dimes and nickels from our poor. It was a fit tribute to his businss tact.

Our journals should improve greatly in the next decade. Let the work and field be studied, a policy marked out, and the greatest good to the greatest number be the aim of each. Get the intelligent sympathy and advice of all connected with publications. Form syndicates and pay for good articles on selected subjects from our best writers and authors. Secure the assistance of some wise, helpful, intelligent, and entusiastic woman. Do your best and success will surely crown your effort.

Before closing we must speak of "Our Women in Journalism." They are admitted to the press association and are in sympathy with the male editors; but few have become independent workers in this noble field of effort, being yet satellites, revolving round the sun of masculine journalism. They still remain willing captives, chained to the chariot wheels of the sterner element, and deem it well if "united they stand." Let us have a few more years of co-operative work. Our women have a great field in literary work. Sex or color does not bar, for neither need to be known. As reporters, women are treated with the courtesy due their sex. They have tact, quick perception, and can readily gain access to both sexes. Again, we are "lookers on in Venice." We are not in the thick of the battle. We have time to think, frame our purposes, and carry them into effect, unlike the editor harassed with both literary and business work and other great responsibilities incident to such an enterprise.

Women can do much to purify and strengthen life through the columns of the daily press, or the weekly, or the monthly journals. Right well do they seem to appreciate their opportunities; and a broad view of life and its purposes will come to them through this source. Let one who desires journalism as her life-work, study to acquire a good knowledge of the English language, and of others, if she so desires, but the English language she must. Be alive to obtain what is news, what will interest. Let the woman select her non de plume, or take her own name if she prefers, and use it always, unless for some special purpose it is changed. Write oftenest for one journal and on one subject or on one line, at least, until a reputation has been established. Work conscientiously, follow the natural bent, and the future will not fail to bring its own reward. Hoping that these few scattered, irregular thoughts on "The Power of the Press" may serve as seed-thoughts to lead to more serious thinking, I bid my readers adieu, believing that no brighter path opens before us, as a race, than that of the journalism of the present age.—*Afro-American Press.*

INDUSTRIAL EDUCATION FOR NEGROES.

BY MRS. JULIA A. HOOKS, MEMPHIS.

INDUSTRIAL education is the lever by which the Negro race is to be lifted up. "Give us more schools of industry," should be the cry of the dark sons and daughters of the South. The able, scholarly, and masterly address of Prof. Booker T. Washington, President and founder of the great Tuskegee Institute of Alabama, delivered here recently, has attracted the attention of our citizens in a most favorable manner. Indeed, no man in the country is better prepared than he to discuss the important topic and show its material worth and practical application as a factor in the solution of the great problem. That man has labored hard and long to develop the race along the lines of industrial pursuits, and he has won for himself and his race merited distinction for the work accomplished. We should all be ready and willing to give earnest heed and cheerful indorsement to his labors. I desire to offer a few thoughts, hopeful that they may be the means of arresting the attention of our young men and women to the worthy subject, who, perhaps, did not have the advantage of listening to the words as they fell eloquently from the lips of that great man.

Before offering my thoughts and suggestions I wish to say that this is one great thing which called forth the most rapturous applause. Prof. Washington, though knowing of the difficulties which the Negroes have had to strive against, made no unsavory mention, no incendiary talk, but kindly advised his people to seek for peace with their neighbors, and cease hoisting the flag of distress. "Drop the bucket down where you are." Grand thought, good advice. It is my humble opinion that our system of education until recently has been largely at fault, and even yet it is to be regretted that so much attention is given to the education of the mind, without the application to matter. I mean this: In the schools where the masses must receive instruction there is no industry taught. The head alone is attended to in utter disregard of the hand. Boys and girls are taught that the only avenues in which to be really useful, that the only really honorable opportunities afforded to "make their mark," is to be considered "smart." Indeed, only "smart" enough to be a learned professor, teacher, or preacher. They are led to think that any other training is degrading and beneath the standard of true dignity. It is a fact that many of our boys and girls, after coming to the city to acquire higher educational advantages, often abhor going back to the country, as they should, to help the poor old father and mother to a better understanding of the worth of the "forty acres, a mule and plow." It is true that most of our children abhor the "sweat of human industry;" they look with disgust on the "horny hand of toil." They are ashamed of the title "servant;" and yet are not the possessors of the requisites to be the master or mistress. What is the use of learning? I insist that the great end of education is to prepare one for usefulness in life; and an education that does not accomplish this is worse than useless.

Prof. Washington knows what is required in this age. It calls for the practical man and the practical woman. And the man who will continue to sit at his desk in his classroom and fancifully dream, or the young woman who will leave the schoolroom, after a long day's hard work, and go butterfly chasing the rest of the afternoon, or spend the evening supinely lying about with the novel or story paper in hand, constantly "dreaming dreams and seeing visions," and then looking for their fulfillment, will awake after the great procession of progress has passed, only to discover the awful dangers of the days spent in idly teaching, and dreaming, and failing to discover the true essentials of practical living. If schooling means anything, it means to prepare one for the highest standard of true greatness in its fullest sense. It is a fallacy to seek knowledge simply for the purpose of being smart. Prof. Washington did not dare discourage higher education; nor do I mean to decry the highest education of the mind, yet I say that I oppose any form of education for my boys that is not to be made practical, and carried into their generous life. Again, much of the education nowadays is misdirected. Boys and girls should be trained with an eye single to the place in life they are to fill. Casting a boy adrift upon the world with a mind stored with classic lore, and most of it only shamly crammed into his brain, and while neither he nor his parrents are prepared to find an honorable means of support for that classic mind, is nothing less than a crime. As a bread winner he is rendered a miserable failure. Idleness and uselessness naturally follow as a sequence. This leads to poverty and crime, which is feeding our jails, thronging our penitentiaries, and swarming the many houses of prostitution—by many considered a necessity. Industrial ignorance and antipathy, more than anything else, is the cause of anarchism, and, indeed, many of the great evils of the day come from the lack, the total ignorance, of industrial habits. Idleness and industrial ignorance is causing our people to lose their patriotism, and the perpetuity of our national life depends upon our knowledge and the usefulness of industrial pursuits.

The only star of hope which is to shed the radiant light to illumine our darkened pathway here in the Southland, and open up a way into a new faith and a new inspiration, lies in the education of the hand as well as the head—"the grasping of matter and bringing from it something." The community has nothing to fear from the intelligent, industrious boy or girl. The man or woman who is an earnest, intelligent, and industrious owner of his "forty acres" and farming tools is not shunned. The vacant lands lying around here are calling to us, "Come and till; come and use us and we will do you good." Let us as patriotic people ask, nay, beg, our legislatures to legislate for industrial education in connection with the free school system, and also let us beg that a compulsory system of this education be demanded of parents and guardians. Then will our youths be thrice armed to combat with America's great evils—immorality, intemperance, ignorance, malice, and prejudice. An educated industry will make a man a truer husband, a kinder father, a better neighbor, and a nobler citizen. An intelligent, industrious woman will be a truer wife, a fonder mother, and a more faithful servant. Our State can better afford to found and give to its citizens of color industrial schools, than schools where tactics and athletics are taught. We have more need of carpenters than athletes, and a prosperous, well-educated farmer is worth more to us and to the State than a hundred well-drilled and disciplined soldiers.

The Negro must look to industry as the bright ray of hope. The few industrial schools where industry is truly and properly taught must be supported. Such opportunities will be the means in many instances of saving from shame and disgrace our boys and will help in preserving the virtue and chastity of our girls. I trust and believe that the many right-thinking colored mothers who listened with marked appreciation to Prof. Washington will treasure the effort put forth by the Whittier Association in bringing him here, and that as they sing the little girl infant to sleep they may look forth to this industrial education as the safeguard which is to protect and save her for future usefulness. On my Sunday mission to the county jail I look with pity and remorse, with sorrow and disgust, upon our poor little boys and girls and our young men and women when I see so many of them with brilliant minds wasting their lives in idleness and profligacy, oftentimes dishonoring their parents, disgracing themselves and their race, bringing trouble and expense upon the State and county by their condition. I sit prayerfully considering and sorrowfully begging my Lord to show me some plan by which I can help uplift my people out of the low estate into which so many hundreds of them have fallen. I can but see a gleam of hope as I look forth to the industrial education, the applying of mind to matter, as the only and great lever which is to lift them up and make them a blessing, rather than a curse, to society; a blessing, rather than a curse, to posterity. Teaching our boys and girls of to-day, who will be the men and women of to-morrow, the true meaning of education is the only hope. Demanding of parents and guardians to see to the proper education of head and hand will prove a future blessing to the Southland's glory and greatness.—*Commercial-Appeal.*

THE NEGRO AS AN ECONOMIST.

HOW HE IS COMING—THE DEPTHS FROM WHICH HE HAS COME.

IT is said that the colored population of Georgia pay taxes on about $40,000,000 worth of real property. The amount of mortgage on the lands of the Georgia Negroes is not stated, but even if it should be one half of the value of the real estate, the result would be the possession by those people of $20,000,000 worth of land, which they have accumulated since the war. It is quite likely, though statistics on the subject are not available, that a similar, if not better, result would be shown in the other Southern States, and the probability is that the Negroes of the South own, free of all encumbrance, perhaps $250,000,000 to $300,000,000 worth of real estate. Such a result as this is probably unprecedented in the history of our civilization. It should be remembered that less than thirty years ago the Negroes started with less than nothing, for as slaves they acquired habits of thriftlessness, of wastefulness that almost unfitted them for the accumulation of property. In one generation they have managed to pile up an aggregate of wealth that is simply enormous. It is true that a considerable percentage of the race still retain the habits of idleness that characterized them as slaves. It is also true that no large percentage exhibit talent for accumulation, but are content to earn from day to day the wages of the day before, trusting to chance for the future of the morrow. But after these deductions have been made, there still remains a large number of them who have exhibited decided financial ability. Starting in the most humble way, with limited intelligence, and exceedingly circumscribed knowledge of the manner in which economy is to be practiced, they have nevertheless gone on from year to year accumulating a little until their savings, as represented by their property, have built churches, have erected school houses, they employ and pay preachers and teachers; and all out of the humble earnings of day laborers. Such results as these deserve honorable mention. When contemplating the race as a mass, it is usual to judge its members by its worst representatives, a method both unjust and untrue. The colored people of the South, as a class, should not be judged by the criminals among them who become conspicuous in the newspapers from the evil deeds that are often visited with swift and terrible justice; they should rather be judged from the honest, hard working men and women who, beginning with nothing, have in the course of one generation accumulated an amount of property that even of our magnificent national wealth forms no inconspicuous portion.—*St. Louis Christian Advocate.*

IMPROVING NEGRO HOMES.

BY CARRIE A. BANISTER, IN THE "NASHVILLE CITIZEN."

NOT long since the subject of improving the homes of the Negroes as a paramount factor in developing better men and women among them was discussed in a leading New York journal, and the habit of considering all Negroes as Negroes and not as men and women intrudes itself as usual. The writer says that the first need of the Negroes is the improvement of the "dark and cheerless abodes" in which these people live. For, says he, the Negroes who live in neat and well kept homes are thrifty and intelligent, self-respecting and respectable; and from this he deduces the conclusion that if the Negroes were placed in better homes they would at once become thrifty and respectable. The true deduction to be reached is that the Negro's thrift and self-respect made the home, and not the home which made the Negro.

The Negro whose soul is free, like every other man, appreciates the sacredness and beauty which must be inseparable from a happy home. On the other hand the Negro debased and brutified by a servitude of centuries, has no comprehension or desire for home in any exalted sense. Perhaps the least desirable legacy bequeathed by slavery to the children of its victims, is the disintegrating and nomadic tendencies of a homeless and non-familied people. The improvement must begin with the people who are to make the homes, who do make them. Quixotic as seems to us there are those among the freedmen whom no wretchedness can impel, and no opportunity inspire, to alter or to make tolerable the places in which they and their families exist. More than one old Negro lives for years in a one or two-room cabin, declining to build another room "kase he won't be gwine to leave."

In the same way the pure air and water of the vast open fields and hill sides call in vain to the denizens of the filthy and over-crowded tenements of the cities. In effecting any improvement all the formative and educative influences which touch the colored people must be called into requisition, the schools, the churches and the press. Of these influences none is so powerful or far-reaching in its results as the industrial school since it educates the whole man. The soul is schooled to higher wants and the hand is skilled to obtain them. When these influences have combined to make a generation of virtuous, clean, industrious women, though they may not shine in society or speak but one language, though they may be ugly in feature and unsophisticated in manner; and by their sides a generation of men who will care for and love their own firesides, what though their names are never heard outside the little limits of their own state or neighborhood, what though their hands are hard with toil, we will not need to discuss the improvement of homes; such women and men will improve their homes of their own volition.

Residence of R. R. Church,
Memphis, Tenn.

SUNSHINE.

VALEDICTORY ESSAY BY SARAH A. PAGE, DELIVERED AT TUGALOO COLLEGE, TUGALOO, MISSISSIPPI.

WHAT would the world be without sunshine—sunshine from above us and from within us. If you can imagine so dark a picture try to think of yourself in a sunless world. Look around you, and see if anything like joy can be awakened by your surroundings. All is dark, dismal and chilly. As we look out upon our now verdant fields and forests, we cannot help thinking of the great body that has furnished light and heat for them and coaxed them to robe themselves in their spring dress. Our woods are full of fragrant flowers. Mother Nature has withheld nothing beautiful from us. But suppose that just as the little plants had peeped up from under the sod they had been deprived of the sunshine. For a time they would have struggled on against adversity, but with so little strength that they would have at last succumbed to the effects of cold and darkness. While living they would have been beautiful. We have seen plants that were deprived of sunshine. Were they rich in the beautiful colors which we see in our woods? No, they could not boast of colors. They were weak, dwarfed and pale. In them we see none of the beauty that characterizes our wild, free flowers. Where the shadow has been predominant, beauty cannot reach its full development.

In this world we are all plants, and what is strange about it is that our sunshine is received in a large measure from others. We, too, must live and grow. And to support life in us we need sunshine.

Let us notice, first, ourselves as sources of light or shadow. We are constantly in the presence of others. Whether we know it or not we are causing them to flourish by the genial rays from our hearts, or we are causing them to wither and fade by the gloominess of our looks and words. The little brothers, sisters, sons and daughters in our homes are tender plants. They need warmth and light to make them vigorous and beautiful. Give them this and you are nourishing the great roots of patience, love, trustfulness and self-reliance.

Through these roots the great tree of manhood and womanhood is to draw its food. They are easily injured now, and too much shade will dwarf them for the rest of their existence. You are putting in the lovely colors such as no artist can portray on his canvas.

Our parents need our sunshine. How could we have reached our present condition without their love and care? Let us show to them that their rays have been absorbed by us and not misspent. Let us throw our brightest beams in their pathway. They have had enough of the dark side of life. It is our great privilege to be the disseminators of light and cheerfulness to them. If we perform our duties faithfully in this respect, we will be a great power in lightening the burdens that will come to them from other sources.

In the school-room, at the counter, at the work bench, there is ever a demand for sunshine. Your pupils are encouraged, your customers pleased if your service is given in a pleasant, light-hearted manner. Look among the happy homes and see if you can find the moody, silent, humdrum man. You will usually find him not in such a home as this, but in the home where shades from unloving hearts prevail. He may mount the ladder of fame but he has lost one of the most precious jewels of life. The happy laborer would not change places with him. He grows hardened and the bright rays which would have made his heart glad cannot at once affect him. He does not understand the worth of this treasure. He must be gradually brought to realize it. You may say there are many great men whose early lives were overshadowed. To this we will agree only in part. However dark may have seemed their way, some struggling sunbeams have reached them at some time, and these few rays, on account of their scarcity, were made more precious. There are lives which seem to have no glimmer of light in them, but many of them have some secret hope, some unknown comforter.

We have been observing this agent as going out from us to others, let us now look at it coming to us from them:

First, how do we secure it? Sunshine may be poured out upon us from others, and we may make ourselves impervious to its effects. We may cherish such gloomy thoughts that we will fail to be benefitted. When others are happy, do not cast a gloom over them by coldness. It freezes the heart of a friend to be observed with coldness when he is happy. We sympathize with others in their sorrow; can we not also share their joys? It adds to their happiness to have others happy.

You feel low-spirited sometimes. You do not to care relate your trouble to others, why then keep up a gloomy appearance? Throw off the shadow and let bright beams radiate from your countenance. If you are naturally of a gloomy disposition you can do no better than to imitate the example of others who are cheerful. If you have some trouble in which your friends can help you, show your appreciation of their kindness.

What a world of darkness this would be, had we no kind friends to share our woes! How different would seem our surroundings. Nearly all our pleasure comes in having others share our feelings. There are innumerable ways in which we can give sunshine. Of some of them we have already spoken. The sharing of joys or sorrows, the pleasant word, or look, the warm handshake, all bear with them a message of cheer, and oh, how soothing to the heart, how welcome to the ear. There are many valuable gifts which we are unable to bestow, but kind deeds, one of the most precious, we can each give in abundance. We have seen faces from which there seemed to radiate all that was true and beautiful. Our world would know less of woe if there were more of such faces. If we are to be constantly sending forth bright rays, we must have a strong reservoir from which to get our supply. The light shines from our faces, but what is the source? Before we can do much toward giving the light to others, we must have within our hearts love and cheerfulness. One word spoken from the heart is worth more than many spoken from the tip of the tongue. "It needs the everflow of heart to give the lips full speech." We can distinguish between the shallow words of pretension and those of heartfelt interest. Surface words are revolting when we are in need of advice or encouragement. The *light* that lighteth all the world must be within us. Drawing from that neverfailing Source, our supply of light is sure. The bright face is an index to the brighter heart. As we look into the faces of others we can judge whether they are usually happy or not. We notice their actions and judge them by their fruit. God judges them by their roots. We may be deceived as to their fruits, but he is never deceived as to the source of their strength.

There is a beautiful custom among the natives of Madura. At evening-tide the mother trims and polishes her lamp and sets it on a table in the centre of the room. As the members of the family gather in, each one pays homage to the light before proceeding with the social joys of the evening. This custom is of course connected with some of their superstitious beliefs, but a lesson may be borne to us from it. What light have we that draws us together and exerts a binding influence upon us? Sunshine is the philosopher's stone that transmutes everything to gold. It is not miserly, but steals into every crevice and tries to awaken its occupants.

Our sunshine should not be sparing, but for every one we meet there should be a bountiful supply. Life is too short for us to indulge in shadows. There will be enough of them howe'er the sunshine falls. In all our lives there must be some shadows, but they may be so regarded that we will be strengthened by them. Our sunshine is then made more glorious by contrast. There will be times when we must, with Longfellow—

> "Be still sad heart and cease repining,
> Behind the cloud is the sun still shining."

Life cannot be one pleasant summer day. We each learn by experience that "some days must be dark and dreary." We might grow tired of the sunshine were there no shadows for contrast. Some flowers need all sunshine, some flourish on very little, and seem to require the shade. Out of seemingly dark recesses some beautiful lives grow, but their light comes from above and dispels all gloom. Their sorrows are borne in patience because they live in anticipation of the light to come. Like those flowers whose faces are constantly turned toward the sun, let us ever look toward the source of our light, hoping thereby to become more radiant and beautiful. To-day brings us to a point in our career which has both its sad and joyous features. When we think of the happy hours spent here with our teachers and fellow students, and when the thought comes to us that these hours have ceased to be, a feeling of regret fills our hearts; but we have not the time to look back, and so as we look off into the future and contemplate the work that is before us, we can but rejoice at the prospect of enlarging our work for the Master. Classmates, our pathway which for some time has been one and the same, to-day separates in many branches. We each pursue a different way, resolving to make the best of it, rejoicing in the sunshine, keeping cheerful in the shadow.

We extend hearty thanks to these kind teachers who have had our interest at heart, and who have striven to aid us in attaining a higher life. Their efforts shall not be lost, for the inspirations which we have received from them we are trying to make part of our lives.

We hope that when report of our actions reaches your ears, you will recognize in them the principles of a noble manhood and womanhood.

Fellow students, to you we must bid adieu. We hope that the good that you receive here may serve to make your path sunny. These opportunities are still yours.

In saying farewell to-day, we do not feel that we are at the end. We have only laid the foundation; our building we have yet to construct. We go forth among our fellow-men to reflect the light that we have received here—to remove the darkness of ignorance and unhappiness; and in so doing we hope to follow out our Master's injunction, to "Shine as lights in the world."

"MAMMY" AND HER PET.

TRUE CHRISTIANITY.

IN the minds of many people religion is associated with gloom. It is something to which they may be compelled to resort to avoid worse evils, but of itself it is without zest or charm. Doubtless the austerity of the Puritan regime has done much to foster this impression. The lines between the church and the world were drawn with precision, and the discrimination was more against external things than against inward dispositions. The old Manichæan notion that matter was inherently sinful, and that material pleasures were seductions of the evil one, colored their conceptions, as they did those of the mediæval church. Gradually, however, the Christian churches have been coming to wiser views. They have been led to see that the world and all it contains is God's world, that he framed his creatures for many grades of enjoyment, and that, other things being equal, he is the truest man who is alive in every faculty of soul and body. We have also come to see that the Christian ideal of life is not one in which the faculties for physical enjoyment are sternly repressed, but one in which all powers are subordinated to spiritual claims and controlled by spiritual motives.

Self-denial has as much place in the Christian life as it ever had; but we have learned to distinguish between self-denial for the sake of conserving the soul's power for some worthy end or for the sake of self-discipline, and self-mortification, as an end in itself. The former is one of the highest manifestations of the Christian spirit; the latter is heathenism. One essential mark of true self-denial is that it is not morose and gloomy. It sees the superiority of the spiritual end it aims to secure, and gladly surrenders the lower good to gain it. It is only the self-mortification which is always unintelligent, and a dash of superstition that is undertoned and repining. The Apostle Paul is an admirable illustration of the true Christian temper. Few man have sacrificed more than he for spiritual ends, but his letters abound with good cheer. Men constantly turn to them for courage. In the parable of the Prodigal Son, the elder son who could say that while his brother who wasted his living, he had never had a kid to make merry with his friends, unconsciously disclosed the real quality of his life. He showed that he had all the time been longing for just such a life as that his brother had led. His brother's life was the kind of life he would have led if he could have given free play to his impulses. Inwardly he had wandered as far from his father as ever his brother had outwardly in miles or riotous excess. His heart had not been enlisted in the home life; it was some small motive of decency or self-interest that kept him respectable. The elder son is a type of the men whose religion is gloomy, and who represent it to others as a distasteful experience. They are not quite in the world, though they long to be, and they do not live in the Spirit.

"The fruit of the Spirit is—joy." The more real one's religion is, the happier, the sunnier he will be. The man who enters into the spirit of Christ will be wary about making external prohibitions for himself or for others. Rather he will seek for himself and others that devotion to the highest things which remands the lower life and its pleasures to their proper place, and, in so doing, finds the deepest satisfactions.—*Boston Watchman.*

Turpentine Farm, Near Savannah, Ga

TEMPERANCE.

TO THE COLORED WORKINGMEN.

EVERY laboring colored man is called upon to choose between the saloon, with its attendant miseries and vices, and the home with its manifold blessings. In the *Journal of United Labor*, the following letter by Mr. T. V. Powderly, is worth your careful consideration. He says, "I know that in the organization of which I am the head there are many good men who drink, but they would be better men if they did not drink. I know that there are thousands in our order who will not agree with me on the question of temperance, but that is their misfortune, for they are wrong, radically wrong. Ten years ago I was hissed becsuse I advised men to let strong drink alone. They threatened to rotten-egg me. I continued to advise men to be temperate, and though I have had no experience that would qualify me to render an opinion on the efficacy of a rotten egg as an ally of the rum-drinker, yet I would prefer to have my exterior decorated from summit to base with the rankest kind of rotten eggs rather than allow one drop of liquid villainy to pass my lips, or have the end of my nose illuminated by the bloom that follows a planting of the seeds of hatred, envy, malice, and damnation, all of which are represented in a solitary glass of gin.

He (the drunkard), robs parents, wife, and children. He robs his aged father and mother through love of drink. He gives for rum what should go for their support. When they murmur, he turns them from his door, and points his contaminated drunken finger toward the poorhouse. He next turns to his wife and robs her of what should be devoted to the keeping of her home in comfort and plenty. He robs her of her wedding ring and pawns it for drink. He turns his daughter from his door in a fit of drunken anger and drives her to the house of prostitution, and then accepts from her hand the proceeds of her shame. To satisfy his love of drink, he takes the price of his child's virtue and innocence from her sin-stained, lust-bejeweled fingers, and with it totters to the bar to pay it to the man 'who does not deny the justness of my position.' I do not arraign the man who drinks because he is poor, but because through being a slave to drink he has made himself and family poor. I do not hate men who drink, for I have carried drunken men to their homes on my back, rather than allow them to remain exposed to the enclement weather. I do not hate the drunkard, he is what drink effected; and while I do not hate the effect, I abhor and loathe the cause.

In the city of New York alone it is estimated that not less than $250,000 a day are spent for drink, $1,500,000 in one week, $75,000,000 in one year. Who will dispute it when I say that one-half of the policemen of New York City are employed to watch the beings who squander $75,000,000? Who will dispute it when I say that the money spent in paying the salaries and expenses of one-half of the police of New York could be saved to the tax-payers if $75,000,000 were not devoted to making drunkards, thieves, prostitutes, and other subjects for the policemen's net to gather in? If $250,000 go over the counters of the rumseller in one day in New York City alone, who will dare to assert that *workingmen* do not pay one-fifth, or $50,000, of that sum? If workingmen in New York City spend $50,000 a day for drink, they spend $300,000 a week, leaving Sunday out. In four weeks they spend $1,200,000—over twice as much money as was paid into the General Assembly of the Knights of Labor in nine years. In six weeks they spend $1,800,000—nearly three times as much money as that army of organized workers, the Knights of Labor, have spent from the day the General Assembly was first called to order up to the present day; and in one year the workingmen of New York City alone will have spent for beer and rum $15,600,000, or enough to purchase and equip a first-class telegraph line of their own; $15,600,000, enough money to invest in such a co-operative enterprise as would forever end the strike and lockout as a means of settling disputes in labor circles."

Ought to be Made Odious.

"Intemperance, like treason," says Cardinal Gibbons, ought to be made odious in the land, and there is a close similarity between the two. The treasonable man endeavors to dethrone the rightful sovereign, and intemperance dethrones reason, the ruler of the soul."

The A. M. E. Zion Church on Temperance.

At the Nineteenth Quadrennial Session of the General Conference of the A. M. E. Zion Church, held in Pittsburg, Pa., May, 1892, the Committee on Temperance submitted the following report, which was unanimously adopted:

"Temperance has narrowed itself down in these days so that at present it refers to the liquor traffic specially. We recognize the fact that while there are many evils to which our country is heir, and many evil spots of degradation and sin which besmirch the garments of fair Columbia—mistress of the West, pride of the world—there are none which so disfigure her fair garments as intemperance, by which are her garments not only besmirched, but in which they are bedraggled and polluted, and by which, if the cause be not curtailed or extirpated, she will be compelled to follow the path of the grand old government which preceded her, and be buried in the great sea of oblivion; be known as a thing of the past, the very action of whose language, mayhap, like Greece and Rome, be forgotten.

We aver that above and beyond all the evils which pervade our fair land, this hydra-headed monster dominates them all, and subverts all things upon which it takes hold to become the menials of its will. It lurks in the lowly hovel, and revels in the palaces of the great; it perverts government from its high purpose, and makes it become a weakly, servile imbecile, unable either to direct the affairs of government, or to promulgate its laws. It desecrates the family altar, despoils the sweet influence of the family circle, rends virtue into shreds, and puts a premium on vice. It impels the infuriated mob to deeds of horror and crime more barbarous, heinous, devilish than those wrought by Nero, evidences of which fact may be seen in the many lynchings of recent occurrence.

Therefore, because of these facts, together with many other vicious influences which it ingenders, the multifarious evils which emanate from it, we, the committee, submit that all means which can be reasonably and legally brought to bear to extirpate this great evil from among the people of our country be endorsed by our connection, and receive its continued support. We further recommend that Zion's ministry give more attention to the great cause of temperance, and that the laity be incited to greater work in a united effort to put under foot the great monster intemperance."

Temperance Resolutions Adopted by the A. M. E. Church.

The African Methodist Episcopal Church at its General Conference, held at Indianapolis, Indiana, adopted the following resolutions:

"*Resolved* 1, That we discourage the manufacture, sale, and use of all alcoholic and malt liquors.

2. "That we discourage the use of *tobacco* by our ministers and people.

3. "That we discourage the use of opium and snuff.

4. "That we endorse the great Prohibition movement in this country, also the work done by the Woman's Christian Temperance Union, and will use all honorable means to suppress the evils growing out of intemperance.

5. "That it shall be a crime for any minister or member of the A. M. E. Church to fight against temperance, and if convicted of this crime he shall lose his place in the Conference and the church."

The Bishops at this same conference said in their address: "We should allow no minister, or member who votes, writes, lectures, or preaches to uphold the rum trade to retain his membership, either in the Conference or in the church. And those who are addicted to strong drink, either ministers or laymen, should have no place among us. Visit our station houses, bridewells, jails, almshouses, and penitentiaries, and you will there witness the effects of this horror of horrors. Rum has dug the grave of the American Indian so deep that it will never be resurrected. If we would escape the same fate as a church and a race, we must be temperate.

"Some of the loftiest intellects have been blasted and blighted by this terrible curse. The use of wine at weddings should never be encouraged by our ministers; it is often the beginning of a blasted life."

Ordinary observation is sufficient evidence to convince any *poor dram drinker* that the use of liquor is detrimental to his interests.

Benjamin Franklin on the Analysis of Beer.

In 1725 Franklin wrote this interesting reminiscence of his apprenticeship in Watt's printing house in London: "I drank only water; the other workmen, nearly fifty in number, were great drinkers of beer. On occasions I carried up and down stairs a large form of types in each hand, when others carried but one in both hands. They wondered to see, from this and several instances, that the water-American, as they called me, was stronger than themselves, who drank strong beer. We had an ale-house boy, who attended always in the house to supply the workmen. My companion at the press drank every day a pint before breakfast, a pint at breakfast with his bread and cheese, a pint between breakfast and dinner, a pint at dinner, a pint in the afternoon about 6 o'clock, and another when he had done his day's work. I thought it a detestable custom, but it was necessary, he supposed, to drink strong beer that he might be strong to labor. I endeavored to convince him that the bodily strength afforded by beer could only be in proportion to the grain or flour of the barley dissolved in the water of which it was made; that there was more flour in a pennyworth of bread, and therefore if he could eat that with a pint of water it would give him more strength than a quart of beer. He drank on, however, and had four or five shillings to pay out of his wages every Saturday night for that vile liquor; an expense I was free from. And thus these poor devils keep themselves always under."

A Temperance Lecture by Rev. J. C. Price, President National Afro-American League.

"Remembering the circumstances in which the Negro was placed by the dreadful institution of slavery it is not to be wondered at that he now cultivates a taste, even a love for alcohol. Yet it is remarkable to note the progress toward sobriety that the race has made in the later years of its emancipation. A colored total abstainer is not a rare person in any community nowadays. The various temperance societies and nearly all the other secret organizations supported by the Afro-American race uniformly require those who seek admission to pledge themselves to be sober men and women, and in most cases to be total abstainers. The drift is more and more in this direction, and hence soberness in the race is constantly on the increase. It is remarkable, too, to observe the steadfastness and persistency with which colored teachers as a rule, hold to the idea that the race is to be uplifted morally, as well as materially and religiously improved, through total abstinence as a chief instrument. It is the rare exception, not the rule, to find a colored teacher who does not hold to this doctrine. The result is that many boys and girls in the school-room all over the South and in other sections as well are being trained to habits of temperance, and will in all probability develop into consistent temperance men and women. And it must not be forgotten that the true and most influential leaders of the race, the ministers, are moulding and shaping the opinions of both old and young in favor of soberness and total abstinence. The unanimity with which the churches of all denominations declare for the temperance reform is most encouraging. It is a very rare thing to find any considerable proportion of the ministry of any religious denomination exerting an influence in behalf of the extension and perpetuation of the liquor traffic. The church as a factor in this race development and elevation is laboring steadfastly and earnestly for the right. It is the one force that checks and holds the individuals of the race from following the evil propensities of their own hearts when every other force proves unavailing. In it is the chief hope for the present as well as the eternal salvation of the Negro. If the church is kept pure it can lift up and give honor and perfect freedom to the freedmen. The race has implicit confidence in the truth and value of God's word. This confidence must not be shaken but must be cultivated by the selection of clergymen well qualified by special training to teach wisely, acceptably and properly. Along with such cultivation will inevitably go a determination to strengthen the temperance cause more and more.

I have watched closely the men who are recognized as the race leaders in various States and localities. It is acknowledged that they are generally shrewd, calculating and hard to circumvent when they attempt political manœuvers. It is my observation that these leaders are strictly reliable and trustworthy when confined in and— however surprising the statement may be to some—that they are generally sober, upright and honest. I confess that in some localities this rule does not apply, but on the whole a more sober class of leaders does not exist in any race than in the Afro-American. One of the evils against which our people have to contend is the crossroads grocery store, to be found all over the Southland—the bane of this section. Here, with no city or town ordinance to make drunkenness an offense and to threaten certain punishment, they congregate and drink their fill, carouse, engage in free fights and do other hurtful and equally unlawful things, while no one dares molest or make afraid, and the grocery keeper finding his trade benefited, encourages the debauchery. This evil instead of becoming less increases. The business of many prosperous towns and villages is being injured seriously by the competition at the cross roads and the resulting vice, violence and impoverishment. The records of the courts would show that crime among our people is traceable to a large majority of cases to a too free exercise of the liquor habit. Of the men belonging to the race who are hanged, I think it entirely reasonable to say that at least four-fifths committed their offenses while under the influence of liquor. But speaking of the race broadly, and duly considering all the unusual circumstances that ought to be taken into consideration, I think it cannot fairly be charged with anything like gross intemperance. It is something out of the usual order to come upon a case of delirium tremens among the Negroes. Comparatively few of them drink anything of consequence during the week, but excessive imbibition is mostly indulged in on Saturdays. With their rigorous physical constitution they are able, in six days of comparative temperance, to resist the undermining effects of the seventh day's spree. Therefore this is not a race of drunkards, and there is abundant reason for believing that with proper education and training it may be made a race of sober people and abstainers.

In all the prohibition and local option contests in the South numbers of colored men have been on the side of temperance and fought valiantly for its success. Many others would have thrown their influence the same way had they not been duped by misguided leaders who raised false cries of alarm, declaring that prohibition was a device to take away their dearly-bought liberty. It is customary to blame the Negroes for the defeats of prohibition in Texas, in the second Atlanta contest, etc.; but it must be remembered that without a large share of the Negro vote prohibition could not have carried in Atlanta at the first trial and would have been lost in hundreds of other fights.

In order to strengthen the cause of temperance in the South nothing is more important than to treat the Negro fairly, to keep faith with him, to permit no pledge to be broken. Once won, the colored man is the most faithful and reliable of allies. It is of course needless to add that the suppy of temperance literature should be kept up and increased. Especially valuable is the work of arousing total abstinence enthusiasm among the students in the various educational institutions—young men (and women too), upon whom the future of the race and its influence for good or evil so largely depends. I am indeed hopeful for the future of the Afro-American race, and particularly hopeful that it will become a positive and influential contributor to the triumph of the temperance reform. It is estimated that Christendom has introduced 70,000 gallons of rum to every missionary. In the great Congo Free State there are *one hundred* drunkards to *one* convert. Under the maddening influence of intoxicating drink sent from New England *two hundred* Congoans slaughtered each other. One gallon of rum caused a fight in which fifty were slain.—*Ram's Horn.*

TOBACCO.

SOON after the discovery of this plant it was introduced into many of the countries of Europe, and soon became an article of luxury. Its use, however, was condemned, and the Sultans of Turkey declared smoking a *crime*, and death of the most cruel kind was fixed as the punishment. In Russia the "noses of the smokers were cut off in the earlier part of the seventeenth century." Its use was described by King James I., of England, as "a custom loathesome to the eye, hateful to the nose, harmful to the brain, dangerous to the lungs, and in the black, stinking fume thereof nearest resembling the horrible Stygian smoke of the pit that is bottomless."

Dr. J. H. Kellogg, M.D., in Health Science Leaflet, No. 216, says: "Chemists, botanists and physicians unite in pronouncing tobacco one of the most deadly poisons known. No other poison with the exception of prussic acid will cause death so quickly, only three or four minutes being required for a fatal dose to produce its full effect. The active principle of tobacco, that is, that to which its narcotic and poisonous properties are due, is nicotine, a heavy, oily substance, which may be separated from the dry leaf of the plant by distillation or infusion. The proportion of nicotine varies from two to eight per cent. A pound of tobacco contains on an average 380 grains of this deadly poison, of which one-tenth of a grain will kill a dog in ten minutes. A case is on record in which a man was killed in thirty seconds by this poison. Hottentots use the oil of tobacco to kill snakes, a single minute drop causing death as quickly as a lightning stroke. It is largely used by gardeners and keepers of green houses to destroy grubs and noxious insects (its proper sphere of usefulness)."

The habit of smoking was discovered on the island of Cuba. The two sailors who were sent by Columbus to explore the island, report that: "Among many other strange and curious discoveries, the natives carried with them lighted fire brands, and puffed smoke from their mouths and noses, which they supposed to be the way the savages had of perfuming themselves. They afterward declared that they 'saw the naked savages twist large leaves together and smoke like devils.' "

The use of tobacco in any form is both filthy and pernicious. "Keep thyself pure," was Paul's injunction to Timothy; and again he says, "Let us cleanse ourselves from all filthiness of the flesh and spirit." "If any man defile the temple of God, him shall God destroy; for the temple of God is holy, which temple ye are." 1 Cor. iii. 17.

HAVE A BANK ACCOUNT.

EVERY man should make a point to lay up a little money for a "rainy day", which we are all liable to encounter when least expected. The best way to do this is to open an account with a savings bank. Accumulated money is always safe; it is always ready to use when needed. Scrape together five dollors, make your deposit, receive your bank book and then resolve to deposit a given sum, small though it be once a month, or once a week, according to circumstances. Nobody knows without trying it, how easy a thing it is to save money when an account with a bank has been opened. With such an account a man feels a desire to enlarge his deposit. It gives him lessons in frugality and economy, weans him from habits of extravagance and is the very best guard in the world against intemperance, dissipation and vice.

VALUE OF OLD COINS.

COMPARATIVELY few people are aware of the value of old coins. These rare and valuable pieces of money turn up when least expected, and many persons have become suddenly worth hundreds and even thousands of dollars by making a lucky find. It is the scarcity of the coin, not its age, that determines its value. Following we give a table of quotations:

RARE AMERICAN COINS QUOTED AT THEIR MARKET VALUE.

Half Cent.

1793 is worth from	$1 00 to $	10 00
1794 " "	10 to	3 00
1795 " "	25 to	5 00
1796 (Plain edge; without pole)	1 00 to	25 00
1796 (" " with pole)	5 00 to	50 00
1802 is worth from	25 to	5 00
1804 stemless wreath, is worth from	05 to	50
1811 is worth from	15 to	2 00
1828 thirteen stars, is worth from	02 to	10
1831 is worth from	1 00 to	8 00
1836 " "	1 00 to	10 00
1840 to 1848 is worth from	1 00 to	10 00
1850 is worth from	05 to	15
1852 " "	2 00 to	4 00
1854 " "	3 00 to	10 00

One Cent (Copper).

1788 is worth from	40 to	65
1793 " "	2 00 to	3 00
1795 " "	75 to	1 00
1799 " "	4 00 to	6 00
1804 " "	1 00 to	25 00
1806 " "	05 to	4 00
1808 " "	05 to	5 00
1809 " "	25 to	7 50
1813 " "	05 to	4 00
1816 " "	01 to	45
1817 " "	02 to	1 00
1827 " "	01 to	2 00
1830 to 1840 (inclusive) is worth from	01 to	1 00
1856 is worth from	1 00 to	3 50

196   AFRO-AMERICAN ENCYCLOPÆDIA.

1861 is worth from ....$	01 to $	05
1863 " "	01 to	10
1865 copper-nickel is worth from.................................	01 to	45
1877 pure nickel is worth from	10 to	1 00
1881 " " " "	10 to	1 00

Two Cents (Bronze).

1864 is worth from	05 to	50
1865 " "	03 to	15
1866 " "	02 to	10
1867 " "	02 to	10
1872 " "	02 to	10
1873 " "	05 to	25

Three Cents (Silver).

1852 is worth from	03 to	25
1854 " "	02 to	40
1855 " "	05 to	2 00
1856 " "	03 to	1 00
1863 " "	03 to	25
1864 " "	03 to	50
1869 " "	03 to	20
1873 " "	03 to	20

Five Cents (Nickel).

1866 is worth from	15 to	50
1867 " "	15 to	50
1869 " "	10 to	20
1870 " "	05 to	10
1883 " "	05 to	10

Five Cents (Silver).

1794 is worth from	1 00 to	10 00
1796 " "	1 00 to	11 00
1797 (fifteen stars) is worth from	50 to	5 00
1801 is worth from	1 00 to	10 00
1802 " "	50 00 to	200 00
1805 " "	2 00 to	20 00
1840 " "	10 to	50
1846 " "	50 to	3 00
1860 " "	05 to	25
1870 to 1873 is worth from	05 to	10

Ten Cents.

1796 is worth from	50 to	5 00
1797 thirteen stars is worth from................................	1 00 to	15 00
1797 sixteen stars is worth from.................................	2 00 to	25 00
1804 is worth from	3 00 to	25 00
1809 " "	1 00 to	5 00
1822 " "	50 to	10 00
1840 " "	10 to	30
1844 " "	10 to	50

THOUGHTS, DOINGS, AND SAYINGS OF THE RACE.

1852 is worth from .....$	10 to $	20
1854 " "	10 to	15
1860 San Francisco mint only is worth from.....	20 to	1 00

TWENTY CENTS.

1877–1878 is worth from.....$	50 to $	1 00

QUARTER DOLLAR.

1796 is worth from	2 00 to	15 00
1804 " "	1 00 to	10 00
1807 " "	25 to	5 00
1822 " "	20 to	2 75
1823 " "	20 00 to	100 00
1832 " "	25 to	1 00
1841 " "	25 to	40
1844 " "	20 to	1 00
1848 " "	25 to	1 00
1853 " "	75 to	6 00
1866, Without In God We Trust, is worth from	40 to	2 75
1871, '72, '73, and '74 are worth from	25 to	35

HALF DOLLAR.

1794 is worth from	1 00 to	15 00
1795 " "	50 to	3 00
1796, fifteen stars, is worth from	10 00 to	100 00
1796, sixteen " " "	20 00 to	110 00
1797 is worth "	20 00 to	100 00
1801 " "	1 00 to	10 00
1802 " "	2 00 to	10 00
1803 " "	50 to	2 00
1805 " "	50 to	1 00
1813 " "	50 to	1 00
1815 " "	1 00 to	4 00
1817, '18, and '19 are worth from	50 to	1 00
1836, milled edged, is " "	75 to	4 75
1838 is worth from	1 00 to	10 00
1852 " "	1 00 to	2 00
1880, '83, and '85 are worth from	50 to	60

DOLLAR.

1794 is worth from	20 00 to	175 00
1801 and 1802 are worth from	1 50 to	10 00
1804 is worth from	175 00 to	575 00
1836 " "	3 00 to	50 00
1838 " "	15 00 to	55 00
1851 and 1852 are worth from	10 00 to	40 00
1853 is worth from	1 25 to	7 50
1854 " "	1 75 to	10 00
1858 " "	15 00 to	35 00
1881 " "	1 00 to	1 50

Dollar (Gold).

1850 to 1855 are worth from	1 15 to	1 30
1863 is worth from	2 75 to	4 75
1864 " "	5 00 to	10 00
1875 " "	4 00 to	14 00
1879 " "	1 10 to	1 90

$2.50 (Gold).

1796 is worth from	5 00 to	12 00
1796, sixteen stars is worth from	13 00 to	40 00
1806, thirteen " " "	10 00 to	20 00
1826 is worth from	10 00 to	35 00
1834 " "	3 00 to	10 00

$3.00 (Gold).

1857 is worth from	3 00 to	6 00
1864 " "	3 00 to	9 00
1875 " "	4 00 to	35 00

$5.00 (Gold).

1795 is worth from	10 00 to	35 00
1797, fifteen stars, is worth from	15 00 to	40 00
1798 is worth from	20 00 to	50 00
1814 " "	50 00 to	150 00
1822 " "	150 00 to	450 00
1829 " "	10 00 to	50 00

$10.00 (Gold).

1795, fifteen stars, is worth from	11 00 to	15 00
1797, sixteen " " "	15 00 to	35 00

$20.00 (Gold).

1890 is worth from	3000 00 to	5000 00

IN Great Brittain and Ireland the Catholics are now a million and one half less than they were fifty years ago.

BUSINESS ENTERPRISES.

EDITORIAL IN "CLEVELAND GAZETTE."

THE Negro needs more and more year by year to launch out into business for himself. The progress made by our people in the South in all lines of business is most commendable. Corporations are growing rapidly on all hands. They are also more united in their efforts than are their brethren in the North and East. Every town where there are three or four hundred colored people ought to have some sort of business enterprise among them. In a great city like this there ought to be many enterprises among colored people. We are glad to note that there are several of our men who are doing good business along their lines of investment. Several groceries, restaurants and barbershops are doing well among us, but they might do better if the colored people would throw their patronage that way. As we have before said in these columns, we need united efforts. We ought to have corporations and partnerships. There are a few partnerships and only one business corporation in Cleveland and that is "The Fraternal Printing and Publishing Co., the owners of *The Voice of the People.* We are the only company owned and operated by colored men, with our own type and press and printing outfit. Our office is to be in the future a training school and the place where our boys and girls who so desire may learn the printing business. At the head of this business are colored men. They are employing colored printers. We are trying to create a business for our people. We are willing to compete with other publishing houses and if we cannot do as good work and as cheaply, then we are willing to have our friends go somewhere else. We have every reason to expect that people who are wanting printing among us will give us a call and get our prices. We urge you also to get the prices of other firms, and should you be able to do better by yourself somewhere else we do not object to your going. We feel that every loyal colored man will give an establishment run by colored men a chance to work for them when they are willing to enter on competitive prices. We are sorry that some of our friends have without getting our prices gone to other firms where no colored men are employed, to get their work done and have had to pay more for it than our regular prices are. We need not talk about making business and employing ourselves unless the race intends to stand by that business. Colored churches are supported by colored people and colored business enterprises will in most cases be supported by colored people. You say we ought to have banks and railroads and printing houses, etc. What have you done to help the Fraternal Printing and Publishing Co. to establish a business and a paper which shall be a credit to the race? What would it profit colored men to build railroads should colored men all go over and ride on a railroad run and operated by white men? Do not ask why we have no more business enterprises until you have done what you can to help those we have. Do not urge colored men to go into business unless you are willing to help them.

W. Q. ATWOOD.

LUMBER AND REAL ESTATE.

THE subject of this sketch was born January 1, 1839, in Wilcox County, Alabama. After the death of his father, his mother moved to Ripley, Ohio, where she landed May 15, 1853. Here he was placed in school where he remained for six years. In the fall of 1859 he went to California, where he followed steamboating, returning to Ripley in 1861. In 1863 he went to Saginaw, Michigan, where he engaged in the lumber and real estate business, in which he has been engaged ever since and has accumulated quite a fortune. His property is estimated at *more than one hundred thousand dollars.*

Landing Fish at Appalachicola, Fla.

BUSINESS MEN AMONG THE RACE.

BY R. F. BOYD.

WE need good, honest, painstaking, courteous and obliging business men in every village, town and city in the South. These men should receive the entire support of the race; and they could not fail to succeed. Our people make money enough to support not only retail houses but wholesale stores as well. Why should not our people spend their money with men of the race? Other races trade with and patronize their own. With the full confidence and patronage of our own people we would soon have rich merchants and capitalists carrying on large business enterprises in every section of this country that would demand the respect and recognition of the world. Then prejudice on the account of color would vanish and the iniquitous legislation against the race in the South would cease, and every unjust law would be wiped from the statutes. I know that it is said colored men will not give the proper respect to their patrons nor will they stick to their business closely. If this was true, there is no reason why it shall be true in the future. Better things are both expected and demanded of us. The dark cloud of ignorance, superstition, jealousy, envy and race hatred which hung over us at the time of our liberation has been rent in twain and is vanishing before education and intelligence. Why not? We live in the most progressive age of the world's history. Here we are in the evening of the nineteenth century, where inventions and discoveries are seen on every hand. Here we have steam cars that carry us along at the rate of more than one hundred miles per hour, telegraphs by which thought flies around the world at the twinkle of an eye, telephones by which we can converse with persons and recognize their voices hundreds of miles away, and gas and electricity meet our gaze wherever we go. Then why should we not change from the false ideas of slavery and walk in the light that God has given us. There is no reason why we should remain longer in the dark. Then let us come together and help one another in every laudable undertaking. In unity there is strength. Don't imagine because a colored man prospers in business, buys a horse and buggy and can turn out with a respectable showing on the public drives that he has the "big head;" but rather be proud of him and his success. Trade with him yourself and pay for what you get. Encourage others to trade with him, talk him up everywhere you go, and point the youth to him as an example of what they may be. Throw away this old spirit of envy, jealousy and race hatred. Cultivate patriotism and race pride. Go several blocks, yes, go a mile if necessary to trade with a good, honest Negro in business. The Irish, Jews, Germans and other peoples are recognized and respected by nations, only as they are united and held together. All races of America are united except ours, in helping one another by their speech, by their pen, by their vote and with their money. We must do the same. In this way only can we rise as a people. I look forward with great hope for the day when our people shall know and do the right. God grant that it shall come speedily.

NEGRO PROGRESS.

THE Negro population of the South will have a complete, all-round exhibit at the Atlanta exposition; and the indications point to something creditable. It ought to be, and everything possible is being done by the directory to make the exhibit full, attractive, and instructive.

The Negro of the South pays taxes on over $300,000,000 worth of real and personal property, indicating that the true value of the race holdings in 1890 was not less than $650,000,000. Practically, every dollar of this has been accummulated in the last thirty years, about the period of a single generation of our colored race; and it shows, as nothing else can show, that the spirit of thrift and enterprise is being imbedded by the Negro, from his white neighbors.

The race has in its possession, certainly, a sound and strong basis of means for displaying its progress, objectively, to the high credit of the colored people and greatly to their benefit.

The *Atlanta Constitution* has taken high and broad ground on this matter, and is doing all in its power to encourage the leading Negroes to take hold of the exposition, and make it what it should be.

All of our leading business men over the South should follow the *Constitution's* lead. If we would make the average Negro a safe voter, good citizen, a representative of Southern acquisitiveness, and common comforts of our civilization, we must stimulate the pride of self-respect of the race, by all proper means.

The Negro is our American citizen; the white race serves its own interest in making him a good and useful man. He fills the rank of one-fifth of the regular army; he absorbs a large per cent. of the Southern school funds. The white people have built colleges for the race, and urged on the leading and wealthy Negroes the creation of industrial schools, for the Negro boys and girls. All of these beneficiencies should have brought forth creditable fruit, and the way to do this is to induce the Negro to display, in the aggregate, specimens of his agricultural and mechanical acheivements.

We hope the Negro exhibit will be something of which the intelligent men and women among them can be justly proud; and it will be that if the white people take in it the kindly, helpful interest they should take.—*Chattanooga Times.*

TRADES FOR YOUR CHILDREN.

THE *Boston Banner* says, "The white man takes his children at an early age and apprentices them to a trade, and when they grow to man's estate, they are armed for the battle of life. The colored man takes his children at an early age and hires them out for a sum of money that is hardly sufficient to buy them shoes; and when they grow to man's estate they are common, yes, very common laborers, eking out a very meager existence, and when old age comes upon them, they go to the poorhouse. Teach your children a trade." Good advice. Heed it.

It is estimated that 12,000,000 square miles of the land area of the globe are still uninhabited.

LEWIS WINTER.

WHOLESALE AND RETAIL, GENERAL AND COMMISSION MERCHANT.

QUIET and unassuming, yet bold and daring in the field of business is the man whose name appears at the head of this sketch. Thirty years of untiring industry and unceasing fidelity to business in this city has placed him at the head of Nashville's most reliable, solid, and successful busines men. His four-story brick business house is in the heart of the city, at the corner of Cherry and Demonbreun streets.

LEWIS WINTER,
Nashville, Tenn.

Mr. Winter has every faculty for the successful management of his large and growing businss. His goods are bought direct from first hands, for spot cash, in large quantities. He pays the farmer or huxter the highest market prices for his goods, and places the same on the best markets in the largest cities in the country—North and South. His integrity is unquestioned. He has acquired an enviable reputation for fair dealing. Mr. Winter employs about one dozen hands, but he gives his business his personal attention.

He was born at Lebanon, Tenn., June 23rd, 1839. At the age of six years he was separated from his mother by that evil institution, slavery. He worked on a farm until 1865, when he came to Nashville and started into business with *forty dollars* as his capital stock. To-day (Sept. 1, 1895), he is variously estimated at from 35,000 to 75,000 dollars.

He is an active, official member of the A. M. E. Church, and belongs to the St. Paul congregation. He was one of the founders, and and the first and only President of the House Banking and Loan Association, the most prosperous and successful association of its kind among the Negroes of America. It has declared a dividend of ten to twenty-five per cent. annually ever since its organization.

Winter Chapel, Lebanon, Tenn., was named in his honor, he having donated the ground. He owns Little Bethel Church, of Nashville, having bought it at public sale. He still holds it subject to redemption. He was a trustee of Wilberforce University for many years. He has twice been a delegate to the General Conference of his church. He is to-day the senior member of the firm L. Winter and Son, and counts his friends by the thousand, without regard to race.

JOHN MITCHELL, JR., EDITOR AND PUBLISHER.

JOHN MITCHELL, JR., was born July 11, 1863, of slave parents. His father was a coachman and his mother a seamstress. He attended the public schools of Richmond and graduated June 15, 1881, at the Richmond Normal and High School. Since that time he has pursued his studies at home, taking the Chautauqua Literary and Scientific Circle four years' course of instruction. Young Mitchell taught during the sessions of 1881–82 and 1882–83 at Fredericksburg, Va., after which he taught one session in the public schools of Richmond, Va. He took entire editorial charge of the Richmond *Planet* in December, 1884, and has held that position ever since.

He served five years as President of the National Afro-American Press Association and declined re-election in Sept., 1894. He was elected to the Common Council of the city of Richmond, in May, 1888; elected to the Board of Aldermen to serve an unexpired term 1890; re-elected for a four years' term in 1892, occupying at present that position. Mr. Mitchell has a natural aptitude for drawing, and the *Planet* gives abundant evidence of his skill. He was awarded a gold medal by the School Board of Virginia for a map of Virginia which he drew. He was awarded another gold medal for scholarship and still another for oratory.

He is a pleasing and forceful speaker, and has received many compliments for his gracefulness upon the rostrum, and the fervid eloquence of his rhetoric. As a debater he has few equals, and his quite pointed thrusts unmarred by scurrilous assertions win the respect of even those with whom he is debating. He is noted for his bravery, and has been designated by high authority the "gamest Negro editor on the continent."

SAMUEL FARRIS was born in Barren County, Ky., March 10, 1845. To avoid the enemy he was taken by his young master in 1861 to Mississippi and placed on a cotton plantation. In 1863 his young master died, when Samuel tried to make his way back to Kentucky, but fell in with a company of rebel soldiers who took him to Montgomeny, Ala. He had a severe spell of sickness at this place and was left in a dying condition. After his recovery he worked on the farm of Capt. Thornton for nearly two years. In 1865 he lit out for Memphis, Tenn., walking most of the way. He reached Memphis in the fall. Mr. Farris engaged in steamboating for a while, but soon changed his occupation for that of draying, in which he continued for thirteen years. He had saved $500 at the end of these long years of toil, and in September, 1878, he engaged in the undertaker's business in which he is still engaged. He was married to Emilene Yose in 1872. In June, 1893, he professed faith in God and joined the A. M. E. Church. He has filled several official positions in the church to which he belongs. He is a trustee at Avery Chapel. He is a temperate, honest, generous and industrious man. Counts his friends by the hundreds of both races. Has a business that is daily increasing. His motto is, "Owe no man anything," and this accounts for his being out of debt. He is worth about $15,000.

SAMUEL FARRIS, Funeral Director,
Memphis, Tenn.

JAMES EDMUND BRYANT was born in Washington, D. C., Dec. 26th, 1848. He was left an orphan at ten years of age. He remained in Washington after the death of his parents until he was fifteen years of age, but during this time was enabled to secure only an ordinary education. On the first of January, 1863, he left Washington as the body servant of James A. Garfield. In 1864, on the 23rd of November, he entered the service of the rebellion, and was made chief drummer boy of the One Hundred and Twenty-sec-

J. E. BRYANT, Barber,
Paducah, Ky.

ond United States Colored Infantry; he was mustered out of service November 23rd, 1865, when he returned to Louisville, Ky. He was soon employed to work on a steamer that plied between Louisville and New Orleans. In May, 1870, the boat was laid up for repairs at Paducah, Ky. Mr. Bryant being an active, energetic man, soon found other employment. He served an apprenticeship as a barber, and at this point, began his success. By close application to business, and econemy, he has accumulated from $10,000 to $15,000, which he has judiciously invested in real estate in Paducah. He is an official member of the A. M. E. Church, and devotes much of his time to religious work. He is liberal, kind-hearted, and true. He loves his race, and wants to see it elevated and refined. Mr. Bryant is not an educated man except in a business sense. His example is worthy of imitation.

C. S. RANDLE,

CONTRACTOR AND BUILDER.

ONE of the enterprising and successful carpenters in the city of Nashville, Tenn., is the subject of this sketch. He is a man of charitable, warm-hearted and generous impulses. All cannot teach nor can they preach; they must therefore go into trades where success awaits them if they will but pursue the methods that were adopted by Mr. Randle early in life. He was born in Bledsoe County, Tennessee, September 22, 1839. He was born a slave. When only eight years old his mother with her five children were sold for debt. When he was about eighteen years old he was again sold. He changed hands several times and was finally brought to Nashville by the soldiers, with two suits of clothes and $2.50 in cash. Mr. Randle secured a position in a restaurant where he worked for his board until he could find employment that was more lucrative. Through the influence of friends, coupled with his own energy, he soon secured a position at $1 per day as porter of a grocery store. After he had accumulated sufficient money he decided to secure an education and entered Fisk University, which was then in its prime. After three years' close application to books, Mr. Randle decided that he had an education sufficient to master his chosen profession. He lost his mother about this time and shortly after married Miss Irene Webb, who has proven to be a helpmate indeed and in truth. By their perseverance and economy they have secured considerable property. He is blessed with three children all of whom he is giving a fine education.

The writer claims Mr. Randle's family as his friends; has known them for many years and can say that he has yet to find a family where there is more supreme happiness. Father, mother and children are worthy of imitation. His property is valued at $15,000.

PROSPEROUS COLORED PEOPLE IN RICHMOND.

THE population of Richmond, Va., is estimated at 100,000, of which 45,000 are colored, of which almost half are in Jackson ward, one of the largest in the city. This ward is controlled by the Negroes. They have property assessed at $650,000 for taxation. This ward has eleven halls, valued at $65,000; it has *ten* churches. It has *four* lawyers, *seven* doctors, and the ward is represented in the City Council by six men, four of whom are Afro-Americans. An armory on West Leigh street is soon to be erected at a cost of $20,000. This part of the city contains many handsome residences, and one not accustomed to seeing such, would be surprised at the uniform richness and neatness in which the "Africa of Richmond" is kept.

"The True Reformer Hall," valued at $20,000, is said to be the most imposing structure in the ward. The Odd Fellows' Hall, valued at $8,000, comes next. All the societies have their halls. Among the property owners of Jackson ward, the following are the most prominent: Mrs. Bettie T. Lewis, $150,000; Mrs. Fannie C. Thompson, $15,000; W. I. Johnson, $13,000; A. Hayes, $12,000; William Lyons, $10,000; John Oliver, $10,000; Dr. S. H. Dismond, $8,000; J. B. Harris, $7,000; William Tennant, $7,000; W. H. White, $7,000; Rev. W. W. Browne, $6,000; Rev. J. E. Jones, $5,000; B. F. Turner, $5,000; Dr. R. E. Jones, $5,000; S. W. Robinson, $5,000.

Many other colored men of wealth in Richmond deserve to be mentioned in this connection, but time and space forbid. The above are only examples of what can be done by the industrious, economical colored men in every city.

WEALTHY COLORED NEW YORK MEN.

THERE are many wealthy colored men who live in New York City. Several who were formerly slaves, count their dollars by the hundred thousands. Four or five physicians in this great metropolis have a practice of eighteen or twenty thousand dollars a year. The late Mrs. Gloster, who lived on Brooklyn Heights, was very wealthy. J. W. Bowen, a member of the Board of Education of Brooklyn, is worth $150,000. Mr. Hasdra, who owns a country seat on the Hudson, has also a bank account of $160,000. Mr. Roselle, recently deceased, left $300,000. Hiram Thomas is worth $100,000. Dr. White, a druggist, owns a cottage at Sea Cliff, and is estimated at $200,000. Joseph Tenych is rated at $300,000. Dr. P. Ray is worth $250,000. Mrs. Daniel Brooks has $200,000. James W. Mars possesses $85,000. Dr. P. Guignon, a druggist, is worth $100,000. A dozen or more others could be named who are worth less than the above down to $25,000.

THE RICHEST COLORED MAN IN GEORGIA is Mr. Harry Todd, of Darien. His personal property and real estate are valued at $500,000. When a youth his "master" died, giving him his freedom. He was kept by the family on a fair salary as assistant overseer. This money was invested in real estate, *slaves* and

Confederate bonds. When the downfall of the Confederacy came he lost all except his lands. He has made his money by raising cotton. He has an interesting family, five children, all well educated and highly respected. He has a summer resort in the mountains and is altogether delightfully situated.

THE RICHEST COLORED MAN IN THE UNITED STATES.

THE richest colored man in the United States probably is Tony Lafon, a quadroon of Creole descent—that is to say, of French Louisiana blood. The lowest estimate of Mr. Lafon's wealth is $1,000,000, and he is more frequently rated at double that amount.

He inherited a moderate fortune, speculated successfully in real estate, and passed gradually to the condition of money-lender and note broker. Like most men of that class, he cannot be said to be popular, and the colored people do not rely upon him as a political leader. Indeed, he is in politics rather more conservative than an old-fashioned white planter, and not at all desirous of seeing the colored people rule the State. He is seventy-three years of age, and even anxious to increase his wealth.

WEALTH OF SOUTHERN NEGROES.

THE wealth of the Negroes in the several Southern States is as follows: Alabama, $9,200,125; Arkansas, $8,010,315; Florida, $7,900,400; Georgia, $10,415,330; Kentucky, $5,900,010; Louisiana, $18,000,528; Mississippi, $13,400,213; Missouri, $6,600,345; North Carolina, $11,010,635; South Carolina, $12,500,000; Texas, $18,000,500; Tennessee, $10,400,200; Virginia, $4,900,000.

THERE are nearly 2,000 women practicing medicine in the United States.

HAVE COURAGE.

IF any race of people on this earth need to have courage it is the Negro.

Have the courage to say "no," when you are tempted to drink.

Have the courage to wear the old suit of clothes, rather than go in debt for a new suit.

Have the courage to acknowledge your ignorance, when asked about something of which you do not know.

Have the courage to pay a debt when you need the money for something else.

Have the courage to be polite though your character may be assailed.

Have the courage to speak the truth, remembering the command, "Thou shalt not lie."

Have the courage to own you are poor, and thus disarm poverty of its sharpest sting.

Have the courage to own you are wrong, when convinced that such is the case.

Have the courage to be good and true and you will always find work to do.

Have the courage to say your prayers, though you may be ridiculed by man.

Have the courage to tell a man why you will not lend him money, instead of whipping the devil around the stump by telling him you havn't a cent "in the world," calling one of your pockets "the world."

Have the courage of your convictions. "According to a mans faith, so be it unto him." This is true on every plane of life, from the lowest to the highest. A man's power in everything is measured by his convictions. The statesman who has the profoundest convictions is surest of bringing others to see as he sees on any question which he discusses before the public. The minister who can most completely identify himself with his people, if he has the courage of his convictions, is the one who is most likely to be successful.

REV. PRESTON TAYLOR.

PASTOR OF THE CHURCH OF DISCIPLES, NASHVILLE, TENN.—GENERAL FINANCIAL AGENT OF A COLLEGE—BIG CONTRACTOR AND THE LEADING UNDERTAKER.

OUR subject is the leading minister of the Church of the Disciples. He was born in Shreveport, La., Nov. 7, 1849. He was born in slavery. His parents were Zed and Betty Taylor. He was carried to Kentucky when a year old; he was a promising boy and shed sunshine wherever he was. At the age of four years he heard his first sermon on the spot where the First Baptist Church now stands in the city of Lexington, Ky., and afterwards told his mother that he would be a preacher some day; so deep was the impression made on his young mind that years have not been able to eradicate it. He was affectionately cared for, and grew up as Samuel of old, ripe for the duties of his life. When the war broke out he saw the soldiers marching and determined to join them at the first opportunity, and so he enlisted in Company G., One Hundred and Sixteenth United States Infantry, in 1864, as a drummer, and was at the Siege of Richmond, Petersburg and the surrender of Lee. His regiment also did garrison duty in Texas, then returned to New Orleans where they did garrison duty until mustered out of the service. He then learned the stone cutter's trade and became skilful in monument work, and also in engraving on marble. He went to Louisville, Ky., and in the leading marble yards found plenty of work, but the white men refused to work with him because of his color. He was offered a situation as train porter on the L. & C. Railroad, and for four years he was classed as one of the best railroad men in the service, and when he resigned he was requested to remain with a promotion to assistant baggage master; but as he could be no longer retained, the officers gave him a strong recommendation and a pass over all the roads for an extensive trip, which he took through the North. He accepted on his return a call to the pastorate of the Christian Church at Mt. Sterling, Ky. He remained there fifteen years, and the Lord prospered him in building up the largest congregation in the State among those of his faith, besides building them the finest brick edifice as a place for the worship of God in that section of the State. During these fifteen years he became known as the leading minister of his church in the United States. Not only in Kentucky has he been instrumental in organizing and building both congregations and meeting houses, but he was unanimously chosen the general evangelist of the United States, which position he held for a number of years besides assisting in the educational work of his race.

He very recently purchased the large spacious college property at New Castle, Ky., which originally cost $18,000, exclusive of the grounds, and at once began the task of paying for it. The school is in operation with a corps of teachers, and has a bright future before it. He is still one of the trustees, and the financial agent of what is now known as the "Christian Bible College," at New Castle. Some idea can be given of this man of push and iron nerve and bold undertakings by giving a passage in his life: When the Big Sandy Rail road was under contract to be completed from Mt. Sterling to Richmond, Va., the contractors refused to hire colored men to work on it, preferring Irish labor. He at once made a bid for sections 3 and 4 and was successful in his bid; he then erected a large commissary and quarters for his men, bought seventy-five head of mules and horses, carts, wagons, cans and all the necessary implements and tools, and with one hundred and fifty colored men he led the way. In fourteen months he completed the two miles of the most difficult part of this great trunk line at a cost of about $75,000.

The President of the road, Mr. C. P. Huntington, said he had built thousands of miles of road, but he never saw a contractor who finished his contract in advance, and so he then was requested by the chief engineer of the works to move his force to another county and help out some of the white contractors. This he did not do. Afterwards he was offered other important contracts, but declined. A syndicate in Nebraska offered him the position of superintendent of their coal mines, but knowing it would take him away from his chosen calling, he declined the offer. For a number of years he was editor of "Our Colored Brethren," a department in the *Christian Standard*, a newspaper published as the organ of his denomination at Cincinnati, Ohio, with a circulation of 50,000 copies a week. He has written for many books and periodicals. He is a member of both

DR. PRESTON TAYLOR,
Nashville, Tenn.

Masonic and Oddfellow Lodges and was State Grand Chaplain of the former and State Grand Master of the latter and held these positions for three years and traveled all over the State, speaking and lecturing. Especially do the Oddfellows owe much to him for their rise and progress in the State of Kentucky, and the order conferred upon him as a mark of honor all the degrees of the ancient institution. He has represented his Lodge in many of the National Conventions of the B. M. C., preaching the annual sermons for a number of years.

I will give another incident that will show the character of this man, how he loves his race, and with what respect he treats them: While serving the church in Nashville in 1886, the choir of the church gained great reputation by taking a prize over every other church choir in the city in a musical contest. The Nashville *American* gave a very flattering account of the results which caused forty-two of the leading citizens of the white race to petition, through the pastor ot the church, for a concert to be given in the Opera House for the special benefit of their friends.

When Mr. Taylor met this Committee they informed him that on the night of the concert the colored people would be expected to take gallery as usual. Mr. Taylor refused deliberately to have anything further to do with the matter, and publicly denounced the whole crowd in his church, which was very satisfactory to the colored citizens who urged him to give a concert nevertheless, and he consented. On the night of the concert there was scarcely standing room for the people, who said they desired to show their appreciation of this manly stand in resenting such overtures, and the result was an increase to the treasury of over two hundred dollars. He is one of the leading men in the community where he lives, commanding the respect of all who know him. A slight idea may be given of his popularity by stating that once when a gold cane was voted for in some entertainment in the city of Nashville his name was submitted by his friends to be voted for, he opposed the suggestion, but nevertheless, when the votes were counted out of the three thousand votes in that large city, he got over two thirds of the number. A quotation from the *Christian Standard*, Cincinnati, Ohio, March 3, 1886, will give some estimate of how he is held by the editor of that paper. A grand party was given for his benefit, and the editor used these words in reference to his absence:

"We have just received an invitation to a tea party at Nashville,

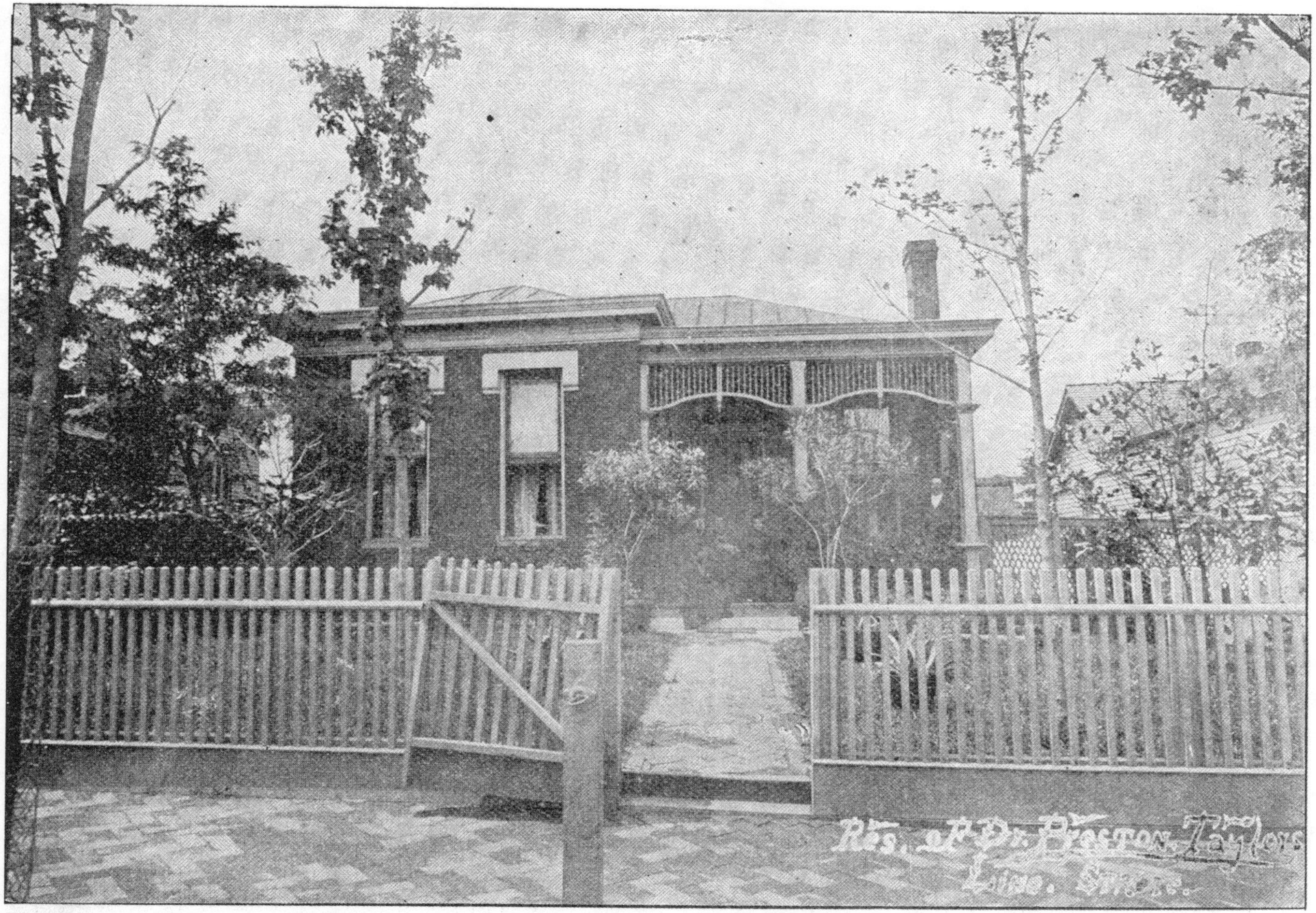
Res. of Dr. Preston Taylor's

Tenn., to be given in honor of Elder Preston Taylor. We would go all that distance, were it possible, to show our respect for the zeal, ability and untiring energy of Preston Taylor. As we cannot go, we take this method of atoning for our absence."

Mr. Taylor is a man who will impress you when you meet him as thoroughly in earnest. He is never idle, always with new plans, warm hearted, generous, sympathetic and a true brother to all men who deserve the cognizance of earnest, faithful workers for Christ.

In the spring of 1888 he embarked in the undertaker's business, and has met with unbounded success; few business men can claim the unanimity of the community as he can, he stands at the head of his profession not only as a funeral director, but as a safe and wise business man. It is said by men competent to know, that he does the largest business of any man of his race engaged in the same business in the country. He owns and occupies the large two-story brick at 449 North Cherry Street; the building is 42x180 feet and it is divided and furnished in the most convenient style, with reception hall, office, chapel, show rooms, supply rooms, trimming rooms, dry rooms, carpenter shops, paint shops and a morgue. In the rear stands a large stable occupied by eighteen head of horses, seven carriages, hearses and all kinds of vehicles used in the undertaker's business. The entire building is lighted with electric lights and fitted up with electric bells. He is the only one in the city that manufactures his own goods. He works sixteen men in his establishment and often is compelled to call in extra help. He has the honor of managing the largest funeral that ever passed through the streets of Nashville, it was the three colored firemen that were killed on January 2, 1892, in a great conflagration. He built a large catafalque with his own men, which held all three of the caskets, which were drawn by six beautiful black horses, followed by sixty carriages, two abreast, accompanied by all the officials of the city, the police and fire departments, the schools, the lodges and citizens by the thousands. In all his business enterprises he ascribes his marvelous success to his Heavenly Father, and he never neglects his chosen calling, the preaching of the word of God. In the last few years he has bought and built one of the most handsome and convenient churches in the city, the Lee Avenue Christian Church, of which he is now the pastor.

TAYLOR & CO.

FUNERAL DIRECTORS.

MRS. GEORGIA GORDON TAYLOR was born in Nashville, Tenn. At an early age she left home with the "Original Fisk Jubilee Singers," traveling extensively in this country and abroad in the interest of Fisk University. Mrs. Taylor possesses a soprano voice of rare quality that is always pleasing and in demand. After retiring from public life she became the wife of Elder Preston Taylor, minister of the Lee Avenue Christian Church at Nashville, Tenn. In this capacity she has proven herself an efficient helpmete in church work, entering into it with all the zeal of an ardent Christian.

REV. J. F. BAULDEN, of Natchez, Mississippi, was the *first* man to petition Congress, asking the right of franchise, and the first Emancipation celebration. The petition was granted and the first celebration took place January 1, 1866. He made the *first* Republican speech that was ever delivered in his town, and was a member of the *first* Republican convention in the State, which met at Vicksburg, July, 1867.

MUSIC AND MORALS.

IN speaking of "Music and Morals" Rev. H. R. Haweis, of London, says: "The Negro is more really musical than the Englishman. Singing very often merrily, with the tears wet upon his ebony cheek, no record of his joy or sorrow passed unaccompanied by a cry of melody or a wail of plaintive and harmonious melancholy. If we could divest ourselves of prejudice, the songs that float down the Ohio River are one in feeling and character with the songs of the Hebrew captives by the waters of Babylon. We find in them the same tale of bereavement and separation, the same irreparable sorrow, the same wild tenderness and passionate sweetness, like music in the night."

MRS. DR. PRESTON TAYLOR,
Nashville, Tenn.

RACE FACTS WORTH KNOWING.

Chicago Afro-Americans pay taxes on three million dollars' worth of property.

In the State of Missouri there are 750 colored teachers and 51,000 colored pupils.

Charleston, S. C., has fifty Afro-American policemen, and under Democratic rule at that.

Washington, D. C., has a Home for Friendless Colored Girls, which has been in existence eight years.

Matthew Lancaster, a well educated Negro of St. Louis, will head a colony of colored people which will take up Brazilian lands.

The National Steamboat Company is the name of the new boat company now being organized in Washington, D. C. It is officered by some of the best colored citizens.

Between 1866 and 1871, the colored people deposited in the Freedman's Savings Bank about $57,000,000.

"Above all, let the Negro know that the elevation of his race can come only and will come surely through the elevation of its women."
—*Senator George F. Hoar.*

President Cleveland has appointed Rev. W. H. Heard, of Pennsylvania, to be Minister to Liberia. He now has charge of a Methodist Church in Harrisburg, Pa.

Mrs. Ida DePriest, of Denver, Col., has been elected Third Vice President of the Colorado State Republican League. Mrs. DePriest is a colored lady.

C. H. Smiley, an Afro-American caterer, of Chicago, has a $100,000 building. He caters for the elite and his establishment is as elegant and complete as any of its kind in the city.

The Woman's League, a progressive organization composed of colored women of Denver, has been admitted to the Colorado State Federation of Clubs.

Capt. W. H. Bentley is one of the most successful military men of Georgia. He has held many positions of trust, and ranks as one of the foremost men of the race.

Miss Kate Crawford, who for many years was a teacher in the Simmons School, St. Louis, Mo., is studying medicine in Ann Arbor, Mich. Miss Crawford was the first colored graduate from the Ann Arbor High School.

Mr. H. D. Smith is the wealthiest colored man of Greensville County, Va. He owns a valuable farm and runs one of the largest sawmills in that section. At one time he represented his people in the State Legislature.

There are two colored steamboat companies in Washington—the National Steamboat Company and the People's Transportation Company.

Rev. Jno. Albert Williams is the first colored man nominated for the city school board of Omaha, Neb.

The third lieutenant of police of Charleston, S. C., is an Afro-American, who is re-elected year after year.

The Afro-American population of Rochester, N. Y., is 900, and only six men and women cannot read and write.

Granville T. Woods, the electrician, mechanical engineer, manufacturer of telephone, telegraph, and electrical instruments, was once a day laborer in Springfield, Ill.

There are two Negroes now studying medicine and engineering in the University of Copenhagen, Denmark; one is at Heidelberg and the other is at Leipsic, Germany.

Mme. Sissieretta Jones has signed a contract with the Walter Damrosch Orchestra Company for a three years' tour to Mexico and Europe, at a salary of $35,000 per year.

In Macon county, Alabama, where the Tuskegee Normal and Industrial Institute is located, there are at present only three people in jail, and all of these are white people. This shows something of the influence of the Tuskegee Institute and the Tuskegee Negro Conference.

Rev. Dr. M. C. B. Mason, of Atlanta, Ga., a colored man, the field agent of Freedman's Aid and Southern Education Society, has been elected assistant secretary of the same, the position which Rev. Dr. J. D. Hartzell (white), of Cincinnati formerly occupied.

There are more than fifty Negro establishments in Atlanta, Ga., representing $100,000 in business employed, giving employment to not less than one hundred persons of the race, and affording them an opportunity to acquire a thorough knowledge of business.

There are 1,416,302 Afro-American children in the public schools of the United States, and in these 1,329,613 are of the public schools of the sixteen Southern States. This is an encouraging showing. A generation ago it was a penitentiary offense in all the South to Educate an Afro-American.

Mr. John W. Wilson is the leading colored clothier of Baltimore, Md. He has a good trade, and keeps on hand a full supply of the latest goods.

Mr. Madison Short is one of the most prominent farmers of Surry County, Virginia. He owns a beautiful farm and has some of the finest horses in the State.

Two books from the pen of Thomas W. Stewart, of Kalamazoo, Mich., will soon make their appearance. One is the "Universal History of the Great Race of Ham," and the other is "The Encyclopædia of the Universal Progress and Achievements of the Great Hametic Race."

Dr. R. F. Boyd, of Nashville, Tenn., recently purchased a three-story brick house on Cedar Street, price $14,000. The building contains twenty-eight rooms. This is the largest transfer of real estate ever given to a colored person in Tennessee.

Says the Cleveland *Gazette:* "William R. Stewart, Esq., of Youngstown, Ohio, one of the brightest of Ohio's young Afro-Americans, has been nominated by the Republicans of Mahoning County as one of their candidates for legislature, and will be elected too, because he is capable, an active Republican and an exemplary citizen."

The American Railway Union, operating principally in the North, denied its privileges to colored operators.

The American Federation of Labor will not grant membership to colored workmen.

An evangelical church in Iowa dissuaded a colored candidate from pressing his application for fellowship.

The Woman's Club of Chicago refused to admit a colored lady of cultured mind and elevated character.

The managers of an ice skating club in Chicago would not sell admissions last week to decent young men of color, though white men and women too need no moral health certificate to gain entrance.

These are not pleasant incidents to refer to, but it is worth while keeping them in mind whenever we are tempted to lambast the South for imposing unequal social burdens on its colored population.—*Ram's Horn.*

Lewis Bates is probably the wealthiest colored man in Chicago, being rated at nearly $500,000. He is entirely uneducated, dresses poorly, and lives like a poor man. He was born a slave nearly seventy years ago. In 1861 he reached Chicago by the "underground railroad," and began by working in a foundry. He soon became an expressman, and at once began investing his savings in real estate. In this he has shown excellent judgment, and nearly all his investments are gilt-edged. Though he spends little money on himself, he is open-hearted and kind. He has no family, and his only heirs are a few very distant relatives.—*N. Y. Tribune.*

The first female student in the world who received a diploma in law was Miss C. B. Ray, a young colored lady of New York city. She graduated at the Howard University, Washington, D. C.

Nation Guards.—The ninth Batallion, Ohio National Guards is composed of three companies of well-drilled Negroes.

"*The Good Jesus Factory.*"—Bishop Taylor, of Africa, says there is a rum factory in Liberia which the natives call "The Good Jesus Factory." Christianity and rum being closely associated in the minds of the natives.

Over thirty-five thousand Negro soldiers have given up their lives in the defense of the United States government.

Fugitive Slave Law.—An act passed by the United States Congress in 1850. It imposed a fine of $1,000 and six months imprisonment on any person harboring slaves or aiding in their escape. It was declared unconstitutional by the United States Supreme Court, February 3, 1855, and was repealed June 13, 1864; it was never fully carried into effect, Massachusetts failing to recognize it.

Emancipation Day, April 16.—An annual commemorative holiday kept by the colored people in the United States, particularly in Washington, D. C., the day being the anniversary of the signing of the Emancipation Proclamation by President Lincoln in 1863.

The first colored school south of Mason and Dixon's line was organized May 20, 1865, in Lexington, Ky. It was established in the same building over which Capt. John Morgan hoisted the first Confederate flag in Kentucky.

The first and only colored Roman Catholic priest in this country is Rev. Augustus Tolton, of Quincy, Illinois.

Slavery in England.—Up to the year 1772 slaves were bought and sold openly in England.

Slavery Abolished.—The total abolition of slavery in the United States was officially announced December 18, 1865.

Black Douglass.—Frederick Douglass, the Great Afro-American orator and philanthropist, was so called to distinguish him from Stephen A. Douglas.

The greatest Negro scholar in the world, Dr. Edward Wilmot Blyden, a full-blooded Negro, and formerly Minister of Liberia to England, is an extensive contributor to English literature.

"*The Black Phalanx,*" written by Col. Joseph T. Wilson, of Va., has had the most extensive sale of any book written by an Afro-American. He is the oldest colored newspaper man now living in Virginia.

The first colored woman to receive the degree of A.M. was Miss Mary Patterson. She graduated in Oberlin College in 1862.

History records the fact that during the late rebellion the Negro soldier participated in more than four hundred engagements.

Jacksonville, Florida, is famous for its numerous colored secret organizations.

The first blood spilt in the war of the revolution was that of a

Negro, Crispus Attucks, who fell in the first charge made on the British troops at Boston, March 5, 1770.

Rev. Lott Carey was born in Virginia in 1780, and died November 10, 1828 in Liberia. He was the first colored American Missionary to Africa.

The first ballot ever cast by a woman in the State of Mississippi was that of Mrs. Lucy Tapley, a colored woman.

There are 300 Negroes in the universities of Europe.

There are over 2,000 colored people employed in the executive departments of the government at Washington.

There were between four and five hundred Negro soldiers who were engaged in the battle of New Orleans.

Dahomey is the smallest State in Africa. It has 4,000 square miles, almost the exact size of Connecticut.

About 6,000 Negroes were connected in different ways with the Confederate Army.

There are 1,928 colored public schools in the "Old Dominion;" the attendance is up to the average, and they are advancing all along the line.

The Presbyterian denomination has 1,622 communicants in Africa.

The first colored regiment to enter the services of the Rebellion was the Fifty-fourth Massachusetts Volunteers.

Rev. H. H. Garnett, of the Presbyterian Church, was the first colored man to preach in the capital of the United States.

The first daily newspaper published by the colored people was the Cairo *Gazette*, owned, edited and published by Hon. W. S. Scott, of Cairo, Ill. The first issue came from the press April 23, 1882.

In 1873, Hon. M. W. Gibbs, of Little Rock, Ark., was elected City Judge, the first colored man in the United States ever elected to such a position.

Hon. J. A. Brown, of Cleveland, commenced life as a laborer on a steamboat, and has risen step by step until his eloquence has reached the legislative halls of the great State of Ohio.

R. C. O. Benjamin was for some time the local editor of the *Daily*

Sun, of Los Angeles, Cal. This was a prominent white paper, and Mr. Benjamin was the first colored man to edit a white journal.

Hon. John M. Langston was the first sanitarian of his race. He was appointed by President U. S. Grant, March 15, 1871, on the Board of Health for the District of Columbia.

The Lone Star Medical Association is the first Negro medical association ever organized in the United States.

S. B. Meyers is the first Afro-American theatrical manager of the United States.

The first and only representative in Congress from the "Old Dominion" was Hon. John M. Langston.

Washington, D. C. has a colored population of 80,000. About 3,000 of them own their own homes, and other real estate valued at $10,000,000.

The census report of 1890 gives the colored scholastic population of the State of North Carolina 216,524, with an enrollment of 116,689, and a daily average attendance of 68,992.

There are 1,820 public school buildings for colored children, valued at $240,402.60.

Albino.—White Negro of the African coast; so named by the Portuguese voyagers.

James Smith, of Columbia, S. C., was the first colored student to enter West Point.

Hon. Jonathan J. Wright, of Columbia, S. C., was the first (and as yet), the only colored associate Justice of the Supreme Court of any State.

Miss Ida Platt, of Chicago, is the first woman of the *race* to be admitted to the bar of any State.

The "Davenport House," of Montgomery, Ala., is finely furnished in all of its apartments. It is owned, patronized, and controlled by colored people.

"Mammy," was the name usually given to the Negro nurse of Southern white children.

The African Methodist Episcopal Church owns church property

to the amount of $5,000,000. This church gave last year for school and church purposes $1,484,784.

Negro Minstrels are Negro musicians, or white men, who often blacken their face and hands, and assume the customs and manners of Negroes, go from place to place singing Negro melodies and playing upon the banjo and "bones." Their humorous parodies upon popular songs, with their manner of singing and their jokes render their entertainments popular among both white and colored.

The increase of colored population in the last decade is greater in Arkansas than that of any other State.

Prof. Booker T. Washington, of Tuskegee, Ala., is the first Afro-American ever invited to address the Boston Unitarian Club, which is one of the most intelligent and wealthy in the United States.

As a historian Geo. W. Williams is to the Negro race what George Bancroft was to the Anglo-Saxon race.

Rev. Harvey Johnson, of Baltimore, was the first representative colored man from the State of Maryland who cast his political fortunes with the Prohibition party.

Theodore D. Miller was the first colored man ever appointed to preach the introductory sermon of the Philadelphia Baptist Association.

The colored Baptists of the United States report a membership of 1,500,000, with 11,000 ordained ministers; 13,000 church buildings, valued at $10,000,000, and 9,000 Sunday schools with more than 500,000 scholars.

Lemuel Haynes was born in Hartford, Conn., July 18, 1753. He graduated from Middleburg College, Vermont, and was the first Negro in the United States to receive the degree, A.M.

In the seventeenth century slaves were sold in most all the New England States. Massachusetts, Rhode Island and Connecticut contained not less than 15,000 in 1764.

According to the latest census resort there are 3,125 deaf and dumb, and 9,610 blind Afro-Americans in this country.

There are 6,535 insane and 10,574 feeble-minded colored people in the United States.

Five thousand Negro soldiers is the official number reported as bearing arms in the Continental Army.—*G. C. R.*

The Negro capitalists of Washington, D. C., have organized a Union Trust and Loan Company under the law of that district.

$200,000 per Month.—There are at least 80,000 Negroes in the National Capital who draw $200,000 per month salaries from the government.

Thirty-five Afro-Americans are employed on the police force in Pittsburgh, Pa.

Rev. O. Summers, colored, is the chaplain of the Legislature of California.

There are about ten Afro-American lawyers in New York, thirteen in Boston, and more than twenty-five in Chicago.

There are 7,309 colored Odd Fellows in the "Old Dominion."

"Blind Tom," the famous pianist, remembers nearly four thousand compositions.

Bishop B. F. Lee, has the pre-eminence in scholarship in the A. M. E. Church.

Slaves were first introduced into the United States in 1619, when a Dutch war vessel entered James River and landed twenty Negroes, who were offered for sale.

In 1869, colored men, for the first time in the history of the District of Columbia, were drawn as jurors, and served with white men.

The colored people of Massachusetts are taxed for property valued at $9,004,122.

Bishop J. W. Hood is credited as being the most Conservative and far-seeing of all the Afro-American Bishops,

Rev. W. B. Derrick enjoys the reputation of being the finest orator of the A. M. E. Church.

Bishop Benjamin W. Arnett, of the A. M. E. Church, is called a "walking encyclopædia."

Alabama appropriates $3,000 annually for the benefit of Tuskegee State Normal.

Maryland appropriates $2,000 annually for the support of a Normal School for the training of colored teachers.

Missouri contributes $5,000 annually to Lincoln Institute for the training of colored teachers.

Virginia, North Carolina, South Carolina, Georgia, Mississippi, and Louisiana, and in fact most all the Southern States make annual contributions for the education of their colored citizens.

Old Midway Church in Liberty county, Georgia, is the most ancient house of worship in the South, having been built in 1752. The midway Society is an organization whose mission it is to perpetuate the historical assciations of the venerable building. Negroes own this structure.

Fully nine-tenths of the colored church members are Methodists and Baptists, and between these two they are pretty equally divided.

Slowly yet surely the slaves of Brazil are being emancipated. Fifteen thousand are annually liberated.

Prof. M. A. Hopkins, of Franklinton, N. C., a colored teacher of marked ability, was appointed by President Cleveland, first term, as Minister to Liberia.

In the State of Missouri there are 750 colored teachers and 51,000 colored pupils.

A. Humbles, a colored man, recently loaned the Baptists of Virginia, $13,000 with which to build a seminary at Lynchburg.

Mrs. Alpha V. Miner, of Kansas City, Mo., has the reputation of being one of the most successful business women of her race in the West. She is quoted at $10,000 and free from debt. She commenced business several years ago as a dressmaker. She now has a dozen or more employees.

The largest silk worm grower in the South is a colored man, S. R. Lowry, near Huntsville, Ala. He took a premium at the New Orleans Exposition over several foreign competitors from China, France, Japan and Italy. Mr. Lowry is of the opinion that the culture of silk in the South will supersede that of cotton.

T. Morris Chester, of New Orleans, was the special war correspondent for the Philadelphia *Daily Press*. He was also the first colored man in the United States to report phonographically the proceedings of the Tenth Grand Triennial Assembly of the Patriarchal Order of Past Grand Masters of the Grand United Order of Odd Fellows in America.

Underground Railroad.—A popular and half-humorous synonym for the numberless methods by which fugitive slaves from the Southern States were aided in escaping to the North, or to British territory during the anti-slavery agitation. William Still, for many years connected with the anti-slavery office in Philadelphia, is author of a book bearing the above title.

Rev. A. E. P. Albert, of New Orleans, is editor of a white paper, the *South Western Christian Advocate*, that is owned by the General Conference of the Methodist Episcopal Church. He is a reliable, able and pleasing writer and his paper is read by more white people than any other paper in the United States.

In 1880 there were only 31 Afro-American journals published in the United States; it 1890 there were 155, and to-day (July 12, 1895) there are over 300. Wonderful strides of journalistic progress!

The "Tennesseans."—They were a popular troup, who established a national reputation, and delighted thousands of intelligent audiences with their popular plantation melodies. With the proceeds obtained by these gifted singers, an elegant and commodious four-story brick structure was added to the Central Tennessee College, which is designed only for the benefit of colored students.

"The most wonderful chapter in the history of education is that which tells the story of the education of the Negroes of the South since 1865. No people were ever helped so much in twenty-five years, and no illiterate people ever learned so fast."—*Bishop Haygood*.

Wiley Jones, of Pine Bluff, Ark., is one of the wealthiest colored men in his State, and is said to be the largest blooded stock breeder of his race. Besides his herds of Durham and Holstein cattle, he has a stable of trotting horses valued at $50,000.

Since the death of Dr. J. C. Price, of Livingstone College, Rev. J. H. Hector, of York, Pa., is the most popular temperance lecturer of the race.

The oldest colored church in the United States is Evan's Chapel, Fayetteville, N. C., (A. M. E. Zion).

The youngest bishop in the United States, and perhaps in the world is Alexander Walters, D.D., of the A. M. E. Zion Church.

The first A. M. E. Zion Church established South of Mason and Dixon line, was St. Peter's, Newberne, N. C., in 1862.

The most prominent layman, so says Anderson, of any colored religious organization in the United States is the Hon. John C. Dancy. He is held in high esteem by all denominations.

The increase of colored population in Tennessee in the last decade is 7.73 per cent.

East Tennessee has a colored population of 12.02 per cent.

Middle Tennessee has a colored population of 24.87 per cent.

West Tennessee has a colored population of 37.24 per cent.

Three counties in Tennessee, Fayette, Haywood, and Shelby, have more colored persons than white.

The colored scholastic population of Tennessee is 176,614, while the daily attendance will average 105,458.

There are 1,609 public colored schools, having 1,745 colored teachers in the State of Tennessee.

The emancipation of slaves in all the French Colonies took place February 4, 1794.

The complete emancipation of slaves in the English Colonies occurred in 1838 and 1839, when more than 800,000 men, besides women and children, were liberated.

Sweden emancipated her slaves in 1846, and this was soon followed (in 1848), by the Danish Colonies proclaiming the freedom of her slaves.

Holland delivered her American Colonies from slavery August 8, 1862.

The African slave trade was closed in this country on the first day of January, 1808.

A gentleman in Brooklyn, N. Y., is building a cottage for the Tuskegee Normal and Industrial Institute to be used for the Young ladies of the Senior Class as a "Model Home," where the latest improved methods of housekeeping will be put in practice during the girls' Senior year.

On the twenty-third day of May, 1881, President Garfield appointed ex-Senator B. K. Bruce, of Mississippi, Register of the United

States Treasury. This was the first colored man whose signature made money of worthless paper.

Dr. Henry Fitzbutler, of Louisville, was born December 22, 1842. He graduated in the Michigan University in 1872. He was granted a charter by the legislature of Kentucky in 1888 to practice medicine, having graduated at the Louisville National Medical College. He was the first regular physician of the Negro race to enter upon the practice of medicine in the State of Kentucky.

The National Republican Convention, held at Philadelphia in June, 1872, received as delegates a number of colored men, and for the first time in the history of presidential conventions, the Negro's voice was heard and applauded.

Charles L. Remond was the first Negro to take the platform as a regular lecturer in the anti-slavery cause, and was no doubt, the ablest representative that the race had till the appearance of Frederick Douglass in 1842.

The Freedman's Journal was issued March 16, 1827, and was the first newspaper published by an Afro-American in the United States.

Hon. Frederick Douglass, in his early life, was a local preacher in the A. M. E. Zion Church.

Prof. William H. Day, of Harrisburg, Pa., is said to be the leading scholar in the A. M. E. Zion Church. He is the only colored man in the United States who enjoys the distinction of presiding over a white school board of a city of 50,000 population. He is also president of the county school board. The unsurpassed excellence of the public school system of Harrisburg is said to be due to his efforts.

Grand United Order of Odd Fellows in America.—This grand institution was founded by Peter Ogden. To-day they enroll a membership in 32 States. Wm. T. Forrester is Grand Master, and Charles B. Wilson, Deputy Grand Master. Total lodges, 2,043; households, 880; total inmates in the 880 households of Ruth, 25,000; councils, 161; patriarchies, 76; male membership, 71,744; whole number of P. G. M.'s and M. V. P.'s, 4,500; total membership in all branches, 98,244.

Mr. J. C. Farley, of Richmond, Va., is one of the finest photographers in the United States. His work has been exhibited at national fairs, taking the premium at many places.

The Afro-American Benevolent Association, of Birmingham, Ala., was organized under the State law and has many worthy features in connection with its management.

In his will, George Washington set his slaves free, and hundreds of other slave owners did the same thing.

Felix Weir, a colored boy of Chicago, 11 years old, is a musical prodigy on the violin. He plays a great many very difficult compositions with sassy grace and skill.

Freedman's Bureau.—Congress passed an act March 3, 1865, organizing in the War Department the "Bureau of the Refuges, Freedmen and Abandoned Lands," which was popularly known as the "Freedmen's Bureau." This remained in operation, with somewhat enlarged powers, until July 1, 1869, when its functions ceased, excepting the educational department, which continued until July 1, 1870, and that for the collection of claims. The bureau exercised a general supervision over the freedmen, protecting their rights, deciding their disputes, aiding them in obtaining work, extending facilities of education, and furnishing them with medical treatment. It was discontinued about five years after its organization, as the chief object for which it was organized had by that time been accomplished.

The "Jubilee Singers."—They were a company of educated Negroes, from Fisk University, Nashville, Tenn., who for seven years of almost continuous labor, both in Europe and America, gave popular entertainments of a species of singing which originated among the slaves of the Southern States. Their efforts were crowned with success, and the proceeds of their concerts were used in purchasing the University grounds, and the building of Jubilee Hall. This building is elegantly located, and is absolutely one of the handsomest structures to be found anywhere in the South.

First Newspaper in the South.—The first race newspaper published in the South was *The Colored American*. It was published in Augusta, Ga., and was edited by J. T. Shuften in 1865. We find the following discription of this paper in *The Afro-American Press:* "It is designed to be a vehicle for the diffusion of *Religious, Political and*

General Intelligence. It will be devoted to the promotion of harmony and good will between the whites and colored people of the South, and uniting in its advocacy of industry and education among all classes; but particularly the class most in need of our agency. It will steadfastly oppose all forms of vice that prey upon society, and give that counsel that tends to virtue, peace, prosperity and happiness."

THE DERIVATION AND NICKNAMES OF THE STATES.

ALABAMA.—The derivation of the name "Alabama," like that of numerous other states, is of Indian origin, and is commonly supposed to signify "Here we rest," and these words are on the States coat-of-arms. It takes its name from its principal river and is generally known as the "Cotton State."

ALASKA is an Indian name and signifies "great land" or "main land." The name is said to have been given by Captain Cook in his voyage of 1778. It was purchased by the United States in May 1867 for $7,200,000.

ARIZONA is supposed to be of uncertain meaning.

ARKANSAS, after its chief river. The meaning is in doubt. By an act of the State Senate in 1881, the true pronunciation of the word was declared to be Ar-kan-saw. Formerly it was so spelled, but the original way has not yet been restored. It was admitted into the Union June 15, 1836. It is called the "Bear State."

CALIFORNIA is of Spanish origin. First permanent settlement made at San Diego, April 11, 1769. Has been supposed to mean "hot furnace," but the term is not applicable, on account of the general climate of the State, which is temperate and healthful. The name is said to have been given to an imaginary island in the Orient, "near the Terrestrial Paradise." In 1535 a company of Spanish explorers supposed they had found this poetic island, or its twin sister and named it accordingly. It is called the "Golden State."

CAROLINAS.—This name was given to a fort not far from Bufort, South Carolina, by Ribault in 1562 in honor of Charles I. of England, or Charles IX., King of France. Is one of the thirteen original

States. Was ratified November 21, 1789. South Carolina is familiarly known as the "Palmetto State," while her neighbor is known as the "Tar State," or "Old North State."

COLORADO is a Spanish word and means "Red or Colored." It was named for the river of the same name. It was admitted into the Union in 1876, just one hundred years after the Declaration of Independence, and hence the favorite nickname—"Centennial State."

CONNECTICUT.—The name is of Indian origin, meaning "Long River," or "upon the long river." The State is sometimes called the "Land of Steady Habits." It became a State January 9, 1788. It is popularly known as the "Nutmeg State," from the jocular slander that its peddlers were in the habit of palming off wooden nutmegs on their customers.

DAKOTAS.—The word Dakota is a name by which the people of the greatest northwestern Indian Confederacies called themselves. It means "leagued." South Dakota was admitted into the Union Nov. 2, 1889. It is sometimes called the "Swiagecat," or "Cayote" State, while her Northern sister has been called the "Sioux," or "Flickertail" State.

DELAWARE.—This name was given first to the bay, next to the river, and lastly to the State, in honor of Lord de la War, Governor of Virginia. It is called the "Blue Hen State," or "Diamond State."

DISTRICT OF COLUMBIA.—Congress, on the 28th of June, 1790, passed an act providing, "that a district of territory on the Potomac, at some place between the mouths of the Eastern Branch and the Connogocheague, be and the same is hereby accepted for the permanent seat of the Government of the United States." Ten miles square was laid out for this purpose, Virginia and Maryland contributing the land.

FLORIDA is the Spanish for "flowery." It is the Spanish name for Easter Sunday, the day on which Ponce de Leon discovered Florida in 1513. It is called the "Peninsular State."

GEORGIA, named in honor of King George II., of England, who granted to General Oglethorpe a charter for same. She was admitted into the Union January 2, 1788. Seceded January, 1861; re-admitted December, 1870. Popularly known as the "Cracker State."

IDAHO.—Indian name and means "Gem of the Mountains," said to refer to the "bright sunshine on the mountain tops, so characteristic of that strangely beautiful country." Admitted as a State, July, 3, 1890.

ILLINOIS, the name of its chief river, and of the confederated tribes dwelling on its banks. The name signifies "a superior class of men." It is one of the most important States in the Union in point of wealth and population. It is appropriately called the "Prairie State" on account of its broad expanse of prairie lands. It is also called the "Sucker State."

INDIANA is sometimes called the "Hoosier State," a term of which the origin has never been satisfactorily explained.

IOWA.—The meaning of this word has been variously interpreted. It is generally conceded, however, to mean "The abode of peace," also "across" or "beyond," and this name is supposed to have been applied by the Illinois tribes to their enemies across the Mississippi river. It is called the "Hawkeye State," and is apparently intended to commemorate the famous chief, Black Hawk.

KANSAS.—This State is called after a tribe of the same name which in the Indian dialect signifies "South Wind." It is popularly known as the "Sunflower State."

KENTUCKY.—Admitted as a State June 1, 1792. It is an Indian name and signifies "Dark and bloody ground." It is sometimes called the "Corn Cracker," but is most generally known as the "Bluegrass State."

LOUISIANA.—Named in honor of Louis the XIV., of France. Popularly known as the "Pelican State."

MAINE signifies the "Main" or "Mainland." From the immense white pine forests it has been given the name of the "Pine Tree State."

MARYLAND, named in honor of Henrietta Maria, Queen of Charles I., of England. It is properly known as "The Old Line State."

MASSACHUSETTS.—This name is of Indian origin, and means "About the Great Hills." The first settlers were known as the "Pilgrims," who landed in a small vessel known as the "Mayflower." Three large bays indent the Eastern shore, and for this reason it is called the "Bay State."

MICHIGAN.—This word signifies "A weir for fish" or "Lake Country." It is called the "Wolverine State."

MINNESOTA after its river of the same name; in the Kakota language, *minne* means "water," and *sotah* means "sky-colored." It is usually called the "Gopher State," but is sometimes called the "North Star State," from the motto on its coat-of-arms.

MISSISSIPPI is from the Indian, Algonquin, *missi-sepe*, "great river." "Father of Waters," the accepted interpretation, and one that has been so popular, is only a fancy. From the frequent bayous formed by the changing of the stream, the State is called by the nickname, "Bayou State."

MISSOURI is of Indian origin and is derived from two words, *missi souri*, signifying "great muddy" (river). It is said to bring down from the "Rockies" so much mud that the water, when taken up in a small vessel, has the appearance of coffee.

MONTANA, a Spanish name, meaning "mountains." It was admitted into the Union Nov. 8, 1889, and is called the "Stubtoe State."

NEBRASKA is an Indian name, meaning "shallow water." It is popularly known as the "Antelope" or "Black Water" State.

NEVADA is of Spanish origin, and from is chief product is known as "The Silver State." The meaning of the word is "white with snow." It took its name from the Sierra Nevada, a range of lofty mountains dividing it from California. It is sometimes called the "Sage Brush State," from the scope of country covered with sage brush.

NEW HAMPSHIRE.—Named after the country of Hampshire, England. From the rocks of the White Mountains, it is called the "Granite State."

NEW JERSEY.—Named after the Isle of Jersey, in the English Channel. Called the "Sharp Backs State."

NEW MEXICO, after Mexico.

NEW YORK—"The Empire State," so call on account of the fact that it takes first rank in population, wealth, and commerce among the States in the Union. It was named for the Duke of York.

OHIO is an Indian word, meaning "beautiful river." This name was first applied to the river between Pittsburg and Cairo, and the first State erected north of this stream was named for it. It is popularly known as the "Buckeye State," from the abundance of buckeye or horse-chestnut trees.

OKLAHOMA is an Indian word, and signifies "beautiful land," or "fine country,' and *so it is*. This beautiful country is increasing rapidly in population and material prosperity

OREGON.—This is a Spanish word from "Oregano." The name signifies "Thyme." It was admitted to the Union February 12, 1859. It is called the "Beaver State."

PENNSYLVANIA is the most celebrated State in the Union for extensive coal beds. It was named in honor of admiral Penn, father of

William Penn. The meaning is Pennis—"Sylva"—woods. It is called the "Keystone State," probably because its name was carved on the keystone of the bridge over Rock Creek, between Washington and Georgetown. She is also the middle of the thirteen original States.

RHODE ISLAND, from her size, is universally known as "Little Rody." The probability is that it was named in honor of the Greek island in the Mediterranean—"Isle of Rhodes."

TENNESSEE is named after her principal river, a Cherokee word, signifying "crooked river," or "river of big bend," and is popularly known as the "Volunteer State."

TEXAS takes her name from a tribe of Indians who passed through that country in 1536. The word is of Indian origin, and signifies "friends." It is called the "Lone Star State," from the device on her flag and shield.

UTAH is named after a tribe of Indians. The word signifies "Mountain Home." Mormans call it the "Deseret," which they claim means "The Land of the Honey-bee."

VERMONT is of French Origin, and is derived from two words— *vert*, green, and *monts*, mountains, hence the nickname, "Green Mountain State."

VIRGINIA.— Commonly called "The Old Dominion," because Charles II. allowed it to call itself the fourth dominion of his empire, that is, England, Scotland, Ireland, and Virginia. The name is in honor of Queen Elizabeth, of England. It is also known as the "Mother of Presidents." Slavery was also first introduced here in 1619.

WASHINGTON was named for the "Father of his Country," and is called the "Chinook State."

WEST VIRGINIA separated from the "Old Dominion" in 1863, and is called the "Little Mountain State."

WISCONSIN, after the name of its chief river, which means "wild rushing channel," "westward flowing," or "Prairie River." It is popularly known as the "Badger State."

WYOMING is an Indian word, said to mean "broad valley."

ABOUT one forth of the population of the world is not under the law of civilization.

MAXIMS, PROVERBS AND PHRASES.

Absence makes the heart grow fonder.—*J. H. Bailey.*
He that hides is no better than he that steals.
He who accuses too many accuses himself.
Brave actions never want a trumpet.
He who does not advance recedes.
Adversity often leads to prosperity.
Adversity tries virtue.
He asks advice in vain who will not follow it.
When advice will not correct the rod will not.
Afflictions are the best blessings in disguise.
He that corrects not youth controls not age.
Give not your alms to a sound-limbed beggar.
Giving alms never lessens the purse.
Angels hear the humblest human cry.—*Bulwer.*
A man is a stark fool all the while he is angry.
A soft answer is a specific cure for anger.
Do not always judge by appearances.—*La Fontaine.*
By hammer and hand all arts do stand.
All asses do not go on four feet.
Even an ass loves to hear himself bray.
It is often better not to see an insult than to avenge it.
A bad tree does not yield good apples.
He is a sorry barber that has but one comb.
It is a base thing to betray a man because he trusted you.
One cannot teach a bear to dance in a day.
Beard was never the true standard for brains.—*T. Fuller.*
A fair face may hide a foul heart.
A thing of beauty is a joy forever.
Beauty may have fair leaves but bitter fruit.
Beauty without virtue is a curse.
A beggar's wallet is never full.
From small beginnings come great things.
What a man desires he easily believes.
Put money in thy purse, but put it honestly.

Better a tooth out than always aching.
Blessings are not valued until gone.
A blind man wishes to show the road.
Boasting renders one ridiculous.
Believe a boaster as you would a liar.
Better buy than borrow.
Borrowing is the mother of trouble.
Much borrowing destroys credit.
Many are brave when the enemy flies.
Every man thinks his own burden the heaviest.
Business neglected is business lost.
A fine cage won't feed the bird.
Keep no more cats than will catch mice.
Change of pasture makes fat calves.
People often change and seldom do better.
A charitable man is the true lover of God.
Cheaply bought, dear in the end.
Cheerful company shortens the miles.
Children are what they are made.
A Christian is the highest style of man.
Better come late to church than never.
Go not to hell for company.
The rotten apple spoils it companions.
Do all you can to be good and you'll be so.
Do not publish people's defects.
A clear conscience is a good pillow.
Contempt is the sharpest reproof.
A contented man is always rich.
Good counsel is not to be paid with gold.
Keep your own counsel.
A man of courage never wants weapons.
A covetous man does nothing that he should till he dies.
Credit is dead; bad pay killed it.
Crosses are ladders which lead to heaven.
To everyone his own cross is heaviest.
A crow is never whiter for often washing.
Curiosity often brings its own punishment.
Every day is not a holiday.
No day passes without some grief.
The longest day is sure to have its night.

If to-day will not, to-morrow may.
Every to-morrow brings its bread.
All death is sudden to the unprepared.
He would be a good one to send for death.
Six feet of earth make all men equal.
A man in debt is stoned every year.
Debt is the worst poverty.
Good deeds remain, all things else perish.
If your desires be endless your cares will be so too.
No one can have all he desires.
Diligence is the mother of success.—*Don Quixote.*
A good dog deserves a good bone.
An old dog cannot alter its way of barking.
Let not the sun look down and say inglorious here he lies.—*Franklin.*
The morning hour has gold in its mouth.
Economy is a great revenue.
A rotten egg cannot be spoiled.
He that endureth is not overcome.
Evils that are passed should not be mourned.
Never do evil that good may come of it.
Who doeth no evil is apt to suspect none.
No great good came without looking after it.
A scalded dog thinks cold water hot.
It is best to be cautious and avoid extremes.
The eye is blind if the mind is absent.
A good face needs no paint.
A single fact is worth a shipload of argument.
Facts are more powerful than words.
Fancy requires much; necessity but little.
A father lives after death in his son.
A father loves his children in hating their faults.
The most faulty are most prone to find fault.
Nothing is easier than fault-finding.—*Robert West.*
He who asks fewest favors is the best received.
Fear is often greater than danger.
The first in the boat has choice of oars.
From great rivers come great fish.
All flowers are not in one garland.
It is a bad soil where no flowers will grow.
A fool alway finds a greater fool that admires him.

A fool thinks nothing right but what he does himself.
Fools for arguments use wagers.
Fools laugh at their own sport.
Young fools think that the old are dotards; but the old have forgotten more than the young fools know.
A wise man will not reprove a fool.
A coward never forgave, it is not his nature.
A man does not seek his luck, luck seeks its man.
Fortune is not far from the brave man's head.
Fortune makes friends and misfortune tries them.
A poor freedom is better than a rich slavery.
Friendship is stronger than kindred.
A true gentleman will respect woman even in her weakness.
God delays, but does not forget.
God helps the sailor, but he must row.
When God says to-day, the devil says to-morrow.
Gossiping and lying go together.
The sweetest grapes hang highest.
Gratitude is the least of virtues; ingratitude the worst of vices.
Grief is satisfied and carried off by tears.
Grief pent up will burst the heart.
The only cure for grief is action.—*George Henry Lewis.*
The handsomest flower is not the sweetest.
Happy is the man that keeps out of strife.
A cool mouth and warm feet live long.—*George Herbert.*
There are no riches like health.
A cheerful countenance betokens a good heart.
A happy heart is better than a full purse.
Help yourself and God will help you.
Help yourself and your friends will help you.
Travel east or travel west, a man's own home is still the best.
There is no place like home even if it is a cellar.
An honest countenance is the best passport.
An honest man does not make himself a dog for the sake of a bone.
An honest man is not the worse because a dog barks at him.
A lady's honor will not bear a soil.
Hope is the poor man's bread.
A good son makes a good husband.
By doing nothing we learn to do evil.
Idleness is the rust of the soul.

Industry is the parent of fortune.
Insolence puts an end to friendship.
Never judge by appearances.
A forced kindness deserves no thanks.
Many kiss the child for the nurse's sake.
A little knowledge is a dangerous thing.
To know everything is to know nothing.
Learning is better than house and land.
Learning refines and elevates the mind.
Life is labor, death is rest.
Little birds may pick a dead lion.
A little pack serves a little peddler.
Little and often make a heap of time.
A living bog is better than a dead lion.
The loss that is not known is no loss.
He loves well who chastises well.
Love is the touchstone of virtue.
Love knows no measure.
A liar is sooner caught than a cripple.
He that hears much hears many lies.
Show me a liar and I'll show you a thief.
There is no vice that hath not its beginning in a lie.—*Dryden.*
You may shut your doors against a thief but not against a liar.
A mad horse must have a sober rider.
Every mad man thinks all other men are mad.
Maidens should be mild and meek, swift to hear and slow to speak.
A man has two ears and one mouth, that he may hear much and speak little.
Men, like cattle, follow him who leads.
Be sure before you marry.
Hasty marriage seldom proveth well.—*Shakespeare.*
Marriage is heaven or hell.
Every fool will be meddling.
The meekness of Moses is better than the strength of Samson.
Small minds are captivated by trifles.—*Ovid.*
A merry heart doeth good like a medicine.—*Bible.*
Mirth and motion prolong life.
Misfortune makes us wise.
The mob has many heads but no brains.
Modesty has more charms than beauty.

A man who is proud of his money has rarely anything else to be proud of.

Money borrowed is soon sorrowed.

A mother is a mother all the days of her life; a father is a father till he gets a new wife.

A good name is rather to be chosen than great riches.—*Bible*.

Better is a neighbor that is near than a brother that is far off.—*Bible*.

It is more noble to pardon than to punish.

Govern your passions, otherwise they will govern you.—*Horace*.

Be patient toward all men.—*St Paul*.

None patient but the wise.

Punctual pay gets willing loan.

Who pays beforehand is served behindhand.

A good pay master needs no security.

Perseverance brings success.

He that hath pity on the poor lendeth to the Lord.—*Bible*.

No dish pleases all palates alike.

An ox and an ass don't yoke well to the same plow.

He who sleeps much learns little.

Sloth is the key to poverty.

Be slow to promise, quick to perform.

The sluggard's convenient season never comes.

A small coin in a big jar makes a great noise.

Small axes fell great trees.

One may smile and smile, and be a villian still.

A snow year, a rich year.

Solitude is of the best society.

The son disgraces himself when he blames his father.

There is a salve for every sore.

A day of sorrow is longer than a month of joy.

Provide for the soul by doing good works.

Early sow, early mow.

He that sows thistles, shall reap thistles.

Sow good works and thou shalt reap gladness.

He that spares vice wrongs virtue.

Who speaks, sows; who listens, reaps.

The brightest of all things, the sun, has its spots.

Rolling stones gather no moss.

Deserve success and you shall command it.

He who succeeds is reputed wise.
Nothing succeeds like success.
It will not always be summer.—*Hesoid.*
The sun shines for all the world.
The sun is the King of torches.—*Western African Negro.*
He that is surety for a stranger shall smart for it.—*Bible.*
He that hateth suretyship is sure.—*Bible.*
There is no sweet without sour.
What so tedious as a twice told tale.—*Homer.*
Great talkers are commonly liars.—*German.*
A thief thinks every man steals.
He who takes no care of little things will not have the care of great ones.
He that has most time has none to lose.
A still tongue makes a wise head.
Put a key on your tongue.
It is better to turn back than go astray.
One never loseth anything by politeness.
No one is poor but he who thinks himself so.
Poor without debt is better than a prince.
The poor sit in Paradise on the first benches.
T'is God's blessing makes the pot boil.
Poverty is the reward of idleness.
He is a fool that praises himself.
Let another man praise thee and not thine own mouth.—*Bible.*
Self praise is odious.
The nobler the blood the less the pride.
Don't promise what you cannot perform.
Providence assists not the idle.
A profitable religion never wants proselytes.
Religious contention is the devil's harvest.
A good name is better than riches.—*Bible.*
Be resolved and the thing is done.—*Chinese.*
Rest is good after the work is done.
Forgetting of a wrong is a mild revenge.
Give me neither poverty or riches.—*Bible.*
He is rich who owes nothing.
The rich man is often poorer than the beggar.
Be sure you are right then go ahead.—*D. Crochett.*
No one is always right.

The nearer to Rome the worst Christians.
On his own saddle one rides the safest.
Salt spilt is never all gathered.
Every one that repeats it adds something to the scandal.
A smooth sea never made a skillful mariner.
The lazy servant takes eight steps to avoid one.
Unwilling service earns no thanks.
He is lost whose shame is lost.
Often shooting hits the mark.
Better be silent than talk ill.
Deep rivers move in silence, shallow brooks are noisy.
Silence is as great an art as speech.
Silence puts an end to quarrels.
Speaking is silver, silence is gold.
All who snore are not asleep.
Travel is the great source of true wisdom.
Travel makes a wise man better, but a fool worse.
The tree must be bent while it is young.
No one gets into trouble without his own help.
If you trust before you try, you may repent before you die.
Trust in God, but keep your powder dry.—*Cromwell*.
Buy the truth and sell it not.—*Bible*.
Truth is better than gold.—*Arabian*.
Every man thinks his own copper gold.
Vanity is the food of fools.—*Swift*.
He who is free from vice himself is the slower to suspect it in others.—*Greek*.
He that forgives gains the victory.
Virtue is a jewel of great price.
A *wager* is a fool's argument.
War makes robbers, and peace hangs them.
Running water carries no poison.
A misty morning may have a fine day.
No garden is without its weeds.
Such a welcome, such a farewell.
Welcome is the best dish in the kitchen.
A wicked companion invites us all to hell.
A wicked man is afraid of his own memory.
The wicked grow worse, and good men grow better from troubles.
A good wife and health are a man's best wealth.

A man can never thrive who has a wasteful wife.
A prudent wife is from the Lord.
It is a mark of wisdom to dislike folly.
He is the wise man who is the honest man.
Wit does not take the place of wisdom.
A silent woman is always more admired than a noisy one.
Better break your word than do worse in keeping it.
Good works will never save you, but you cannot be saved without them.
Youth looks forward and age backward.
Too much zeal spoils all.
Zeal is fit only for wise men, but is found mostly in fools.

THE GREAT NEED OF NEGRO FARMERS.

WE want educated farmers who will own their lands, stock and farming implements. We want farmers who will highly appreciate their calling and study all the latest improved methods of tilling the soil and supply themselves with the best implements in the market. We want farmers who will raise fine stock and cattle, fruits and vegetables for our own and foreign markets. Let the world know where, who we are and what we are doing. As a rule our young men who come to the cities from the farm are ashamed to be known as farmers. They consider farming menial—below the profession. In this they are wrong. No profession can be higher and more honorable than that of farming. The farmer feeds all of the professions. But for the farmer there would be no professions. He supports the people and all other callings; and just as the farmer is successful in producing plenty, all other business is prosperous; and just in proportion as he fails all suffer.

The farmer deserves to be honored, for we are all dependent upon him for that which supports life, bread. Every farmer should be proud of his calling, and by his appreciation of it compel others to respect it. If you will go over the history of all the great men and women of the world you will find that most of them were born and reared on the farm. The purest men and women of to-day are on the farm free from the crazes of city society. Not only our bread and what we eat come from the farm, our clothing as well. Who but the farmer settles our new States and Territories, clears away the forests and makes the waste places to blossom? He plows and sows and reaps and mows for us. Then don't despise the farmer; if you have no employment in the city go to the farm. Thousands of our people lie around the cities and towns, living from hand to mouth in old cellars, dilapidated stables, closely packed tenement houses, not fit for human habitation, often at the point of starvation and often compelled to steal and beg to keep the "wolf from the door," that might make an independent living by going to the country and working farm lands.

Some say that those who own the lands will not pay a fair price; then there is greater reason why we should own lands ourselves. Work and save your money and buy lands. If the price is too high where you live go somewhere else. If you cannot buy a big farm buy a little one. Buy one or more acres and cultivate every inch of it and add more to it when you can. Off an acre-and-a-half strawberry patch, nine miles from Nashville, Mr. John Goodrich picked 1,485 gallons, which brought him $303.75. He commenced picking May 4, 1895, and finished May 29. Land in his vicinity, equally as productive can be had from $15 to $25 per acre. There are thousands of acres of land in Texas, Arkansas and the Western States that can be bought for a trifle. Go in colonies and buy their lands, withstand a few hardships and become independent and useful, patriotic citizens. The homestead lands are not all taken yet. Go out and possess these lands that are free to all who comply with the laws. The poor Germans, Bohemians, Italians and other peoples of the continent come to this country and settle on these homestead lands and in a few years they are independent. We can do the same. Then let us lay aside extravagance, low, base, useless and expensive habits and begin anew. Let us begin at the farm with thrift energy and intelligence to demonstrate our worth. Let us economize and get money and property of our own. "Get money, not to hide away in a hedge, nor for a train attendant, but for the glorious privilege of being independent."

THE African ostrich has but two toes on each foot, and one of them has but one claw.

Cotton Picking in Mississippi.

CHRISTIAN TRUTH IN SLAVE SONGS.

REV. C. J. RYDER, D.D.

THE INFLUENCE OF SLAVERY IN THE SONGS OF NATIONS.

The Purpose of this Paper.—The oldest psalm in the whole collection of these marvelous sacred songs is the ninetieth (XC.). It was born in the heart of a man who had felt the bitter hardship of slavery. "They made their lives bitter with hard bondage," was the pitiful record of his race in Egypt. Moses, the author of this psalm, knew well of those wretched experiences of slavery. The influence of those dark days, and the thirty-eight years wandering in the wilderness, oppressed the Poet General of Israel, and he exclaimed "We are consumed by thine anger, and by thy wrath are we troubled. For all our days are passed away in thy wrath." It was the influence of slavery in the songs of the Israelite nation. You can trace the same effects in the sacred writings after each captivity. The experience of slavery colored their religious songs, as it touched their national life and moulded their nation's history.

It would be a most interesting study to follow out this same line of investigation and note how the suppression of national independence, the subjugation of any people, has colored their religious thought, and found expression in their sacred songs. It is my purpose, however, only to note the fact of this influence, not to illustrate it.

The growth or development of sacred songs is an interesting study. Take some familiar hymns. We sing "Hail to the Lord's anointed," written by James Montgomery, in 1822. "Jesus shall Reign Where'er the Sun," written by Isaac Watts, in 1819. "Rescue the Perishing," by Fanny Crosby. "My Country 'tis of Thee," written by Rev. S. F. Smith, in 1832. Eighteen Christian centuries stand behind these sacred hymns. Each mighty century contributed its rich gifts to the development of the races whose blood flowed in the veins of Montgomery or Watts or Crosby or Smith. There is evolution of Christian song. Now in studying these old slave songs, we touch hands with heathen Africa. Two hundred and fifty years of enforced bondage and thirty years of freedom are all that separate those who sung these songs from barbarism. We cannot expect to find the models of expression that eighteen centuries of free Christian development have produced. We shall discover crude, weird, quaint words, and often fantastic music. But this study and analysis throws light upon race development, and proves, I think, that the great truths of the Christian faith comforted and uplifted the humble, ignorant slave just as truly as the wealthy, and intelligent, and refined.

"The best commentary on the Scripture is the Scripture," said a learned divine. So the best commentary on the Negro is the Negro. We have done almost everything with and for the Negro, except let him speak for himself. We preach at him; we hold him up as a remarkable example of total depravity, of hopeless corruption, or as rich in his religious nature. We tell of his terrible degration, or his wonderful progress, as the whim may strike us. We do everything except let him speak for himself.

This paper is a humble effort on the part of the writer to let the Negro speak for himself concerning his religious faith. These three introductory considerations just mentioned are of importance in studying the slave songs of our own bondmen.

1st. The influence of slavery in coloring their Christian songs. 2nd. The evolution of sacred songs. 3rd. The value of the Negro's views of the Negro.

Turning aside from the statistics of church growth, let us ask the question, What is there among the Negroes of the South to build upon in Christian work? Have they correct ideas of the great fundamental truths of Christianity? What was the theology of the plantation? What are the fundamental elements in the religious thought of these freed slaves? Must we recast their conceptions of religious truth, or only seek to intellectualize that which is spiritually discerned? What are the religious conceptions of these uneducated Negroes? What was the theology of the slaves?

The answer to this question determines largely the future of our church work among the mass of colored people. The progress will be painfully slow, if we must lay the foundations of religious truth before we can build the super-structure of church work. But if we discover that they hold evangelical truth substantially correct, we have a great advantage.

"They that do His will shall know of the doctrine," we read.

These poor Negroes walking never in the full day of opportunity of religious truth communed with God in the night of their oppression and wrong, and it is marvelous how wonderfully he revealed himself to them. They have no polemic literature, no dogmatic theology. We learn of one old colored preacher who had a trial for heresy on his hands, because he preached against stealing chickens!

Indeed they had no literature at all as a race, but coming out from these two and a half centuries of bondage they have brought with them a whole body of *Christian song*. Like the Homeric plays or the Scotch ballads, these Negro songs, which came from their hearts and grew out of their religious experiences, were preserved by being repeated—handed down by word of mouth from father to son, from mother to child.

> "The triumph note that Marian sung,
> The joy of uncaged birds;
> Softening with Africa's mellow tongue
> Their broken Saxon words."

Now do these plantation hymns give evidence that the great fundamental doctrines of evangelical Christianity were held by these humble people in their days of slavery? In pushing our Christian work in the South, can we assume this fact? It is not only a very interesting question in ethnology and race history, but also of great importance in our missionary enterprises to know just what these humble people learned of God's truth in the school house of slavery, having little human instruction but communing with God's Spirit. That we may discover the answer to this question, let us arrange somewhat systematically these old plantation melodies, these songs that were never written, but that burst from the hearts of the slaves when crushed under the weight of their bondage.

They could not read nor write. But let us remember that our own race is indebted for its highest poetic expression of Christian truth in the early centuries to one who could not read, Ceadmon Monk, of Whitley. He was the greatest Anglo-Saxon poet and father of English song. He gave us our first Paradise Lost, equal, in many respects, to John Milton's greatest book.

1. These slave songs teach, beyond doubt, that the slaves held to the truth of Divine Sovereignty. We repeat in our churches the beautiful language of the Apostle's Creed: "I believe in God the Father Almighty, Maker of Heaven and Earth." So do these hum-

ble Negroes believe. This great truth bursts forth from their lips in jubilant song.

> "Didn't my Lord deliver Daniel,
> D'liver Daniel, d'liver Daniel?
> Didn't my Lord deliver Daniel,
> And why not every man?"

What a strange pathetic appeal to this Divine Ruler are these words in the hymn, "Keep me from sinking down:"

> "I bless the Lord I'm gwine to die;
> Keep me from sinking down.
> I'm gwine to judgment by-and-bye;
> Keep me from sinking down.
> "O Lord, O my Lord! O my good Lord!
> Keep me from sinking down."

It suggests to one Jean Ingelow's "Brothers and a Sermon," and the touching prayer of the old fisherman to whom the Lord Jesus came in the night season.

> "O, Lord, good Lord,
> I am a broken down poor man, a fool
> To speak to thee." . . .
> "O Lord, our Lord,
> How great is thy compassion. Come, good Lord,
> For we will open. Come this night, good Lord;
> Stand at the door and knock."
> "Only the wind knocks at my door, Oh, loud and long it knocks,
> The only thing God made that has a mind to enter in."

Yea, thus the old man spake. These were the last words of his aged mouth.

But one did knock. One came to sup with him, that humble, weak, old man; knocked at his door in the rough pauses of the laboring wind.

And when the neighbors came the morrow morn they said:

"He looks as he had woke and seen the face of Christ, and with that rapturous smile held out his arms, to come to Him."

The appeal of these Negroes was to Divine Justice, not to fickle human passion, and they rejoiced in view of such a judgment day. "God, the Father Almighty," they held to, they gloried in and no mystery of suffering ever dimmed their faith. We can assume its existence and build upon it in pushing our church work among them in the Southland.

Calvinism seems to have crept in at the very basis of their doctrinal views. Original sin finds recognition in the following odd song:

> "Old Satan thinks he'll get us all,
> Yes, my Lord;
> Because in Adam we did fall,
> Yes, my Lord."

Whether they hold to the federal headship of Adam, I cannot state positively. If they adopted Professor Shedd's theory that the whole race was actually, physically present in Adam and consciously sinned, it would be another argument for the unity of the human race, or else hint very strongly that Adam was slightly off color.

2. Again these slaves held to the Divinity of Christ—crudely stated, imperfectly discerned, but tenaciously maintained. Among their plantation hymns, illustrating this, I refer to only two or three.

> "Just stand right still and steady yourself,
> I know that my Redeemer lives.
> Oh, just let me tell you about God his self,
> I know that my Redeemer lives."

Or another, the refrain of which runs:

> "Reign, Oh, reign; Oh, reign my Savior!
> Reign, Oh, reign; Oh, reign my Lord."

Or still another:

> "Why, He's the Lord of lords,
> And the King of kings.
> Why, Jesus Christ is the first and last,
> No one can work like Him."

3. There is little in their songs concerning the Holy Spirit. The Father and Son were relations that they could understand. The more mysterious work and personality of the Holy Spirit they did not so easily grasp. But they did not doubt that God was with them and that the Lord Jesus Christ was their companion.

4. The Atonement, the Son of God dying for them to open the way of salvation, was a truth most precious to them in their life of painful neglect or bitter persecution. Their plantation melodies are full of this truth. One, however, will illustrate the fact as well as a dozen. And what more beautiful than that with the refrain,

> "I've been redeemed, I've been redeemed,
> Been washed in the blood of the Lamb."

If we turn from Theology proper to Anthropology, we find here the fundamental truths entering into their religious conceptions. They thoroughly believe in human freedom of the will, if not of the person, and in human responsibility. They sung as they swayed back and forth in their weird gatherings at night, under the old pine forests, or on a hillock in the midst of some swampy jungle, these words:

> "Don't you want to be a soldier, soldier, soldier,
> Don't you want to be a soldier in the year of jubilee?
> Then you must rise and shine and give God the glory, glory,
> Rise and shine and give God the glory in the year of jubilee."

They believe that they must "work out their own salvation with fear and trembling," but they never forget that "it is God that worketh in them both to will and to do of his good pleasure."

The personality of Satan they never doubted, and his ability to tempt human souls is illustrated in many of their hymns. They sing at Tougaloo, Miss., a hymn which especially emphasizes this fact. The refrain goes,

> "Old Satan, he wears de hypocrite shoe,
> If you don't mind, he slip it on you."

A warning that is not limited in its application to the Southern Negroes.

5. Again, how tenaciously they hold to the doctrine of Conversion and Regeneration, the union of the Divine and human in this great change of the soul, is abundantly proved.

> "Run to Jesus, shun the danger,
> I don't expect to stay much longer here."

Here is illustrated human effort, *conversion*, turning to Jesus. This hymn is especially interesting, for Hon. Frederick Douglass told us that these words, "Run to Jesus," sung on the plantation where he was a slave, first suggested to him the thought of escaping from slavery, "Praying with his feet," as he put it.

But carrying out the thought further, we find their idea of conversion and regeneration, and the joy of a new born soul illustrated in the following quaint hymn, "The Angels Done Changed My Name."

> "I went to the hillside, I went to pray;
> I knew the angels done changed my name,
> Done changed my name for the coming day;
> I knew the angels done changed my name.

> "I looked at my hands, my hands was new,
> I knowed the angels done changed my name;
> I looked at my feet and my feet was too,
> Thank God the angels done changed my name."

Souls that sung and felt that, knew the experiences of the great apostle, when he said, "Wherefore if any man is in Christ Jesus, he is a new creature; the old things are passed away; behold, they are become new." 2 Cor. v. 17. N. V.

But if we go a little deeper into philosophy or doctrinal analysis, we discover the familiar old doctrine of the "perseverance of the saints." Did they hold it? Did they sing it? Listen as they sing of the poor inch-worm:

> "T'was inch by inch I sought the Lord,
>   Jesus will come by-and-by,
> And inch by inch he blessed my soul,
>   Jesus will come by-and-by.
>
> We'll inch and inch and inch along,
>   Jesus will come by-and-by,
> And inch and inch till we gets home,
>   Jesus will come by-and-by.
>
> Keep inching along, keep inching along;
>   Jesus will come by-and-by;
> Keep inching along like the poor inch worm,
>   Jesus will come by-and-by."

Now, I submit that this quaint old plantation song not only teaches the "perseverance of the saints," but aptly illustrates about the rate of progress most of us make, "Inching along like the poor inch worm."

But they believe that conversion should change their lives. It is not true that they entirely neglect ethics in their religious conceptions. Take this hymn as evidence:

> "You say you're aiming for the skies,
>   View the land, view the land;
> Why don't you stop your telling lies?
>   Oh, view the heavenly land.
>
> You say your Lord has set you free,
>   View the land, view the land;
> Why don't you let your neighbors be?
>   Oh, view the heavenly land."

6. Their views on eschatology were also sound. They believed in future punishment and future rewards. The former is strange. It would seem as if this whole race of Lazaruses, who received only the crumbs that fell from their rich masters' tables would feel that they experienced their share of evil in this world. But, no! they held firmly to the idea that sin must be punished and incorporated this idea into their songs. Many of their melodies illustrate this. None better, perhaps, than the one beginning:

> "My Lord, what a mourning, what a mourning,
>   When the stars begin to fall;
> You'll hear the sinners mourn,
>   When the stars begin to fall."

But their hope in future rewards, or, better, blessings bestowed by a Heavenly Father, was bright and fadeless. We who were born in freedom can never realize how jubilant was the Christian slave in view of death. It was release. It was victory.

Heinrich Heine, the witty scholar and poet, speaking of his return to the Bible and its sources of consolation in the last years of his life, uses the following remarkable language:

"The re-awakening of my religious feelings I owe to that Holy Book, the Bible. Astonishing! that after I have whirled about all my life over all the dance-floors of philosophy, and yielded myself to all the orgies of the intellect . . . without satisfaction, I now find myself on the same standpoint where poor Uncle Tom stands— on that of the Bible. I kneel down by my black brother in the same prayer! What a humiliation! . . . Poor Tom, indeed, seems to have seen deeper things in the Holy Book than I. The poor Negro slave reads with his back and understands better than we do." Heine had discovered the truth that physical suffering often brings clearer spiritual vision. Paul scourged, was Paul triumphant. John in exile, was John in the Spirit. These physical hardships prepared the Apostle the better for the glories of the spiritual revelation. So these Negro slaves had no light on earth, but the glories of the Son of Righteousness burst through their gloom, and lighted and warmed and thrilled them. In view of death they broke in triumphant song as they sang of

> "Those bright mansions above,
>   Bright mansions above:
> Lord, I want to live up yonder,
>   In bright mansions above."

Their life was full of misery here, but they looked forward with confident expectation and sang:

> " Wait a little while, then we'll sing the new song;
>   Wait a little while.
> My heavenly home is bright and fair,
>   We will sing the new song.
> No pain nor sorrow enters there,
>   Then we'll sing the new song."

We can understand some of the references in their songs to peculiar victories and delights in the heavenly country, only by understanding the customs that prevailed in times of slavery. Take this one: The young men of neighboring plantations were accustomed to organize and ride over the country to watch the Negroes at night. There might be some one escaping or possibly a danger of general uprising. Now the slaves must avoid these "patroles," as they called them. Even when going out at night for prayer or their revival services, they must avoid detection.

One old Negro told me that he used to hide in the smoke house to pray. A Negro woman related in a most interesting manner her experiences on her master's plantation in attending revival meetings on the river side at night, creeping out from her cabin to avoid the patrol and hounds. Now, in this heavenly country, to which these humble people looked forward, one great blessing would come to them, there would be no "patroles" nor hounds. In daylight fair and full, before the hosts of the redeemed, they could sing and pray and shout. How they gloried in this thought in their songs!

> "Shine, shine, I'll meet you in that morning,
> O my soul's going to shine, to shine;
> I'm going to sit down at a welcome table,
> Shine, shine, my soul's going to shine."

> "I'm going to walk all about that city,
> Shine, shine, my soul's going to shine."

Or, another, the refrain of which runs:

> "Chiluns, chiluns, we all shall be free,
> Chiluns, chiluns, we all shall be free,
> When the Lord shall appear."

Or that other sweet, weird song that charmed crowded audiences on both sides of the ocean, and that Mr. Gladstone himself called for whenever he heard the Jubilee singers in England. "Swing low, sweet chairot, coming for to carry me home."

> "I looked over Jordan, and what did I see?
> Coming for to carry me home.
> A band of angels coming after me,
> Coming for to carry me home."

To those who were crowded in unwholesome dungeons, waiting the auction block, or were packed in the foul hole of some Mississippi steamer, to be released only as they went to the miseries of sugar plantations or rice swamps, crudely mingled with their ideas of heaven was the comfortable thought that they would be no longer harassed and annoyed and crowded, and they sung:

> "For my Lord says there's room enough,
> Room enough in the heavens for you,
> My Lord says there's room enough,
> Don't stay away."

But my object is not to illustrate their hymns, but to get if possible from them their conceptions of fundamental religious truth.

One other thought. These hymns are remarkable not only for what they contain, but also for their omissions. 1st. We have in these plantation songs no mariolatry. Many Negroes belonged to Catholic masters. In Louisiana, about New Orleans, I have attended many meetings held by these Negroes. I have never heard, nor have I found anywhere in these plantation melodies, any which sung the praises of the Virgin. Such a figment of a theological brain does not have power in it. It needs the truth to take hold of humble souls and become an inspiration in their songs. 2d. We note with wonder the entire absence of all vindictiveness in these melodies. This certainly is a marvelous fact. Downtrodden, abused, sold from kindred, outraged in every way; it would seem more than human if there did not run through these songs, coming from their bleeding hearts, an undertone of vindictive satisfaction that their masters must suffer under a just God due recompense for these bitter cruelties, but you scarcely find a trace of it. There seems a hint of it in "Turn back Pharoah's army, Hallelu!"

> "When Moses smote the water,
> The children all passed over,
> And turned back Pharoah's army, Hallelu!
> And turned back Pharoah's army, Hallelu!

> "When Pharoah crossed the water,
> The waters came together,
> And drowned ole Pharoah's army, Hallelu!
> And drowned ole Pharoah's army, Hallelu!"

But this is rather the triumphant song of a black Miriam, taking the timbrel as she "sings unto the Lord, for he hath triumphed gloriously, the horse and the rider hath he thrown into the sea." This Negro song heralded the victory of God over his enemies, not over theirs. And we find them, even in the crude language of these plantation songs evidence that among these uneducated millions of Negroes there is a sound and wholesome belief in the great fundamental truths of Christianity. 1st. That God governs the world. 2d.

That Christ is divine. 3d. The fact of the necessity and efficacy of the Atonement. 4th. Man's lost and ruined condition. 5th. The need and possibility of conversion and regeneration. 6th. Progress in the Christian life. 7th. Future punishment of sin and the rewards of faith and obedience. We mark also the absence of the mischievous doctrines of the Romish Church, and also all vindictive bitterness.

We can assume that these truths are in the hearts of the people whom we seek to reach as we push forward our church work. For around us there lie unreached millions of black Americans; across the ocean the uncounted millions of heathen Africa; these are to be saved under God by the *Negroes of America*. What a prospect! What an inspiring work! What a blessed God-given opportunity to the churches of America!

You remember that scene between Cassy and Uncle Tom, unmatched in other profane literature, when Cassy having unsuccessfully urged Uncle Tom to kill that monster Legree, determined to do it herself. With flashing eyes, her blood boiling with passion long suppressed, the abused Creole woman, robbed of womanhood, exclaims, "His time is come, and I'll have his heart's blood!"

"No, no, no," said Tom, holding his small hands which were clenched with spasmodic violence. "No, ye poor lost soul, that ye mustn't do. The dear, blessed Lord never shed no blood but his own, and that he poured out for us when we was his enemies. Lord, help us to follow his steps, and love our enemies."

"Love," said Cassy, with a fierce glare; "love *such* enemies! It isn't in flesh and blood."

"No, Miss, it isn't," said Tom, looking up; "but he gives it to us, and that's the victory. When we can love and pray over all, and through all, the battle's past and the victory's come, glory be to God!" And, with streaming eyes and choking voice, the black man looked up to heaven.

"And this, Oh, Africa! latest called of nations, called to the crown of thorns, the scourge, the bloody sweat, the cross of agony, this is to be thy victory; by this shalt thou reign with Christ when his kingdom shall come on earth."

NATURE.

BY ELIZABETH L. JACKSON.

COME with me into the haunts of nature. Hand in hand let us tread her rural solitudes, roam through her beautiful valleys and majestic forests, climb her sublime mountains and, standing upon their lofty peaks, behold the world with its ever-changing scenery stretched out before us; descend into her seas and view the beautiful, wonderful things there. Let us wander through her lovely dells and beautiful meadows, sprinkled with the lovely daisies and modest violets; across the babbling brook, over hill and dale, by murmuring rill and gurgling spring, over rolling prairie and level field; now through fields of ice and snow and now through balmy fields radiant with blossoms and fruit; now where the north wind whistles over treeless plains and now where the south wind gently stirs the lovely flowers and whispers softly through the beautiful trees dressed in green.

The coal that gives us heat, the iron that supplies so many needs, the gold, silver and diamonds we use for ornament, the copper that is put to so many uses, and many other useful metals have been cradled in the bosom of the earth for ages. How harmonious is nature in all her workings, from the earth in whose bosom countless riches have been locked for ages to the beautiful sky, radiant by day with the refulgent rays of the sun and by night spangled with the lovely stars and bathed in the pure, pale light of the moon; from the murmuring rills and babbling brooks to broad rivers flowing between their fertile banks; from the lakes to the sea, whose waves roll over priceless treasures; from the mountains, rearing their proud heads heavenward, to the valleys in their peaceful rest; from the snowbound North to the sunny South.

How sublime yet how awful are the hurricanes that sweep houses from their track, uproot the giants of the forest, lay low even the rocks in their path; the cyclones that rise and dip, and dip and rise, carrying houses and trees in their course; the storms whose lightnings flash and thunders roar; the volcanoes belching forth fire, smoke, lava and rocks.

As we contemplate the work and workings of nature, who, we ask, made the laws that govern nature? As we stand by Niagara and hear its booming thunder, who, we ask, gathered the mighty waters and sent them whirling, rushing and leaping a hundred feet downward? Who guides the sun in his cause? Who gives the moon her stated time to rise and set? Who guides the stars in their trackless path across the sky? To all these questions we answer God. His are the laws that govern nature; his the hand that holds back the boundless billows of the deep, that gives the tints to the lovely flowers and the color to the fragile ferns. In nature's haunts can be found food for the artist, thought for the poet, ideas for the sculptor, inspiration for the musician, reflection for the thoughtful.

To the lover of nature she is beautiful at all times; as beautiful when the earth is wrapped in her winding sheet of snow and the branches of the trees are bending beneath icy freight, and glistening in the sunlight like diamonds as when the trees are dressed in green and laden with blossoms and fruit, when the wheat fields are gently stirring in the soft summer breeze, and the corn gently rustles in the playful zephyrs, and when the hay fields are filled with fragrant, new-mown hay. If you be a true student of nature, you should study when the winds blow bleak and cold, as well as when the soft summer zephyrs woo you to indolence and ease. There is much that we may study in nature. Here we find a lofty oak, proud, strong, defying the storms that rage and roar about it; the tender ivy clinging closer as it mounts higher, teaching us the lesson as we mount higher in our Christian life to cling closer to God.

By studying nature you can be better able to fulfill the duties that rest upon you, for by this study the mind is exalted and purified. Study nature, make nature a daily study; study nature so that in her humblest children beauty may be found. If we study nature thus earnestly, and submit ourselves to the will of Him whose laws govern nature, when we come to cross the dark river we will sweetly glide from the arms of nature to the arms of nature's God.

HUMANE EDUCATION.

BY MISS C. M. THOMPSON.

HOW many of us know that blinders are almost intolerable "and cause thousands of accidents because the horses are thus prevented from seeing behind them?" How many men who hire a hack on Sunday—or any other time for that matter—think that in their zeal to get their money's worth out of the turnout, they are driving some poor, tired horse until he is almost ready to drop from exhaustion? How many boys and girls know that constant twitching at the reins, indulged in by most inexperienced drivers, is almost unbearable by the poor horse? Ah! it is facts such as these that we should impress upon the children's minds and hearts. To every true teacher, minister and parent come with irresistible force the words of Longfellow:

> "How can I teach my children gentleness
> And mercy to the weak, and reverence
> For life, which, in its weakness or excess,
> Is still a gleam of God's omnipotence?"

Allow me to quote here from *Our Dumb Animals*, a monthly paper published by the Massachusetts Society for the Prevention of Cruelty to Animals.

"*Query.*—What is the use of teaching kindness to animals in schools and in Sunday schools? *Answer.*—The eminent French teacher, Du Sailly, says that when he began to teach kindness to animals in his school, he found that his pupils became not only kinder to animals but kinder to each other. In a large Scottish public school at Edinburgh, out of about seven thousand pupils carefully taught kindness to the lower animals, it was found that not one had ever been charged, after going out into active life, with any criminal offense in any court. Out of two thousand criminals inquired of in American prisons some years ago, it was found that only twelve had any pet animal during their childhood. Edward Everett Hale says: 'We are all in the same boat, both animals and men. You cannot promote kindness to the one without benefiting the other.' Every kind act we do, every kind word we speak, which adds to the happiness of others also adds to our own happiness; and when we teach the boy and girl to be doing these kind acts and saying these kind words a hundred times a day to the lower animals, are we not teaching that which will make their own lives happier?"

I have quoted thus extensively because I want to get this matter before you in the strongest light possible, and I see no better way than by using George T. Angell's vigorous words. It makes my heart ache to see how the lower creation is misused and abused by man, the proud monarch of them all. How useful are these creatures to us—how dependent upon them are we for so many articles of food, clothing and shelter! How grateful, too, are they for any kindness! We have never found a Judas among the lower creation. What more useful friend has man than the cow—and how cruelly is it often dealt with! Says George T. Angell, President of the American Humane Education Society: "I have stood in slaughter houses and witnessed scenes which compelled me to leave or drop fainting on the floor. I have seen hundreds of cattle compelled to stand and see other cattle killed and dressed right before their eyes and knowing that their turn was coming next." Great God! how horrible! Do all of us, who, following the craze made the fashion by Izaak Walton, know that the fish we lucky anglers take out of the stream suffer from lacerated mouths and the removal from their native element, and should be put out of pain at once by a sharp blow on the back of the head? Indeed, it is a law as unalterable as nature that "every pain which an animal suffers before dying poisons the meat." How many boys, and girls too, are given to robbing birds' nests? Would not "a word in season" work wonders in opening their eyes to the cruelty of such conduct? The wanton slaughter of birds in order to procure feathers for ornament seems about to depopulate the forests, and it is a grand move on the part of the Princess of Wales, the Dutchess of Portland and other ladies of high rank, who, in order to stop this cruel work have pledged themselves to wear no feathers save those of the ostrich, "now, henceforth and forever." The dog, called by some, man's most faithful friend; the cat, beloved by such men as Cardinals Wolsey and Richelieu; the toad, rendered illustrious by Shakespeare, which with its fellow sufferers, the bat and the owl, destroy myriads of insects which infest the fields and would blight vegetation—all these have proved their friendship to man "by their works," and he should have gratitude enough to treat them with some little consideration.

"The quality of mercy is not strained," says Portia; and even when we are compelled to kill creatures that are harmful, we need not cause them unneccessary suffering. "Kind hearts are more than coronets," sings Tennyson; and it should be the aim of every instructor of youth to make his pupils kind-hearted. Kindness to animals indeed begets kindness to our fellow-men, and the cruelty fostered in the heart by some act of unkindness to a defenseless animal will break out some day in cruelty to one's fellow-men. Teach the young people kindness to animals. Petition the School Board, if it be necessary, to allow you to form Bands of Mercy among your pupils. Train their young minds to be compassionate, to be forbearing, to be merciful. Constitute yourself the champion of the weak, and arouse in them a chivalrous regard for the defenseless. The lessons learned from you relating to the mercy to be excised toward the dumb beasts may develop into the deep-rooted, abiding principle which shall keep them from doing acts of violence and bloodshed. There is a bond between humanity and the lower creation which few of us acknowledge, and none of us can comprehend. Kindness grows by what it feeds upon, and so does cruelty. Knowing this, how untiringly we should strive to inculcate kindness into the minds and hearts of our pupils! Implant in them the spirit of kindness, and the influence will be felt to all eternity. In the words of Sidney Herbert:

> "Open thy lips and speak;
> Protect the dumb and weak;
>   Their cause maintain.
> Why should we them abuse?
> Why these kind friends misuse?
> O let us never choose
>   To give them pain."

A grand, cultivated brain is a great thing, but a grand, cultivated heart is better. It is well to know the Rule of Three, it is well to be able to analyze water, it is well to know all about the government and people of Tahiti, it is well to be able to tell the distance to the sun and to "call the stars by name," but it is far, far better to be a good, true, noble man or woman, with heart "full of the milk of human kindness," and life spent in harmony with God's own plan. Our ambition should be to make good citizens, rather than brilliant scholars. Work upon the children's better natures, so that they will become imbued with the spirit of kindness, and show it in every act of their lives. So may we lessen much suffering, and have a conscience and mind at ease.

> "A man of kindness to his best is kind,
> But brutal actions show a brutal mind.
> Remember, He who made thee, made the brute;
> Who gave *thee* speech and reason formed *him* mute.
> He can't complain, but God's all-seeing eye
> Beholds *thy* cruelty and hears *his* cry;
> He was designed thy servant, not thy drudge,
> And know that *his* creator is *thy* judge.

MRS. LILLIE ENGLAND LOVINGGOOD, was born in Louisville, Ky., in 1871. After successfully passing through the public schools of Louisville, she spent two years at Knoxville College finishing the normal course. Her career at college was marked with great success. Earnest, studious, diligent, she ranked among the best students of the school, loved and respected by all. In 1889 she won the A. E. T. Draper medal of the college for general scholarship and elocution. After her graduation she taught successfully in the public schools of Birmingham, Ala., until Christmas, 1894, when she was happily united in wedlock to Prof. R. S. Lovinggood, a graduate of Clark University, Atlanta, Ga., who was then and is now Principal of Cameron Public School, of Birmingham, Ala. In 1894, she passed an examination which entitled her to a life-time license to teach in Birmingham, Ala. Mrs. Lovinggood is a constant and voluminous reader, devouring dry history with almost as great relish as "Hypatia" or "Le Miserables." She is a devoted Christian and an excellent musician. She has become imbued with the feeling that she has a great mission to perform in the elevation of the race on the line of literary work, social purity, economy, etc. May we not confidently expect great things from this able young lady of the race?

THE product of the wax tree of the Andes cannot be distinguished from beeswax.

WOMAN'S WORK IN THE ELEVATION OF THE RACE.

BY MRS. LILLIE ENGLAND LOVINGGOOD, BIRMINGHAM, ALA.

IN speaking of the race, we speak in general terms, and by it we mean the race of mankind, Jew or Gentile, black or white, male or female. We conceive of no inherent difference in the races. Are not all men prompted by the same impulses of right and wrong, love and hate, happiness and misery? Did our beneficent Father in the creation when he commanded the first man and the first woman "go forth and multiply" have it in his heart to make any discrimination in his children? Were we not all created in his own image? We all sprang from the same great Spirit, however much men may seek to deny the fact. Our physical make-up is the same, no matter from what nation we sprang. It is unnecessary to expatiate on the advantages of the higher civilization, how it makes one nation become the ruler of another, *et cetera*. The fact remains that we carry within us, be we ever so savage, the possibilities of greatness. It takes only the advantages of the higher civilization to bring to a happy fruition these latent possibilities.

Since the Ruler and Maker of the universe made us all of one blood, all that he did was for the good of all mankind. So it is, the race is a general term. Whatever of good one nation has accomplished is of help and profit to another. We all profit by the experiences of others. The road to greatness is by emulating the example of those truly great and good. The male of the human race has from the earliest times been its main benefactor in whatever line we take it. He has given us our laws, has explored from the earliest ages the vast fields of the sciences, has reveled in the mysteries of ancient lore; in fact he has well-nigh had a monopoly of everything, and rather enjoyed monopolizing all the fields of usefulness and learning. So much so that the many restrictions thrown around woman had well-nigh crushed out all ambition or desire to be anything but a slave to man's wishes. Her sphere of action was proscribed. Only here and there in the history of the earlier times do we find an occasional woman chafing in her bonds, longing for a breath of free air, and finally escaping the thraldom of ignorance.

In enumerating some of those women who have been of inspiration to a people we cannot refrain from mentioning Miriam, the Jewess and Prophetess of Israel. Her very name was an inspiration to the Jews; the Queen of Sheba, Sappho the Greek, and Joan of Arc, have played conspicuous parts in the history of the world. Charles Kingsley gives us an excellent illustration of the character of woman in his Hypatia.

In more recent times the work and labors of Florence Nightingale, have been of an incalculable value to the world. Woman played a drastic part in the anti-slavery cause in this country. There were Lydia Maria Childs and Harriet Beecher Stowe who fairly electrified two continents by their graphic and realistic portraiture of slave life and its attendant horrors. Miss Frances E. Willard in the temperance cause, Susan B. Anthony and her co-laborers have worked for Woman's Suffrage, and the cause grows. Already woman has a full ballot in a number of our States and many vote on school questions in quite a number of other States. They have surmounted almost insuperable barriers and are now taken for their true worth.

Let us now speak more specifically of the Negro woman. What are her possibilities for usefulness? Is she less capable than other women? To all of which we affirm she is as capable as her sister in white. She is fired with the same ambitions, her sense of right and wrong are just as acute, she experiences the same emotions of love and hate, joy and sorrow. Her piety and love for God are as sincere.

What has she done? We have some among the race who have run well. Sojourner Truth stood at the side of Douglas and Garrison; Phylis Wheatley, by her intellectual power, extorted praises for her literary genius. The work of Miss Ida B. Wells cannot be estimated. There are others, worthy women, that could be named.

The Negro woman, while being capable, is less fortunate than her white sister. She lacks money, a very necessary factor; then, too, prejudice prevails. But shall her poverty make the Negro woman less active? Shall prejudice dampen, and finally quench her ambition? Is it possible that she will sit down merely lamenting her sad condition, and make no effort to the amelioration of it? No. She must bestir herself and be up and doing. It is a case of Mahomet and the mountain. If the mountain will not come to you, then you must go to the mountain.

We have need for good, faithful women, women of broad culture, women with sympathy for the distressed condition of our people. Many there are longing and thirsting for knowledge, desiring to be fed. What then can she do? What is her duty?

1. If the hand that rocks the cradle rules the world, the home is a great field for woman. The Negro race need homes, not hovels and pens. Christian character is built most largely there. Beautify the home, make it cheerful and cultured. Be economical in expenditures. Cultivate economy in all lines. Be thrifty and industrious housewives.

2. We do not confine woman's work to the home. Her sphere is any where she can do good. As women are doing most of the teaching now, here is a vast field for her activity that should be well cultivated. Next to the home the school room is probably the greatest factor in character building. As Daniel Webster once said: "If we work upon marble, it will perish; if we work upon brass, time will efface it; if we rear temples they will crumble into dust; but if we work upon immortal minds, if we imbue them with principals, with a just fear of God and love of our fellow man, we engrave on those tablets something that will brighten to all eternity." Teachers, be faithful.

3. Reform in mode as well as quality of dressing. Dress neatly and well if your income will allow. One can always be neat and clean, however. It is certainly a miserable mistake that makes the majority of our people think that they must dress so as to be conspicuous for blocks away, wearing hats that are veritable flower gardens. Tight lacing should be abandoned by all sensible women.

4. Social Purity among our Girls. The thinking, solid women of our race ought to take some steps to save the young girls of our race, especially that vast throng in the larger cities, who have no gentle home influences; thousands are being dragged down to destruction every year. Raise the fallen, and so fulfill the law of Christ.

5. Industrial Schools. Teach dressmaking, cooking and housewifery generally. These can be established with little or no capital. One may be mentioned who has entered this field, **Lucy Laney**, of Augusta, Ga.

6. Professional and Literary Work. Women should study medicine, law, music, elocution and become the best in those professions. Write books, poetry, history, etc. Do not be content to be ornamental alone. Let us not cultivate our tastes for the merely frivo-

lous. Let us rather rejoice in doing good for our weaker brothers and sisters. The good results of labor for good will bid us hope for a better and brighter future, a future in which the homes of refinement and culture will predominate. Is it too much to hope for such a happy result after years of self-denial and toil? We think not.

The women of the race then, whatever parent, teacher or in whatever sphere of life their lot is cast should pursue that plain path of duty. Some will say, "What recompense shall I have for all my years of self-denial and toils? our people are ungrateful, etc." True, they are a little ungrateful; and true there is nothing "so unkind as man's ingratitude;" yet our duty is obvious and we would be very selfish if we held back for that consideration. What is done should not be done with a view to notoriety, but with the desire to accomplish good results from our labors. Sometime in the near or distant future our reward will come if we faint not. We urge the women of the race to action. The words of the sweet singer, Longfellow, are wonderfully befitting:

> "Let us then be up and doing
> With a heart for any fate;
> Still achieving, still pursuing,
> Learn to labor and to wait."

THE EMANCIPATION OF WOMAN.

BY LUCINDA W. GAMBLE.

FROM time immemorial, woman has been a subject for voice and pen. Volumes have been written on the progress of woman. Speeches many have been delivered in defense of her rights. Biographies of great women have been written. Why has so much attention been paid to woman? It is because of the importance of the influence she has had in shaping the history of the world. In the different stages of the world's history, the regard in which woman has been held has varied greatly. In the earliest stages she was very highly regarded. Some of the earlier people were noted for the respect and attention they paid to their women. Later this regard seemed to fade away and women were respected only in so far as they could be made use of to aid the men, and to provide for their happiness. The idea of woman being created for anything other than to be a slave for man was lost sight of. She was denied the privilege of every accomplishment, especially that of learning. For awhile learning was locked up, so, to say, from the mass of the people, but it was not so effectually locked up that it remained out of their reach. Gradually it became unlocked and within reach of the people, at least the sterner element of the people. It was not thought necessary for those of the weaker element to have much of an education. At first it was thought they might become too knowing and wise.

All efforts were turned to educate the boys; to teach them trades; in short to thoroughly equip them for fighting life's battles. The young girls were refused admittance to colleges and all higher institutions of learning. Some colleges to this day refuse to admit women. But such an advance has been made, such a change has wrought, that now a woman can stand almost on a level with man, and so she should. Truly it has been said that the degree of civilization reaching a people is measured by the respect and attention it pays to its women. Since woman has been allowed to influence the affairs of the world, what has she not done? Since she has been allowed to know and learn something of the world in which she lives, its people, customs, manners, art, literature and music, has she not been an invaluable factor in the world's progress?

We now find woman engaged in almost every profession. Her influence is felt in every avenue of life. We find her not unhonorably filling the lawyer's position. We find her successful as physician and druggist. How invaluable is she for the success of many of the newspapers and journals of the day; many of which must thank women for their high moral tone, and often for their best articles and editorials. Literature is very greatly indebted to woman. The deep love of purity, truth, and honor so deeply implanted in the nature of every true woman has been very vividly shown in many of the best works of literature we possess. If time permitted, noted instances might be cited.

Her influence in music and art has been of the greatest importance. The influence of woman in her immediate surroundings in the social world and in the religious world cannot but be seen and appreciated. How often has she, by her encouragement and advice, been of invaluable service in times of great distress and doubt. Yet with all the power which has gradually become hers, she has lost none of her charms, none of her grace and sweetness of nature. The hope of a nation lies in its children. Where do we find the most conscientious, sympathetic teachers and trainers of these children? The granting to woman the aforenamed privileges has in no way made her less fit to reign like a queen in that most blessed place of all places, "Home." "The hand that rocks the cradle rules the world." Should not the owner of that hand be allowed every means to become all that is necessary to make the world better? Is she not better prepared by the power and privileges she is gradually gaining? Is she not enabled to be a far better help-mate and companion to man? thousands of whom have woman to thank for the success they have made in life. Truly we may adopt a quotation of the illustrious poet Tennyson, and say:

"Yet I doubt not through the ages one increasing purpose runs,
Widened is the path of woman with the process of the suns."

—*Omaha Enterprise.*

ADVICE TO YOUNG LADIES.

BY MRS. M. A. McCURDY.

IT is a deplorable fact that, too often many of our women and girls forget what are the real qualifications of a lady, and as such is the case, girls who are compelled to earn their own living, and who have not an over-abundance of money to spend upon clothes, are, it seems, too often apt to spend that little foolishly in a vain display of cheap finery. A girl would look much more ladylike dressed neatly and plainly, with no attempt at ornamentation, which, at the best, give to a lady a cheap and tawdry appearance.

A true lady is, to a great extent, judged by her conversation and behavior when on the street or in any public conveyance. To hear a woman or a girl talk loudly on the street or in a street car, is a practice quite unbecoming and disagreeable, because it is common.

Our girls should beware of the company they keep, for "on the choice of friends our good or evil name depends," and the girl who is seen with common, ill-bred, or rude companions, no matter how ladylike she herself may be, will, as a rule, be judged by them.

The books and papers that a girl reads has much to do in forming her habits and character of conversation. If she reads the poor and trashy books which she finds exposed for sale on many newspaper stands, her mental life will, of necessity, partake of the character of the poor, unwholesome food with which she feeds it. If on the other hand she reads instructive and interesting books and papers, which she may obtain at no greater cost, she will be laying the sure foundation of a good, useful, and happy life in the future.

The question of girls' amusement is a very important one at the present time, because of the silly and vicious attractions that are being offered on every hand, and mothers should see that their girls are not present on all occasions, regardless of the fact that they are accompanied by some intimate gentleman friend, because true enjoyment is not to be found in continually attending places of amusement, but rather in living a quiet, wholesome life, doing one's duty from day to day, reading useful and inspiring books, doing our daily work, striving to do service for Christ on any and all occasions. Then let our girls be modest in their dress, careful as to what and to whom she talks, choice in her selection of books and companions, moderate as to her indulgence in amusements, and she will find that she will not only win the approval of all who causually come in contact with her, but the Lord will greatly bless her, and open ways for her to fit herself for usefulness in honored positions in the ranks of true ladies.

OUR DUTIES.

AS CONCERNS THE FUTURE OF BOYS AND GIRLS.

BY MISS A. C. DAVIS.

DOUBTLESS, there is a calling for every person born unto the world. In infancy the signs of the future man are stamped upon the features, and if we could read them many would be overcome with doubts and discouragements. But God has so limited our knowledge that we are left without a glimmer of the future at that age. Day by day the brooklet winds its way to the mighty deep. Just so we are making our way to man and womanhood, and erelong we will reach the honor which boys and girls so much desire. When a lad, thoughtless and indifferent, he frolics over the compass of life wholly without a thought of the future. We must entreat, coax and sometimes scold, for fear that he will stray from the way in which God said he must be brought. Watch him as he takes a peep into manhood. He begins to think, What must I be when I grow to manhood? What must I do to sustain life? Generally, the first thing to be thought of is a teacher, a preacher, a lawyer, a doctor, etc. There are almost numberless occupations equally as good but considered of less importance. This somehow creeps into the mind at an early age and it has been the means of many a shipwreck in life. "All work is honorable," says one. Then why not be a farmer, a carpenter, a blacksmith, with strong and brawny arms? No! I would rather lean against the sunny side of some building than to soil my already rough hands or disfigure my tattered apparel. There are battles in life which are just as hard for a teacher, a lawyer, or a doctor to fight as the peasant. Do not understand us to say that they should not aspire for said positions, for such are needed in our land and country. But there are many who have been mistaken in their calling. They have not the ability to discharge their duty, to do honor to their position, to make the hearts of those who placed them there glad. Hence it is necessary that the matter be given much thought and prayer. We think when a boy or girl has grown old enough to choose his or her path in this world's "broad field of battle," he or she should have at least a common education mingled with Christianity and a heart full of beautiful thoughts from the lips of a Christian mother. Then he has a guide, sword and shield, and he is prepared to stand the many temptations of the world. Mothers, you are entrusted with these precious gems, which we might call the ruling powers of the world. See that you do not allow them to be led astray and at last they will have a higher calling, probably a call to the duties which angels now perform.

There is a duty for each of us, and why not begin in early life? Young men, creation would be incomplete without you. From the beginning, God made you ruler over every living thing. Do you properly appreciate the kingdom over which you reign? We know that these thoughts do not take hold on you in boyhood, but there is a time when they are fully realized and yet neglected. God has called you because you are strong. Then exercise that strength, both spiritually and temporally.

Young women, there is a duty for you to perform also. It has been well said that "It is easy to judge what the men are, when you know what the women are." Oh, the word woman! We pause to think of the purity and innocence which existed in her when first placed in the garden of Eden. Make society good by your true Christian character, live so that the world may be better for your having lived in it. The path of duty in this world is not all gloom or sadness or darkness and it is only when we turn to the right or left that we are lacerated by piercing thorns and concealed dangers. When we learn that doing our duty will help some poor, weak one, it will strengthen us and we will do more in the interests of our brothers and sisters. When we have a task to perform, we should go about it with a cheerful heart, with an eye single to doing our best; then duty becomes a pleasure. Now having attained man and womanhood let us aim to be first in the pursuit of our life's work; we cannot reach the topmost round at once, and if we get there at all there must be something in us worthy of the upper rounds. Can we ask Him to be our guide who noticed the falling of a sparrow to the ground? Do so; then we will not choose the wrong path, we will not stumble in our darkest hours. We will not think solely of our slavery, of our closing hour or how we will spend the evening, but will put our mind on our duties and resolve that they shall have the best that is in us; and by-and-bye, we shall enjoy the reward which is laid up for the finally faithful.—*Woman's World.*

OBJECT OF EDUCATION,

MORALLY AND PHYSICALLY.

BY LENA R. GOLFIN.

THAT man is a creature of habit no one can deny. What the little child observes its mother do, it instinctively tries to copy. The infant mind is very much like a plate overspread with wax; smooth and unimpressed, yet so sensitive that each touch is mirrored there. Hence we see how important that the whole atmosphere of the home life be such as to leave only impressions for good upon the children committed to our care—education we call it. Our mental, moral and physical growth, to be in harmony, should all grow equally. Were we to educate one to the exclusion of the others we could not expect to build up a perfect man or woman. The prime object in all education is the amelioration of our race; it is the lever that moves the world.

The body is the home of the soul and of the intellect, and it is all important that that dwelling place be a pure and perfect one. In order that it may be so, we must guard our lives and educate each member of our body by strict cleanliness and exercise. We can do much to improve a deformed body, and it is our duty, by athletic exercise, to develop and perfect ourselves. For this reason some system of gymnastics should be enforced in our schools. Then, with a healthful body and pure soul, a sound and cultivated mind, who can say how high we may ultimately rise? In this nineteenth century it is the all-important object in life. Without it we are objects of commiseration and pity. With the proper appreciation and seizure of the opportunities offered us, there is practically no limit to the greatness, goodness and grandeur we can attain. The child is thrice blessed who has a cultivated mother, for she forms the infant mind. She is the God-given guardian of the little feet as they totter in infancy and she teaches the tongue to lisp its first phrases. Be she as great morally as intellectually she it is who teaches it to lisp its first prayer to Him who sitteth between the Cherubim and whose fatherly love is over us all. How grand a thing it is to train the mind; to awaken high and noble impulses, and to lead the child from a contemplation of nature up to nature's God.

God's written word, and the Sunday school, with its excellent system of moral training, where God-fearing men and women strive to lead us to a higher moral plane, where that great command is inculcated, "Love the Lord thy God with all thy soul, with all thy mind and with all thy strength, and thy neighbor as thyself," where lessons of self-forgetfulness are taught and where the soul is enabled to rise on wings of faith from the gross scenes of earth to revel in the bliss of a brighter and better soul. Education raises a nation from barbarism to the highest degree of civilization. All culture must needs be of slow growth to be enduring. We must "make haste slowly." "Line upon line, here a little, there a little" must be our motto. As an instance of what education can do to lift an individual out of the depths and set him upon the proud pinnacle of fame, I refer to the life and history of that great and good man, Frederick Douglass, the noted orator and diplomat, who died at Washington, February 20, 1895. Let his example be followed by all youths in our land. May we ever hold in view the advancement of ourselves, both as individuals and as a whole, until we stand the equal of any.

LIBERTY.

[An essay by Miss Katherine Mitchell, of Washington, D. C., read before the Epworth League at Ebenezer.]

WHAT is liberty? Liberty is a solemn and glorious thought, and when liberty comes it is welcomed. Liberty is something that you and I, and each of us should appreciate as though it was a jewel to us, and that it is. Some of our ancestors had no liberty, and of course they were not a free people, but to-day we have liberty, and are a free people; we must be serious, for we have to do the greatest thing that ever was done in the world, What is it? that is to govern ourselves. Our mothers and fathers have said to us, "The hour is most serious with you children when it passes from parental control into free man and womanhood." Then is our time for thought, and we must bind the righteous law upon ourselves more strongly than our parent ever bound it upon us, and where a people leaves the band of servitude and enters the ground of freedom, that ground must be fenced with law, must be tilled with wisdom, and must be hallowed with prayer. The court of justice, the free school, the holy church must be built there to entrench, defend, and to keep the sacred heritage.

Liberty, I say is a solemn thing. The world up to this day has regarded it as a boon and not as a bond. I believe there is nothing in the present crisis of human affairs, no point in the great human welfare on which our ideas need to be cleared up, to be advanced, to be raised to a higher standard as this grand, terrible responsibility of liberty. In the universe there is no trust so awful as moral freedom, and all good civil freedom depends upon the use of that. But look at it; around every human, every rational being is drawn a circle, the space within is cleared from obstruction, or at least from all restraint. It is sacred to the being, him or herself, who stands there, it is secured and consecrated to his or her own responsibility. May I say it? God himself does not penetrate there with any absolute power. He compels the winds and waves to obey him, compels animal instinct to obey him, but he does not compel man and woman to obey him; that sphere he leaves free; he brings influences to bear upon it, but the last, final, and solemn question between right and wrong he leaves to themselves. Oh! instead of madly delighting in his or her freedom, we could imagine a man or a woman to protest, to complain, to tremble that such a prerogative is accorded to them, but it is accorded to him, and nothing but willing obedience can discharge that solemn trust; nothing but a heroism greater than that which fights battles, and pours out its blood on its country's altars; the heroism of self-renunciation and self-control. We, the young Negro people, should think that it is an honor to us for the Hon. Frederick Douglass to continue speaking of slavery and refreshing our minds of the injustice done to our fathers and mothers. Why? So we can know for ourselves what our parents have been through for us, make us feel that we should be slaves for our parents.

Come that liberty, come none that does not lead to that, come, the liberty that shall strike off every chain, not only of iron laws, but of painful construction of fears, of enslaving passion, of mad self-will; the liberty of perfect truth and love, of holy truth and glad obedience. Come, the liberty that we shall appreciate higher than anything that ever was given to us.

EXTRAVAGANCE.

LIVING beyond his income has been the ruin of many a man. Extravagance is a disease, and be it said to their shame, many professing Christians have caught it. Cotton plaids are no more worn; girls must have silks, and the dressmaker's bill is long as a security debt, and quite as hard to pay. Show and style have bankrupted many a wealthy man, and a poor man who tries to keep apace with so-called "society," is simply a fool. "Cut your coat according to your cloth," is the advice of a philosopher. Spurgeon says, "debtors can hardly help being liars, for they promise to pay when they know they cannot, and when they have made up a lot of false excuses they promise again, and so they lie as fast as a horse can trot." Now if owing leads to lying, who shall say it is not a most evil thing? Of course, there are exceptions to the rule, and I do not want to bear hard upon an honest man who is brought down by sickness or heavy losses; but take the rule as a rule, and you will find debt to be a great dismal swamp, a huge mud hole, a dirty ditch. Happy is the man who gets out of it after once tumbling in, but happiest of all is he who has been by God's goodness kept out of the mire altogether. If you once ask the devil to dinner it will be hard to get him out of the house again. Better have nothing to do with him. When a hen has laid one egg she is likely to lay another; when a man is in debt once he is likely to get into it again; better keep clear of it from the first. He who gets in for a penny will soon be in for a pound. Never owe a dime and you will never owe a dollar."

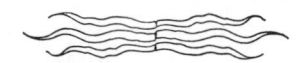

PHILOSOPHY.

A LECTURE BY REV. WILLIAM D. JOHNSON, A.B., A.M., D.D., SECRETARY OF EDUCATION OF THE AFRICAN METHODIST EPISCOPAL CHURCH, ATHENS, GEORGIA.

[Delivered before the Scientific and Literary Institute of the Georgia Conferences, in Bethel A. M. E. Church, Atlanta, Ga., May 24, 1893.]

LOOK out of the window and tell me what you see," were the words of Prof. J. P. Shorter to his class at Wilberforce University last year, during the summer school. One said: "I see a cow;" another, "I see a tree;" a third, "I see a house." "No," said the Professor, "the answer is I see one." Then he proceeded to show that there is no such thing as a concrete number. That same, "one" can be fitted to anything, and we can just as well say, "One man, one horse, one child," etc. Therefore, just what it is behind the appearance of things, and that makes them what they are, it has been the object of philosophy to find out.

PHILOSOPHY DEFINED.

The word philosophy is derived from the Greek *phileo*, to love, and *sophia*, wisdom, and means the love of wisdom. But what is wisdom? You say, wisdom is the best application of knowledge. Still, going into the etymology of the word, we find it made up of the German *wissen*, to know, and the Latin *domus*, a house. Hence, wisdom means knowing what is in the house. The real man lives in several houses—first, in his own body; next, in the clothing he wears; then the house proper; next, the community; the state; after these in time and space; but, above all else, in God; for says the Apostle, "In him we live and move, and have our being." Philosophy, therefore, is an inquiry into the cause and nature of things.

THE PHILOSOPHICAL METHOD.

The word "search" expresses the mode of philosophical operations. It contains the idea of the Latin *circum*, a circle. Circus is the ring where the show performs. Curriculum, the race course, from *curro*, to run, is the notion adopted by the schools to include their range of studies, and you are expected to know all the subjects contained. The primary school, normal school, the college, each has its curriculum, rising higher and growing wider, until we reach the university courses, leading to the highest branches of studies.

"All knowledge begins with the ability to distinguish one thing from another." Therefore, it is said a little child cannot tell its right hand from its left. With this first knowledge, we start out classifying and arranging things until, step by step, we traverse the great fields of art, science, and philosophy. Search, investigate, are the words of command in philosophy. The second word means—follow in the tracks of what you want; and the first one tells how far you are to go.

We are all familiar with the parable of the woman mentioned in the Bible, having a hundred pieces of silver and lost one. She forgot the value of the others in the desire to find the piece that was lost. She drew her circle and determined to investigate. This she did by thinking out a plan and following it. Said she, "I have not been down town, nor into the yard; therefore it must be in this house. I will look all through the house." She did not find it. Next she said, "I shall move every piece of furniture in the house," but was still unsuccessful. "Now," said the woman, taking up her broom, "I shall sweep the entire house, every corner and crevice till I find it." That was fortunate for the house, for some people's houses never in years get such a cleaning up. By this method it was not long till she found it. Then, said she, "Go out and tell my neighbors to come and rejoice with me, for I have found my piece that was lost." This is the same spirit that animated the great philosopher who, after a long and weary search, exclaimed, "Eureka"—I have found it—and this has ever since been the triumphant shout of the successful searcher after truth.

The Field of Philosophy.

Lord Bacon divided the whole field of thought into three knowledges—Nature, Man and God. The knowledge of nature is science with its several great branches—astronomy, geography, geology, biology, etc. The knowledge of man gives us the field of philosophy proper, showing the relations of man to man, to nature and to God. Here we have the great departments of mental philosophy, moral philosophy, political economy, æsthetics, etc. And, lastly, the knowledge of God gives us theology with its sweeping divisions, including theology proper, God in his essential nature, and his relations to the universe; second, anthropology—man in his constitution and relations to God and the universe; and thirdly, soteriology—man as a sinner and the plan of salvation by a Savior. There is no essential difference between science and philosophy. "Science is systematized knowledge." It gives all that may be known upon a particular subject. It is like a bunch of fish—when you lift up the string you raise the whole bunch. "Philosophy is unified knowledge." It embraces every science, and seeks to explore the universe. It is a system of systems, so that when a man has adopted a system of philosophy, there is nothing you can bring to him that he cannot explain by his system of philosophy.

The Reign of Law.

Science and philosophy agree in the fact that everything is included in a reign of law. What then is law? Ask any lawyer and you will get the greatest and simplest definition—"Law is a rule of action." The first law then, is that everything must go. A minister told me that he fell in love with his wife at first sight, and married after six months' acquaintance. "But," said he, "during that whole time I went to see her every day. At four o'clock I was always there." Some young men do not choose that delightful hour to visit, but go later. One young man after a long visit lingered at the gate and the girl began to cry. He said, "Dear, don't cry; I will come to see you again." But she cried on. "O darling, don't cry so; I will be sure to come again." Still she cried. At last he said, "Love, did I not tell you I would soon come again to see you?" And through her tears she replied, "Yes, but I am afraid you never will go; that is what is the matter with me." We must all go. The great sun in the heavens; the moon in her silver orbit; the stars in their glory, keeping time to the celestial music; the winds, the waters, the flowers, the dull clod, iron and flashing steel wherever found—all are moving upon their appointed rounds.

Law shows how things must go. That way they must go or become the means of their own destruction. They are like the railroad trains, the cars must go upon the rails or move at their peril. By examining the term law, we find its essential idea to be what is laid down, fixed. By observing things going we see how they go, how they develop; and by induction, we conclude they will always go that way. That is the law of the thing. When God created the world, he imposed or fixed in each particular thing the law of its being. Take the fire, it is the law of fire that it will always go upward. Try to make the flame burn downward, it goes out, and after much smoke you have no fire. It is the law of water that it will run downward. Try to make water run up hill, and you will have much mud, and after a while you will have to get out of the way of the angry waters. Just so, rising into the range of philosophy, we observe people in their social relations, through long times and various circumstances. Then, taking each one by the hand, in the words of the blessed Savior, we say: "Thou shalt love the Lord thy God with all thy heart and with all thy soul and with all thy mind." This is the first and great commandment. And the second is like unto it: "Thou shalt love thy neighbor as thyself." "On these two commandments hang all the law and the prophets." "Love is the fulfilling of the law." It is the law of the highest social development; and in families, communities, and states, people will be virtuous and happy just in proportion as this law is obeyed. On the other hand, try to reverse it, and misery, crime, and suffering will increase until you create a hell upon earth.

Practical Philosophy.

Uncle Jim was once asked a great question. It was: "If you had to be blown up which would you choose, to be blown up on the railroad or on the steamboat?" "Well," said Uncle Jim, "I don't want to be blowed up no way; but if I had to be blowed up, I would rather be blowed up on the railroad; because, you see, if you is blowed up on the railroad, dar you is, but if you is blowed up on the steamboat, whar is you?" He was practical in his philosophy.

Philosophy teaches us the proper use of knowledge in the explanation of phenomena, and in the practical affairs of life. Not long since a man was telling me about a rabbit. The rabbit said: "I don't blame the man that caught me, but the man that jumped me up." It was noted as a first fact in nature that everything must go. We find it true, however, that man in his physical constitution is composed of matter, and in him as elsewhere, matter has its essential principle called *inertia;* hence man has a tendency to get in one place and stay there. It is a scientific fact that all motion is based upon resistance. From this is derived the familiar formula that "action and reaction are equal." Also, the greater the resistance, the greater will be the motion that is set up. Suppose we put a ball into a gun, and put in a very loose wadding of cotton. The ball will not go very far. But suppose we put in a good charge of powder, then a stout wadding, and ram down the ball so tight that we say to it: "You never shall get out of here!" When shot off the explosion will be terrific, and the ball will leave the gun with corresponding force.

Col. Ingersoll says: "It is not the man who has conquered every time that can boast as a man of courage, but the one who has been whipped the oftenest, and yet comes up to try it again." Bishop A. Grant, D.D., on the same line, says: "If a man wants to know his own strength, he need not measure himself. He needs only to size up the fellows who are pulling against him to find out how strong he is."

THE NEGRO PROBLEM.

When we come to consider the Negro, no race has probably been so oppressed with opposition and resistance. It has been like piling upon us the entire mountain system of the country. Yet, what are the facts? If the Negro had been a weak race, it must evidently have been crushed under this weight of slavery, ostracism, caste, and persecution. If he only survived he would by the law of action and reaction, be as strong as the combined weight of his opposition. But we find that as a race we have been more than equal to the surroundings, for our rapid advance since emancipation, in the march of progress, has become a wonder to the world. Before freedom we used to hear it said: "A nation that has once tasted of liberty can never be re-enslaved." We do not hear it now, but can say it for our own benefit.

BUSINESS.

All movements take place under the law of supply and demand. According to this law "things must move from where they are abundant to where they are needed." The movements of populations come under the same general law. The Negro has been blamed for his lack of integrity and business success. But along these lines there is a mighty improvement. I have just returned from a trip through Tennessee, Arkansas, and Mississippi, and I will tell you something of our people in these States. At the corner of Gilmer and D streets in Chattanooga, Tenn., is the magnificent "Conyers Block," built by Mr. J. F. Conyers, a colored man who left Atlanta six years ago. It is built of fine brick, with marble trimmings, and is three stories high. There are four stores on the first floor; on the second floor eighteen rooms, arranged in suits; and on the third floor is a beautiful hall 72x45 feet, handsomely arranged, and lighted with elegant chandeliers. This building cost $30,000.

In Little Rock, Ark., at the corner of Ninth and Gaines streets, is the "Jones Building," taking up half a block, a three story brick building, with nine stores beneath, the rooms above affording meeting places for all societies in the State. On the corner is the handsome drug store, with George E. Jones in raised letters on the iron doorstep.

There is a colored drug clerk, and four colored physicians with offices in this building. Mr. Jones has several other business places, and is a large owner of real estate.

At Pine Bluff, Ark., we paid a visit to the stables of Mr. Wiley Jones, the owner of the street railroads and other business in that city. He has two horses valued at $10,000 each, and several others at $5,000. To a question, he replied: "I own $50,000 in horse flesh." On leaving, a gentleman said: "Why don't you ask Mr. Jones how much he is worth?" "I do not like to," said I, "but if it pleases Mr. Jones I would like to know." He said: "They tax us pretty lively here, so you may just put me down at $200,000."

At Natchez, Miss., I was in the splendid offices of the "Interstate Mutual Benefit Association," and of the "Mississippi Co-operative Benefit Association." Both are in the great building, corner of Main and Union streets. To look in here you would never suppose that such business places were controlled by colored men. Col. G. F. Bowles is General Manager of the "Interstate Mutual Benefit Association." It employs eighteen men, colored and white, in the building, and has five hundred agents, and an authorized capital of $5,000,000. They print four weekly newspapers, and have more than $5,000 worth of new printing material. Mr. Lewis J. Winston is General Manager of the "Mississippi Co-operative Benefit Association. They employ five men in the office, have twelve traveling agents, and $80,000 out on loan. The authorized capital is $10,000,000. This business is represented by a weekly paper called the *Natchez Reporter*.

EDUCATION.

"Revolutions never go backward." In the matter of education, to say nothing of the race, what has the A. M. E. Church done in this direction? It may almost be said that the A. M. E. Church was born of the new educational movement. The church began its formation in 1787, and in 1796 Bishop Allen had not only commenced the day school work, but had supplemented it with both the Sabbath school and the night school. When Bishop Allen moved into the blacksmith shop, the whole African M. E. Church, as it now is, was wrapped up in him, in an undeveloped form. All of our five hundred thousand members, two hundred thousand Sabbath school children, with $8,-000,000 worth of property, are the outcome of the forces put in operation by him. What shall we say then of the long and herculean labors of the venerable Bishop Payne, Bishops Cain and Dickerson, Bishops Brown and Campbell, Wayman and Ward, to say nothing of the great educational works of our younger Bishops Turner, Gaines, Tanner, Lee, Salter, Handy, of Bishop B. W. Arnett, D.D., President of the Board of Education, and of Bishop Abraham Grant, D.D., your own presiding officer, "the noblest Roman of them all?" These efforts have resulted in Wilberforce Univerity, Allen University, Paul Quinn and Morris Brown Colleges, the Western University, Edward Waters College, and the whole column of forty schools of the A. M. E. Church. In 1892, we had thirty-eight schools; one hundred and thirty-four teachers; four thousand and fourteen students; three hundred and seventy graduates; with $502,650 worth of property under our educational banner.

The Law of Progress.

It is the law of every successful organism, or organization, that every part shall work for the good of the whole. Any failure to do so imperils the life of the organism, or threatens the existence of the organization. This result is not goverened by the will of man, but is a law of life laid down by the Creator. The human race is one organic whole, and every nation is a member of the one body of humanity, subject to a common life and destiny. And when, through the full operation of education and religious rectitude, the peoples of the earth shall be brought into harmonious relations, it will be realized that the good of one is the good of all, so that no man in the universe can be benefited, without extending a part of that benefit to every member of the race.

There is no mistake about the residence of the Negro in America. It is to be hoped that, through the superior advantages and achievements of the race in this great land, "the heart of the fathers may be turned to the children, and the heart of the children turned to their fathers," so that the touch of kinship may lead us as descendants of Africa, to spread the light of Christian education and civilization upon her benighted shores. But just now, the attention of our people is needed at home. I say "home," for as a part of the American people, "we are here to stay"—here in a country set apart as the world's arena for all nations to work out the problem of human liberty. We are among the oldest inhabitants of the land, and everybody wants us to remain. We have a glorious record in peace and in war. We have been raised to the full grade of citizenship, and admitted into the highest functions of the nation. And this is not all—the labor, the business, the art, the science, the philosophy, and the religious teachings of the United States, and the Christian civilization are so many irresistible forces sustaining the claims of American Negroes to full recognition in the common heritage of humanity—a humanity glorified and exalted by the life and teachings of Christ.

Let us, as Negroes, educate—let us survive—let us live up to our opportunities of doing good to ourselves and to others—so shall we work out a glorious destiny upon earth, and contribute our share of the good and great immortals out of every nation, that shall take their places among "the spirits of just men made perfect who are without fault before the throne."

UNIVERSITIES AND COLLEGES.

NAMES OF THE LEADING UNIVERSITIES AND COLLEGES FOR THE BENEFIT OF COLORED PEOPLE, SHOWING THEIR LOCALITY.

1. Jones University..........................Tuscaloosa, Ala.
2. Talladega College (Con.)....................Talladega, Ala.
3. Emerson Institute (Con.)...................Mobile, Ala.
4. Tuscaloosa Institute (Pres.)...............Tuscaloosa, Ala.
5. Tuskegee Normal and Industrial School....Tuskegee, Ala.
6. Central Alabama Academy..................Huntsville, Ala.
7. Philander Smith College (Meth.)..........Little Rock, Ark.
8. Haygood Seminary (Meth.).................Washington, Ark.
9. Helena Normal (Con.).....................Helena, Ark.

10. Wayland Seminary (Bap.), valued at $150,000. Washington, D. C.
11. High and Normal School..................Barton, Fla.
12. Cookman Academy (Meth.), valued at $30,000. Jacksonville, Fla.
13. Florida Academy ....Jacksonville, Fla.
14. Normal School (Con.) ....Orange Park, Fla.
15. Edward Waters College (Meth.)...........Jacksonville, Fla.
16. Atlanta University......................Atlanta, Ga.
17. Clark University (Meth.), valued at $350,000. Atlanta, Ga.
18. Gammon Theological Sem. (Meth.) $100,000. Atlanta, Ga.
19. Atlanta Seminary (Bap.), valued at $50,000. . Atlanta, Ga.
20. Spelman Seminary (Bap), value $147,000.... Atlanta, Ga.
21. Walker Institute (Bap.)..................Augusta, Ga.
22. Paine Institute (Meth.)..................Augusta, Ga.
23. Beach Institute (Con.)...................Savannah, Ga.
24. Dorchester Academy (Con.)..............McIntosh, Ga.
25. Ballard Normal Institute (Con.)..........Macon, Ga.
26. Allen Normal and Industrial School.......Thomasville, Ga.
27. The Holsey Institute (Meth.).............Lumber City, Ga.
28. Chandler Normal (Con.)..................Lexington, Ky.
29. Atkinson College........................Madisonville, Ky.
30. Berea College (Bap.)....................Berea, Ky.
31. Eckstein Norton University (Bap.).........Cane Spring, Ky.
32. Leland University.......................New Orleans, La.
33. New Orleans Univ. (Meth.), value $100,000..New Orleans, La.
34. Southern University ....New Orleans, La.
35. Straight University (Con.)................New Orleans, La.
36. Bebee Institute..........................New Orleans, La.
37. Homer Institute.........................Homer, La.
38. Gilbert Academy (Meth.), value $50,000.....Winstead, La.
39. Morgan College (Meth.), value $100,000.....Baltimore, Md:
40. Jackson College (Bap.), value $35,000.......Jackson, Miss.
41. Meridian Academy.......................Meridian, Miss.
42. Rust University (Meth.), value $55,000.....Holly Springs, Miss.
43. Tougaloo University (Con.)................Tougaloo, Miss.
44. Alcorn Agricultural and Mechanical College. Rodney, Miss.
45. George Smith College (Meth.) $50,000.......Sedalia, Mo.
46. Western Baptist College..................Macon, Mo.
47. Gregory Institute........................Wilmington, N. C.
48. Washburn Seminary.....................Beaufort, S. C.
49. Riddle University (Pres.).................Charlotte, N. C.

50. Shaw University (Bap.) valued at $175,000..Raleigh, N. C.
51. Livingstone College (Meth.)................Salisbury, N. C.
52. Bennett College (Meth.)....................Greensboro, N. C.
53. The Agricultural and Mechanical College...Greensboro, N. C.
54. Shiloh Institute...........................Warrenton, N. C.
55. Carr Academy..............................Norwood, N. C.
56. Skyland Institute.........................Blowing Rock, N. C.
57. Saluda Seminary...........................Saluda, N. C.
58. Wilberforce University (Meth.)............Wilberforce, Ohio.
59. Allen University..........................Columbia, S. C.
60. Claffin University........................Orangeburg, S. C.
61. Brewer Normal.............................Greenwood, S. C.
62. Avery Institute (Con.)....................Charleston, S. C.
63. Benedict College (Bap.)...................Columbia, S. C.
64. Central Tennessee College (Meth.) $125,000. Nashville, Tenn.
65. Rodger Williams College (Bap.) $225,000....Nashville, Tenn.
66. Fisk University (Con.) $350,000............Nashville, Tenn.
67. Le Moyne Institute (Con.).................Memphis, Tenn.
68. Lane Institute (Meth.)....................Jackson, Tenn.
69. West Tennessee Academy................Mason, Tenn.
70. Morristown Academy....................Morristown, Tenn.
71. Samuel Houston College..................Austin, Texas.
72. Bishop College (Bap.).....................Marshall, Texas.
73. Wiley University (Meth.)..................Marshall, Texas.
74. Hartshorn Memorial (Bap.) $45,000.........Richmond, Va.
75. Virginia Seminary.........................Lynchburg, Va.
76. Morgan College Annex......................Lynchburg, Va.
77. The Virginia Baptist Seminary.............Lynchburg, Va.
78. Female Seminary...........................Burksville, Va.
79. Hampton Normal and Agricultural Institute.Hampton, Va.
80. Virginia Normal and Collegiate Institute...Petersburg, Va.

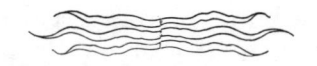

CENTRAL TENNESSEE COLLEGE.

THE Central Tennessee College is situated in the southeastern part of Nashville, on Maple street. This location was chosen because at the time of its purchase no other more suitable property could be bought for a school for the Freedmen, either in Nashville, or any of the principal towns of Middle Tennessee. The school was originally begun as a school for "Refugees," or "Contrabands." In 1865, as soon as the smoke of battle had cleared away, the Missionary Society of the Methodist Episcopal Church appropriated ten thousand dollars for the purpose of establishing a school for the Freedmen in the South. Bishop D. W. Clark, D.D., to whom the matter was referred, visited Nashville, and determined to locate the school in this city. Under his directions the school was opened in Clark Chapel, formerly Andrew Chapel, of the M. E. Church, South, which had been purchased for this purpose, and also for religious services. The school was under the supervision of Rev. John Seys and O. O. Knight, with other assistants. During the year 1865-6, the church became too small. Early in the year 1866 a board of trusees was selected, and a charter from the Legislature of Tennessee was secured. The school was then moved into a building known as the "Gun Factory," on South College street, where it remained for two years. This building had been used by the Federal Army as a hospital, and the Government returned it to the owners. This made it necessary to seek another location. Attempts were made to purchase property, but there being prejudice by the white people against having a school for Negroes in their neighborhood, it was no easy matter to secure such property as was desirable. At length the present site on Maple street was purchased, and the school moved, in 1868, into the only building on the ground, which was entirely inadequate to accommodate the students who attended during the year. The building was repaired during the year, and the chapel and boarding hall erected by the Freedmen's Bureau. These buildings afforded ample room for the school for several years. In 1872 the number of students was such that additional buildings became necessary, and a band of students, known as the Tennes-

MEHARRY MEDICAL DEPARTMENT.

CENTRAL TENNESSEE COLLEGE,
Nashville, Tenn.

seans, sung in the North, and raised nearly all the money for the large, four-story building, which is now the main school building. Other buildings have been added, as the Model School and Webster Hall, the latter used for industrial purposes and dormitories, the blacksmith, carpenter, and machine shops. Other buildings and grounds have been added by purchase. Rev. Bishop Walden has recently purchased what is known as the Hurley Place, joining on the rear of the original purchase, which, with other additions, gives ample grounds for other buildings, which are greatly needed to meet the requirements of the literary departments and African Training School. In 1880 the building for the Meharry Medical Department was opened, and in 1880 the Dental and Pharmaceutical building was first used for these departments.

In its early history, the college was only a primary school. The object was to prepare teachers and preachers as rapidly as possible, to meet the great need for both classes among the colored people. There was an intense desire among the colored people for some education. Some wished to learn to read so they could read the Bible; some because the white folks had given so much time to educate their children, hence, if good for white, it was good for black folks; some because it would help them in business, and some, few in number, because they believed they had minds capable of development, and education would add to their power of usefulness. The school was at first composed of pupils of varying ages, from the "tot" three or four years old to the octogenarian. Children, parents, and grandparents were in the same classes, and the primer, spelling book and first reader were the principal text-books used. As time passed by, these gave place to the higher readers, arithmetics, geographys, grammars, and to pedagogics. Then as these were mastered, the preparatory studies, higher mathematics, natural science, languages, and the full college course of study was introduced. This was the work of years. The first college graduate was Miss Araminta P. Martin, in 1878, who was a member of the school almost from the first, who graduated with honor, and was employed as teacher of Mathematics, Latin, and History until her death in 1883.

As the students advanced in their studies, the query arose, What shall we do? Some said, "We want to be doctors," but there was no medical school open to colored students in the Mississippi Valley. The Meharry family, living in Indiana and Ohio, who were deeply interested in the education of the Freedmen, furnished the means with which the Medical Department was opened in 1875, with Drs. W. J. Sneed and G. W. Hubbard as faculty. This department has had a very prosperous history. The faculty now numbers fifteen, and the students from the first class of eight to one hundred and twenty-one. The Pharmaceutical and Dental Departments have been prosperous. From these departments there have been graduated in Medicine, two hundred and sixty-four; in Dentistry, twenty-one, and thirty in Pharmacy, making a total of three hundred and fifteen.

The Law Department was opened in 1879, with the Hon. John Lawrence in charge. He devoted much care and labor to the instruction of the young men who were desirous of preparing themselves for practice in any of the courts of the States. There have been twenty-five graduates in the law course. Some of them have won very honorable positions in the estimation of the members of the Bar in the courts where they have practiced. They have been fairly well received by the white lawyers, where they have proved themselves competent for the discharge of the duties of an attorney. This department has been of slow growth. The young men who enter this profession must be well prepared to meet their antagonists in trials, where prejudice is so strong against the color line as it is in most parts of the United States. The crowded condition of the profession, and the ease with which white lawyers can be retained, if the fee is only sufficient, make it quite problematical whether the young colored lawyer may not starve before he can get a paying practice. The department, however, seems to be steadily growing, and has already proved that the well educated colored attorney, who is wise in his deportment toward all, and industrious in his preparation of his cases can succeed.

The great need of intelligent preachers for the colored people at the close of the war made it necessary to try to provide for this want as soon as practicable. Hence the earliest work done by the various schools of the church was to provide biblical instruction, and such other theological training as the candidates for the ministry were capable of receiving. The charter of the college requires that a Biblical Department shall be maintained at all times. This department was opened the first year of the school and Rev. John Seys gave such instruction as the candidates were capable of receiving. The course of study was enlarged from time to time so as to embrace the ordinary studies of the theological seminary. The degree of Bachelor of Divinity has been conferred on those who have secured the A.B., before graduating in this department. While only a few have finished the whole course of study in this department, many have enjoyed the privilege of the instructions given, and have been made more useful by the partial course of study which they have been enabled to take. The graduates of this department have occupied very honorable and useful positions in the denominations to which they belong.

The colored people have a musical element in their make up, which was wonderfully manifest in the days of slavery. The strangely moving melodies which they sung in their religious meetings, and also in their cabins, were sources of the great power of endurance which was a striking characteristic of their slave life. These melodies inspired as they were wedded to words as peculiar as themselves, emotion, hope, faith, resignation, joy and through the clouds that shrouded their final triumph and freedom. These songs were sung in the school. Vocal music was taught in the school from its beginning without extra charge, the whole school being considered in music which is demanded everywhere. It is required in the home, the church, the social circle, in the school room, in peace and in war, on earth and in heaven. Music is a science. It must be studied. The Musical Department at first was to direct in the singing the old-time melodies. Then the music of the Sunday school and church was brought in. Soon the desire for instrumental music was expressed, and the parlor organ and piano were added to the course in music. The young people made commendable progress in this delightful art, and soon from humble homes could be heard from these instruments the strains of Sunday school or church music. This was followed by the more difficult music of American and European composers till at length the works of the most renowned authors were executed with great skill and excellent taste by the students in this department. Instruction on the violin has been given and a number of efficient performers on this famed instrument has been developed. Instruction is offered on all orchestral instruments. Voice culture has received considerable attention, and the promise is, that the best voices of the future, and the most renowned singers and musicians in this country may be from among the descendants of the freedmen. The study of harmony and musical composition is a part of the full course. The students make excellent progress in composition, and it would not surprise the world if from this same people should come in the future some of the world's greatest composers. The students have furnished the music for all public occasions, almost from the beginning of the school. Many have become proficient as teachers of vocal and instrumental music. Miss Lula Evans, of Franklin, Tenn., was the first graduate of this course in 1894. The department has the advantage of the best methods of instruction, and is rapidly growing in favor with all who seek its advantages.

The Industrial Department was openend with the carpenter shop, in 1884. Mr. C. S. Randals was the first superintendent. Since that time there have been over two hundred different students who have learned something of the use of tools, and their care, as well as considerable knowledge of the trade. A number have made such progress as to make their living at the trade.

In the blacksmith shop, over fifty have learned how to do much that is done by blacksmiths. In the tin shop, about forty different students have had lessons in soldering and making the usual variety of tin vessels. In the sewing classes over five hundred girls have learned how to do plain sewing, many others, more elaborate needle work, and quite a number have learned the art of dress-making, and are able to make a livelihood in this useful avocation. There has been a class of twenty-four in cooking who made rapid progress in bread making, and other culinary arts. There have been fifty students in the classes of Phonography, who have made some excellent shorthand and typewriters, doing good work for their employers.

This rapid survey of the Industrial Department gives only a cursory view of what has been done. How many homes will be made better, more tidy, more healthful, happier by the lessons taught in this department will be difficult to estimate. But that many will be more useful, more able to meet the responsibilities of life and bear life's burdens more cheerfully and discharge its duties more successfully, cannot be a matter of doubt. The college has been in operation for more than a quarter of a century. It began as a primary school. It is now, in fact, a university. It has sent forth graduates from every department. The English, the Normal, the Preparatory, the College, the Theological, the Medical, the Dental, the Pharmaceutical, the Law, the Musical, the Industrial, the African Training School, have all given their graduates to the world. The world has, we trust, been made better by them, as they have entered upon their fields of labor. In the school room they are successful. They fill the place of primary, intermediate and grammar grades. They are principals of city and high schools. They are professors in colleges and presidents of colleges and universities, and they fill these positions with ability and success. The graduates of the Theological Department have filled the most important pulpits in their respective churches. They have represented their brethren in the highest judicatories of their churches. They have filled the places of agents, secretaries and editors, and have been successful preachers of the gospel of Christ. The graduates of the Law Department have made a favorable impression on the courts where they have practiced, and have given satisfactory evidence that the colored attorney will be able, in the near future, to stand side by side with the best representatives of the bar.

The graduates of the Medical Department have been received with favor in all parts of the country. They have shown themselves capable of discharging the high functions of physicians, dentists, pharmacists. They are recognized by the white doctors as worthy members of this distinguished profession. They have been successful practitioners in their several departments and have made themselves useful to a large area of our country. That they have done good is admitted on all hands. They have given instruction to their patients in reference to the laws of health, also in regard to their homes and methods of improving them. They have attended the people in sickness, and by faithful work have reduced in some places the death rate of the colored people, and have met a great need of intelligent physicians for a poverty-stricken people.

The aim of the school in all departments has been to prepare the students for the practical duties of life. Care has been taken to infuse as far as possible the idea that education and Christianity are very closely related, and that education without religion is not the kind that will best prepare young people for a successful life. Thoroughness in all school work is the aim in teaching and the monthly examinations are intended to aid in securing this end. While the great need of teachers has made it necessary to pay attention to the normal classes, and the necessity for improved preaching rendered important the theological work, the college course has not been forgotten, as leaders of the people must have the best intellectual culture as well as the highest moral character. The college authorities favor a full college course for all who propose to enter any of the professions, and all the students will be encouraged to take the full classical course whenever practicable.

The annual enrollment of students has varied from 150 in 1869 to 676 in 1892. The entire number of students from the organization in 1865 is over 5,000. The number of teachers has increased from three in 1867 to forty-four in 1895. This school is supported by the contributions of Christian people; its education must be distinctly Christian. While under the auspices of the Methodist Episcopal Church, the principles of the Bible are taught without special reference to denominational dogmas. It is expected that students entering any of its departments will cheerfully comply with such regulations as have been found salutary in the past history of the school. The use of tobacco and all intoxicants are forbidden, and such attendance on religious services is required, as a well-regulated Christian family might reasonably require of all its members.

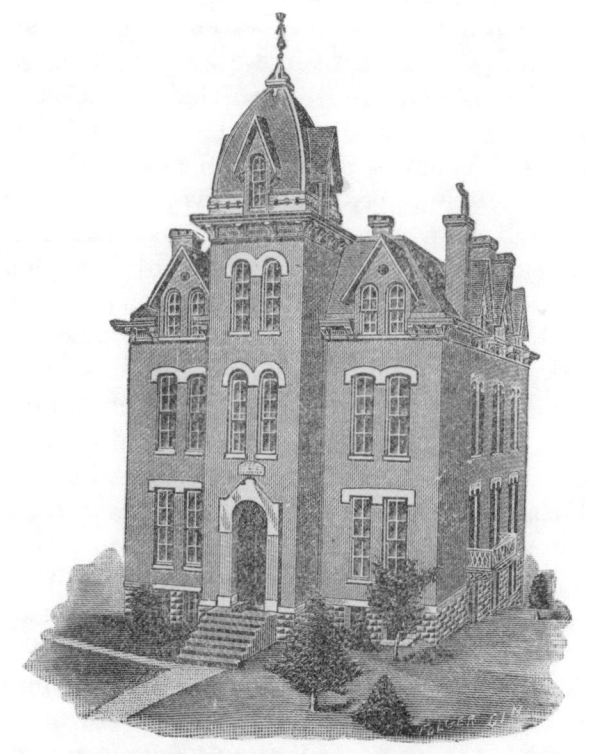

MEHARRY MEDICAL COLLEGE,

The Meharry Medical College was organized as the Medical Department of Central Tennessee College, Nashville, Tenn., in October, 1876. It takes its name from the noble and philanthropic family for whom it is called. The first members of this family who lived in the United States were Alexander and Jane Meharry who were of Scotch-Irish descent, and came to this country in 1794. They lived in Pennsylvania until 1798 when they fitted out a flat boat and floated down the Ohio river and landed at Manchester, Adams county, Ohio. Here, in what was then a dense wilderness, they cleared the forest, built their humble cabin, and raised a family of eight children. The father was suddenly killed on his way home from a camp meeting in 1813 and the care of the family then devolved on the mother who was a woman of great force of character and deep piety.

When the boys grew to manhood, most of them moved to Indiana where they soon had comfortable homes of their own, and by industry and economy accumulated a considerable amount of property. Five of these boys have aided in establishing and supporting Meharry Medical College. Alexander was a minister in the Methodist Episcopal Church; he was admitted to the Ohio Conference in 1841, and for thirty-seven years did faithful work as itinerant minister, presiding elder and financial agent of Wesleyan Female College, of Cincinnati, and the Ohio Wesleyan University. He died at Eaton, Ohio, in 1878; and after his death his widow faithfully carried out the benevolent plans of her deceased husband. Hugh and Jesse died many years ago, leaving most of their property for benevolent purposes. David has recently passed from his labor tn his reward, while Samuel is still living in Lafayette, Ind.

This Institution from the beginning has been under the care of the Freedmen's Aid Society of the Methodist Episcopal Church and its former secretary, Rev. R. S. Rust, D.D., and his successors, Drs. Hartzell and Hamilton have been its firm friends and supporters. We are indebted to the John F. Slater Fund, through its agents, Bishop A. G. Haygood and Dr. J. L. M. Curry for timely and valuaable assistance for many years. This college was the first one opened in the Southern States for the education of colored physicians, and since it was organized 432 students have been enrolled, 263 of whom have received the degree of M.D., and most of them are now engaged in the successful practice of their profession in the Southern States. They have been cordially received by the white physicians who have counseled with them in dangerous cases and assisted in difficult surgical operations.

The success which has attended the labors of the Alumni has been most encouraging, and the professional reputation they have acquired is such as any college might well be proud of. Four of the the graduates have been appointed United States Pension Examiners; one has been Medical Director of the Texas State Colored Asylum for the Blind; two are Professors at the Medical Department of New Orleans University and several are lecturers in different schools and colleges. They have been unusually successful in passing the different County, District and State Medical Examinations before which they have appeared; as far as heard from, every graduate of the class of 1895 has passed with honor the required examinations. A large number have purchased homes of their own, and their professional income is probably greater than that of any other class of colored citizens. There are seventeen members of the faculty, nearly half of whom are graduates of this college.

The character and appearance of the college buildings will be seen by examining the engravings which accompany this article; they are located at the corner of Maple and Chestnut streets and are on the line of the city electric railroad. The main building is constructed of brick, is forty feet wide and sixty feet in length, and four stories in height, including the basement. The ground floor is used as laboratories for practical work in chemistry; the second story for office, museum and dwelling apartments; the third floor contains a lecture room of sufficient size to accommodate one hundred students, recitation room and cabinet of materia medica; the fourth floor is fitted for dormitories.

An additional building has been erected for practical demonstrations in anatomy. The Dental and Pharmaceutical Hall contains a clinical amphitheater capable of seating two hundred students, a Dental Infirmary, Dental Laboratory, two rooms for pharmaceutical work, a laboratory for analytical chemistry and a museum. It requires four sessions of five months each to complete the course of study, which is as follows:

First Year.—During the first year's attendance students will be required to recite daily in Anatomy, Chemistry and Physiology, and work two hours a day in the Chemical Laboratory for ten weeks.

Second Year.—Daily recitations in Anatomy, Materia Medica and Therapeutics; Physiology completed; Analytical Chemistry, with two hours' work a day for ten weeks in the laboratory; Prescription writing; Urinalysis, Toxicology, Elements of Botany and Dissecting.

Third Year.—Medical Chemistry, Materia Medica and Therapeutics completed; Theory and Practice of Medicine; Elements of Pharmacy, Pathology, Bandaging, Physical Diagnosis, Microscopy, Bacteriology, Hygiene, Obstetrics, Medical Jurisprudence and Dissecting.

Fourth Year.—Surgery, Diseases of the Genito-Urinary Organs, Dermatology, Gynæcology, Practice of Medicine, Medical Ethics, Electro-Therapeutics, Mental Diseases, Ophthalmology, Otology, Laryngology, Dissecting, and Review of Anatomy.

Dr. Georgia L. Patton, who graduated in 1893, has for the past two years been serving as a self-supporting medical missionary at Monrovia, Liberia, where she has done most excellent work in that difficult and onerous field of labor. It is expected that in the years to come, many young men and women will be trained in this college for missionary work in the Dark Continent.

MEHARY DENTAL AND PHARMACEUTICAL HALL.

The Meharry Dental Department was opened in 1885, and since that time twenty-two have completed a course in Dentistry and received the degree of Doctor of Dental Surgery.

It was once supposed that the colored people rarely required the services of a dentist. However, that may have been in the past, it is not true now. There is a large and rapidly increasing demand for this kind of work, and in every large city in the South a good colored dentist will find plenty of work, and at least fair remuneration. A most promising and useful field is now open in this profession, and we hope, in years to come, our alumni will occupy it with honor to themselves and credit to their race. This school is now a member of the "American Association of Dental Faculties," and its diplomas receive due recognition wherever they are presented.

Dental Operating Room.

The Meharry Pharmaceutical Department has been in successful operation for five years, during which time thirty-one students have finished a course in Pharmacy, and have been fitted for the responsible position of practical druggists.

There is an increasing demand for well qualified colored Pharmacists; and there is a promising outlook for this department in the future. It requires two years to complete this course.

PHARMACEUTICAL LABORATORY.

During the past session one hundred and two medical, twelve dental, and sixteen pharmaceutical students were enrolled.

The tuition in each of these departments is thirty dollars per session. G. W. Hubbard, M.D., has been the Dean of this college since it was first established, nineteen years ago, and to him all inquiries concerning it should be addressed.

TROY PORTER. The subject of this sketch was born in Fayette county, Kentucky, April 15, 1855. He moved to Illinois early in life, learned the trade of plumbing, gas and steam fitting, and after the expiration of ten years he had accumulated enough to establish a business for himself. His intelligence, industry, and attention to business, made for him a friend of every citizen in Paris. He was appointed superintendent of the water works in 1883, and in 1885 was elected town clerk of Paris, which was the first colored man in the county to be elected to this position.

TOUGALOO UNIVERSITY, TOUGALOO, MISS.

BY PRESIDENT F. G. WOODWORTH, D.D.

THE chartered schools of the American Missionary Association, though doing an essentially similar work, are yet strongly individualized. Tougaloo University is emphatically the black belt plantation school of the Association, located in the country, in midst of America's darkest Africa, touching that by far most

MANSION.

numerous and important class on which the future of the Negroes mainly rests—the plantation Negroes. Forming the bulk of the colored population, least tinged with white blood, they are at once the most ignorant and the most hopeful class. Within seven miles of Jackson, the State capital, on the Illinois Central road, easily accessible, not only from Mississippi, but from large regions of Louisiana and Arkansas, it draws pupils from a wide area and sends its trained teachers and graduates to a region still wider. Its location is healthful and one of beauty, and removed from town distractions and temptations, it is admirably situated for efficient work. The school was established in the autumn of 1869, and

GIRLS' DORMITORY.

BALLARD HALL.

the early reports show a surrounding region which in its drunkenness, fighting and iniquity, is quite in contrast with tne present condition of affairs. Five hundred acres of land were purchased and with them a fine mansion (page 307) then not many years old, intended for the finest plantation house of the State and built for a bride who came not. As the illustration shows, it is a handsome structure—the only one with any decided architectural pretensions in the place. It served at first for school rooms and dormitory purposes, and has been thus used during most of the life of the school. Now it contains the offices of president and treasurer, the main library—which greatly needs more books—music rooms, the doctor's office, teachers' rooms and the president's home. There are

BOYS' DORMITORY, STRIEBY HALL.

now nine large buildings for school use, with several smaller ones. The next oldest of the large buildings is the girls' dormitory, just south of the mansion, where is the common dining room, with the necessary kitchen, laundry and bake house appliances, and dormitory room for several teachers and eighty to ninety girls.

Washington Hall, built just north of the mansion about the time of the *girls' dormitory*, was burned some years ago, and now on its site stands the Ballard Building, containing the study and recitation rooms of the grammar and intermediate departments, which lead up to the normal and the chapel, where all general exercises and Sabbath services are held. One of the greatest needs of the school is a church building, that can be specially devoted to religious purposes. There is a grand chance for a memorial building. A little northeast

THE PLANTATION BARN.

of Ballard is the *boys' dormitory, Strieby Hall*, erected in 1882, a brick structure 112x40 feet, and three stories high, with a basement which has a laundry and bathrooms. In this building the normal and higher work is carried on, with a fairly good physical and chemical laboratory and reference library, but needing great enlargement and additional facilities. The normal work is of chief importance, for the future of the race lies largely with the trained teachers of the common schools. Those who have gone from Tougaloo have won golden opinions from both races and do a work which in its scope and missionary character multiplies greatly the influence of the supporters of the school. Strieby has, by crowding, dormitory room for seventy to eighty boys. A separate building for normal work is greatly needed, one having a library, reading room, recitation room, museums and laboratories. Just northwest of Strieby is the large *barn*, which, with the picture of the cattle, will suggest the large agricultural department of the school with its stock, garden, fruit raising, etc. Here, too, a building is greatly needed for the farm boys and a foreman, where a special course of instruction can be given in fitting out good farmers. Not a few graduates and former students have been successful in the conduct of farms and market gardens, some of them in connection with teaching. Back of the mansion is a little and not at all beautiful building that has been a slave pen, day nursery for slave children; then, under the American Missionary Association, a dormitory known as Boston Hall, then a carpentry class room, then girls' "Industrial Cottage" and is now dignified as *Bible Hall*, and houses the theological department, which was established two years ago. This department has the beginning of a library, but needs books and maps very greatly, and has two courses based on the English Bible, one of two and one of four years. Though having this year but few pupils in the regular course, it is doing very thorough work. The evening class for outside preachers has been for some

BIBLE HALL.

years a power for good. A glance at the picture will convince anyone that theology should have better quarters. Who will give them? *Berkshire Cottage*, of which a picture is given, accommodates the industrial training work of the girls. Here are class-rooms for needlework and cookery, with courses extending over four years, and which all girls in the grammar

BERKSHIRE COTTAGE.

grades are as much obliged to take as they are the English branches. To the normal girls special instruction in dressmaking is given. Berkshire, besides accommodating several teachers, has a kitchen, dining and sitting room, and several bedrooms, devoted to practical housekeeping, where, at present, four girls at a time keep house practically for six weeks at a time, so becoming competent for homemakers. Not far from this cattage is the Ballard shop building, where the manual training of the boys is carried on. Here to the small boys of the Hand school instruction in knife work is given, and to the boys of all higher grades

BALLARD MANUAL TRAINING SHOP.

CARPENTRY.

careful instruction, in accordance with the best manual training methods, in wood-working, with excellent accommodations for more than twenty boys at a time, forging, at which eight at a time can work, and mechanical and architectural drawing, with tables and tools for two dozen. The outcome of this work and of the girls' industries, teachers of which are supported by the Slater Fund, which has done, and is doing, so grand a work, has been most satisfactory and encouraging in the skill manifested, the increased earning capacity imparted, the greater ability to gain and maintain homes, and the development of character.

One other picture, the Hand Primary building, suggests the practical

FORGING.

work of the Normal Department, for here the Normal students have practice during the two closing years of their course, gathering pupils from surrounding cabins.

Underneath all the work of the school is the dominating thought of the development of Christian character. The preaching, the Sabbath school, with its class prayer meeting directed by the Sabbath school teachers, the religious societies, the Covenant for Christian service, the personal influence of teachers and older pupils, all tend in that direction with most blessed results. Upon the surrounding region growing influence is exerted through the four Sabbath schools from two to four miles away, in which teachers and students from the University assist. A picture of one of the schools, McCharity, is given here. Mention should also be made of "Tougaloo University Addition to Tougaloo." One hundred and twenty acres of land have been divided into five-acre house lots, which are being sold at $100 each to former students and those who wish to educate children at the University. In a few years it is expected that a fine community will be there.

Around three great fundamental ideas the work of Tougaloo, with its nearly 400 students and 23 instructors, with its theological, college preparatory, normal, agricultural, industrial, musical and nurse-training departments, its religious work, is grouped and carried on

DANIEL HAND KINDERGARTEN AND PRIMARY SCHOOL.

with notable success. These are the development of the family and home, leadership and pure religious life. Who will endow a chair? Who will endow the University and perpetuate one's influence in a most fruitful way? Successful as Tougaloo has been, its largest, widest work is yet to come.

NOTE BY SECRETARY BEARD.

It would quite repay those who would study the problem of saving these children of the rural districts of the black belt to go far out of their way to visit Tougaloo. They should take time for it, to ride over its broad acres of cultivated land, its cotton fields, its fields of sugar cane and corn, its hay fields, all under the care of those who are being educated. They should see its shops for iron working, wood working, and its varied other industries. They should see those who work by day, diligent students at the books all the long evenings until late. They should see the self-help of all. They

McCHARITY SUNDAY SCHOOL MISSION, OF TOUGALOO.

should go through the grades and notice the quality of the work done and its character, its classes in mathematics and in languages, and its work in the physical sciences. It is a great school —Tougaloo—and if people could see it, they would quote it more for its economy and efficiency. Not always are efficiency and economy found pulling equally in the same harness.

HISTORY OF LIVINGSTONE COLLEGE.

BY PROF. B. A. JOHNSON, A.M.

AMONG the evidences of Negro ability to establish and control great institutions, we have no better example than the Livingstone College. In a quiet, antiquated looking town of historic connection with those stirring times of our American Revolution, is the town of Salisbury, N. C., and in this town is Livingstone College —the pride of a great church and the honor of a noble race.

October the 9th, 1882, the first session of Livingstone College began on its present grounds in the town of Salisbury, N. C. It was then known as Zion Wesley Institute—later it was called Zion Wesley College, and in '86 or '87 became Livingstone College in honor of the African explorer—David Livingtone. It may not be out of place to mention here that the president and faculty felt that in the scope of the work the institution aimed to do, it would be less hampered by the new name. The wisdom of this has doubtless been seen by those intimately associated with the college. As to the early history of the institution the writer wishes to insert the following account, taken from a paper read by Bishop Harris at the Decennial Celebration at the commencement, in May, '93:

"Livingtone College is a monument of the intense yearning of the A. M. E. Zion Church for a thorough education of her children. It also teaches the fact that to maintain an institution of the high grade to which Livingstone College has attained, earnestness and self-sacrifice are required not only of the teachers, but also of the students, and of the church which is to maintain it.

Incorporated in 1879 under the name of Zion Wesley Institute, and depending almost exclusively upon the collections from the churches in the bounds of the North Carolina Conference, after two sessions at Concord, N. C., it was compelled to close its doors. Livingstone College, the successor of Zion Wesley Institute, would not now be in existence, but for the fact that at the close of the Ecumenical Methodist Conference, held in England, in May, 1881, the able and far-seeing Bishop President of the Board of Trustees of Zion Wesley Insti-

BIRD'S EYE VIEW OF LIVINGSTONE COLLEGE—BUILDINGS AND GROUNDS.

tute, saw the swelling of the tide, which, taken at the flood, would lead on to fortune. He prevailed upon Rev. J. C. Price, a delegate to the conference from the A. M. E. Zion Church, to remain in Europe and solicit funds for the Institute, then holding its second session under the instruction of Prof. A. S. Richardson.

"The agent thus selected, already known as an eloquent orator by his speeches during the session of the Ecumenical Conference, was heartily welcomed everywhere, and by well directed plans, secured an amount which finally footed up to $9,100. Seeing the agent so highly successful, the trustees of the Institute, though offered a tract of seven acres by the church at Concord N. C., concluded that Salisbury would be a more favorable site, and located the Institution at that place.

"In the spring of 1882, Bishops J. W. Hood and T. H. Lomax, trustees, visited Salisbury, and with $3,000 from England, supplemented by $1,000 donated by business men of Salisbury, with the influence of Mr. M. L. Holmes, purchased the premises we now occupy. It consisted of a two-story building, with a basement, containing ten rooms, with forty acres of land, the total cost of which was $4,600.

"In September, 1882, at the bishops' meeting at Chester, S. C., Zion Wesley Institute came under the fostering care of the entire connection. Mr. Price made a complete report of his doings in Great Britain. A suitable remuneration was voted him, and the faculty chosen, with Rev. J. C. Price, President; Rev. C. R. Harris and Prof. E. Moore, as Assistant Teachers, and Mrs. M. E. Harris, as Matron.

"In the next month, October 9th, 1882, was opened on its premises in Salisbury with five day students the first day. About the middle of the month in came our first student from abroad, Miss Lizzie Williams, Newbern, N. C. A week or so later, five students were sent from Beaufort, N. C., by one of the trustees of the Institute, who was so zealous in securing students that some of them were unprepared to pay their board. How erroneous and damaging the presumption that an unendowed school is able to give instruction and board free. We kept them, however, and did the best we could, but the precedent was a bad one, and hundreds, if not thousands of dollars are now due the institution for unpaid board of students.

"Students from town and from abroad continued to come. A pressing need arose—the want of room. The girls were crowded in rooms having two beds each, and were sometimes obliged to sleep three in a bed. A new building, 16x40, was erected for the boys. This session closed with ninety-three students.

The President being required to travel and solicit donations, another teacher was needed. A friend of the President, Rev. W. H. Goler, attended our commencement, or closing exercises, as they were then modestly called. He preached the annual sermon and at the conclusion of the address of the orator of the day, Bishop S. T. Jones added encouraging words. He became one of the members of the faculty at the next session.

At the end of the first term of the second session the number of students enrolled was one hundred and twenty. Hence, the building for the boys was given to the girls, and the boys had to be provided for as best we could in renting houses, one of these being named by the students the White House, and the other the Black House. How they had to tramp through mud and snow that winter. But with characteristic gallantry, they willingly gave up the comfortable building erected for them to the gentler sisterhood.

If I mistake not, the summer of 1883 was occupied in erecting an addition (42x56) to the original ten-room house for a chapel, a dining room, and dormitories for girls. The chief donor to the fund for this building was the "railroad king," C. P. Huntington, whose picture you may see in the center of the group in the rear of the chapel. Hence the name Huntington Hall given to the building.

It will be remembered by those who are acquainted with the history of Livingstone College, that too much can hardly be said of the work of Bishop Harris in helping to establish this institution. The entire dimensions of the building mentioned above are 91x38, four stories high including the basement.

In the fall of 1885, the necessity for more buildings caused Dr. Price to visit the Pacific coast. After lecturing about four months, he secured the donation of $5,000 from the late Senator Leland Stanford and $1,000 from Mrs. Mark Hopkins. The entire amount collected by Dr. Price on the coast was about $9,000. Only a little over $1,000 was needed to make up the sum of $20,000. The Hon. Wm. E. Dodge, who had assisted Mr. Price through school, promised him a donation of $5,000 if he should raise that sum. Dr. Price lost no time in securing the residue, and Mr. Dodge kept his word.

In March, 1886, ground was broken for the erection of a dormitory for boys—Dodge Hall—a four-story brick building, 60x40, and a four-story brick, 100x40, for girls, known as Hopkins Hall, forming a nucleus to Stanford Seminary. It will be observed that these buildings are named for their principal donors.

In 1887, Mr. Stephen F. Ballard, of New York, erected the Ballard Industrial Hall, 66x39, and fitted it up with complete outfits for the departments of carpentry, shoemaking and printing. The entire valuation of the buildings and grounds (now about fifty acres), is estimated at $100,000.

The aim of the school has been to give a thorough literary training to colored young men and women. The industrial feature has not been neglected, although in the past two years the school has not been able to do as much in that line as formerly. The reason of this has been the withdrawal of the Slater Fund. However, this department has been operating with such means as the officers have been able to obtain. The students in the carpentry shop make and repair all the furniture used in the school, such as bedsteads, chairs, tables, desks, washstands and dressers. The printing office is well equipped and during the past year much minute and pamphlet work has been done beside the publishing of the college journal, which is now conceded to be one of the best, if not the best college magazine published by a colored institution in the country. The institution has been running but little over a decade. It boasts, however, of a prominence equal to any institution in the South founded and sustained by colored men. The character of its graduates and the showing they have made bespeak the thoroughness of its work. In fact the officers of the institution while recognizing the need and the cry for the industrial training of the Negro have stoutly maintained that industrial education should not supplant the higher educational development of the Negro. The success of the 108 graduates since 1885 has been sufficient argument for them to hold this point.

The young men who have entered the ministry are all prominent in the great church under whose auspices the school works. Many of the largest and most prominent churches in the connection are held by them and they have merited each place. In the law and in medicine they are not behind, and in the school room as teachers, many brilliant records have been made by its young men and women. As teachers they are in demand and in most cases give entire satisfaction. The work of the great Dr. Price in his efforts to lift the race to a higher plane of intellectual and moral development is well known on both sides of the Atlantic. To speak of Livingstone and its aim, is to speak of the one great desire of its lamented president.

So thoroughly wedded was he to this idea and its development through the work of Livingstone College that no honor in church or State, however tempting the emolument attached to it, could induce him to give it up. His great influence rests upon his successor and his associates, ten in number. These are making noble self-sacrifices to carry on the work.

The maintenance of this work is wonderful when it is remembered that Livingstone has no endowment fund for teachers; no scholarship fund for students, and only a small appropriation from the church that is supposed to support it. And only a little over half of this is received annually to carry on the work and pay teachers.

The last commencement was one of the most successful and brilliant in the history of the institution. Dr. W. H. Goler, the new president, took charge with a vim and purpose that delighted all. His ability, his friendship for and acquaintance with Dr. Price and his experience in the work obtained under that great leader give him a confidence that makes success doubly sure.

The present session has opened with the most flattering outlook. During the past five or six years the school has averaged an enrollment of over two hundred students. The enrollment one year was about three hundred. Students representing New England, Michigan, Missouri, Kentucky and all the States along the coast from Massachusetts to Florida as well as Alabama, Mississippi, Louisiana, Arkansas and Tennessee have been enrolled. Besides these representatives of Liberia, West Coast of Africa and the West Indies are among the number.

The death of Dr. Price, which occurred October 25th, 1893, was a great blow to Livingstone. Its friends within and without were thrown into a state of anxiety for its future. But many believed that Price's work was accomplished when he demonstrated to the world his practical production of his great lecture, "Negro Capabilities." When Livingstone started the world had not learned that a college could be established and controlled entirely by Negroes. The school is the argument and the proof. Price is gone but the school is going on and it is doing nobly and well its part in swelling the stream of workers for God and humanity.—*The A. M. E. Zion Quarterly Review.*

FISK UNIVERSITY.

THE work of founding Fisk University was begun in October, 1865; the Fisk School was opened January 6, 1866. It was founded and is still fostered by the American Missionary Association of New York City. The University has just held its thirtieth annual commencement. The educational work was begun with a race just emancipated by our great civil war and the first department established was the common English. There have since been organized the following departments: College preparatory, normal, college and theological. The University also has a department of music, which, during the past year, has had 116 pupils. Departments of medicine and law will be established in due time. In the Industrial Department, printing, carpenter work, plain sewing, dress making, cooking and nursing are taught. The average attendance during the past five years has exceeded five hundred.

EQUIPMENT.

The University campus contains thirty-five acres, most favorably located for beauty and health, one mile and a quarter in a straight line northwest of the State House. The property of the University is valued at $350,000. The accompanying pictures of the four principal buildings will convey a more vivid impression of their size and architectural beauty than any description can do.

JUBILEE HALL.

This is the "Home" for young women and for the female teachers. It is surrounded by eight acres of land, beautifully ornamentd by trees and shrubbery. This building was erected with funds earned by the famous Jubilee Singers, who left the University October 6, 1871, under the leadership of Mr. George L. White, Treasurer. They spent seven years of continuous labor in the United States, Great Britain and Ireland, Holland, Germany and Switzerland.

JUBILEE HALL.

LIVINGSTONE MISSIONARY HALL.

This building was erected, principally, through the gift of $60,000 by Mrs. Valeria G. Stone, of Malden, Mass. It is the "Home" for young men, but the first two stories are now used for chapel, library and recitation rooms. When the great recitation hall is erected on the central square midway between Jubilee Hall and Livingstone Hall, the entire work of instruction will be transferred from Livingstone Hall.

FISK MEMORIAL CHAPEL.

This chapel was secured through the legacy of $25,000 in railroad bonds left the University by Gen. Clinton B. Fisk, which netted with interest nearly $30,000. This Memorial Chapel gives a perfect audience room for one thousand persons in the regular seats.

THEOLOGICAL HALL.

The cost of this handsome building was about $25,000. The money was furnished partly by the band of Jubilee Singers, which pleaded for it during the fall and winter of 1890-91, and partly by the American Missionary Association.

THE GYMNASIUM AND SHOP.

Fisk University was the first institution for colored youth to establish a gymnasium for the physical training of students. The main floor of this building is devoted to this purpose and the basement is a large and well-equipped shop for instruction in wood working.

APPARATUS AND MUSEUM.

The University has made a good beginning in securing the necessary apparatus for instruction in the various branches of natural science. Laboratory work in elementary chemistry and mineralogy is now systemized and established. The museum contains a well-arranged collection of over three thousand specimens in natural history, geology, mineralogy and ethnology.

LIBRARY AND READING ROOM.

The library now contains 5,227 bound volumes and a large number of pamphlets. The reading room is an adjunct of the library and this year has been provided with twenty-five of the best periodicals and thirty-five newspapers.

Livingstone Missionary Hall.

F

AIMS.

Fisk University aims to be a great center of the best Christian educational forces for the training of colored youth. During the thirty years since its founding, the faculty and trustees have held unfalteringly to this purpose and all plans have been laid for providing the best possible advatages for the "Higher Education." The University in all its methods seeks to develop character and to give its students a thorough preparation for the practical duties of life.

THE ALUMNI.

The Alumni are making a record of useful services to which Fisk points with pride as ample vindication of the wisdom of founding a University for the Negroes of the South in the very dawn of their freedom. Christian education accomplishes the same beneficent results in the case of the Negro that it does in the case of other races. College and university education are a vital necessity to the study and permanent advance of any race or class of humanity.

REV. E. M. CRAVATH, D.D., *President*.
REV. A. K. SPENCE, M.A., *Dean*.
REV. E. C. STICKEL, M.A., *Treasurer*.

REV. CHARLES E. ALEXANDER, Memphis, Tenn. The subject of this sketch was born of slave parents in Princeton, Ky., on Jan. 31, 1853, was transferred by sale to Mississippi where he remained until the breaking out of the war, when he, with his parents, ran away to Memphis, remaining in Memphis until after the war; he then attended school at Nashville where he graduated in the Normal class in 1876; he was then elected Principal of the Mason Preparatory School where he spent fourteen successful years as the principal of that school. Many of the young men are now in professional life in this and other cities. He is now the present Pastor of Centenary M. E. Church.